The Search
for the Girl
with
the Blue Eyes

By Jess Stearn

The Search for the Girl with the Blue Eyes
Edgar Cayce—The Sleeping Prophet
Yoga, Youth, and Reincarnation
The Grapevine
The Door to the Future
The Sixth Man
The Wasted Years
Sisters of the Night

The Search for the Girl with the Blue Eyes

A Venture into Reincarnation

Jess Stearn

ASSOCIATION FOR
RESEARCH AND
ENLIGHTENMENT

A.R.E. Press • Virginia Beach • Virginia

A.R.E. Press
Sixty-Eighth & Atlantic Avenue
P.O. Box 656
Virginia Beach, VA 23451-0656

Library of Congress Cataloging-in-Publication Data
Stearn, Jess.
The search for the girl with the blue eyes / by Jess Stearn.
    p.   cm.
Originally published : Garden City, N.Y. : Doubleday, 1968.
ISBN 0-87604-395-3
    1. MacIver, Joanne. 2. Reincarnation—Canada—Biogra-
phy. I. Title.
BL520.M33S74   1998
133.9'01'35—dc21   97-27335

Cover design by Lightbourne Images

The wind bloweth where it listeth, and thou hearest the sound thereof, but canst not tell whence it cometh, and whither it goeth: So is every one that is born of the Spirit.

John 3:8

Overture

THE TELEPHONE RANG WITH a curious insistence. It was my editor, Lee Barker, in New York. As I was preparing my excuses for not having finished the manuscript in my typewriter, his voice broke in over a secretary's. "I have something exciting for you," he said, brushing aside my half-formed apologies.

I quickly conjured images of a new panacea for cancer, another Russian espionage plot, perhaps the truth about Vietnam.

"It's bigger than Bridey Murphy," he said.

A sudden curtain rang down, and my voice must have betrayed my disappointment: "Reincarnation?"

"A much better case," he went on, unabashed. "This girl lived and died only a generation or two ago in Canada, only a few miles from where she lived before."

As I thought of the hardheaded practical New England Puritan on the other end of the phone, I could hardly restrain a laugh. "And who," I asked, "is your authority?"

He was cool and unruffled. "It's another of those regressions under hypnosis, but this one can be checked out with people still living, with landscapes and sites still recognizable. A perfect case."

"But I don't believe in reincarnation," I protested mildly.

His voice boomed back. "Precisely. You will check this out like any other story."

Even as he spoke, I wondered how this could be possible. In three recent books, in the metaphysical area, I had dealt with evidence for reincarnation, without turning up anything I thought conclusive. I agreed it was a plausible explanation for the apparent injustices permitted by a presumably benevolent deity, but it seemed to me it was postulated to accommodate the human need for a significant existence.

"We can talk about it in New York," I said dubiously.

"Fine," he said. "I have a report from our man in Toronto who's sold on the case."

"Why not send it on to me?" I suggested.

My editor, known for objectivity, had edited Morey Bernstein's *Bridey Murphy* into a dazzling best-seller a few years before, without half the enthusiasm that he now revealed.

And yet I was not sure of his innermost feelings—nor of mine. For while I had not accepted reincarnation, despite many claims of remembrance from a past life, I had, through psychic research, begun to realize there was more to life than so often met the eye.

By coincidence, perhaps, I had spent an interesting evening only a short time before with the original Bridey Murphy and her three charming children. And I discovered that Virginia Tighe, regressed by Morey Bernstein into a previous life in Ireland, actually didn't believe in reincarnation herself, but attributed her remembrance of things past under hypnosis to genetic memory.

"Just as the salmon remembers the river its ancestors

swam up to spawn, or fledgling swallows the flight south, so I may have remembered," she said.

Whatever it was, I had witnessed many dramatic cases of remembrance squeezed out of man's mysterious—and mystifying—subconscious.

Here I was in Virginia Beach, finishing up a book on the amazing mystic Edgar Cayce, who, in trance, had discussed past lives in Atlantis, Egypt, India, and other lands of antiquity with the same matter-of-factness and clarity of detail that some would discuss contemporary affairs in London, Paris, or New York. Only the week before, I had watched a dark, handsome professor of philosophy from the University of Ceylon skillfully regress a middle-aged subject, successively, to young adulthood, childhood, the womb, and before. Marveling, I watched as the woman scratched her name in response to his command—the handwriting reflecting the determined flourish of youth and the undisciplined scrawl of childhood—and then, further regressed in time, to a presumed previous life, revealing not only a different script but, lo and behold, an entirely different name.

Professor K. N. Jayatilleke had seen nothing unusual in the performance. He had regressed many people and felt they were all reliving some phase of a previous life. With a shrug, he observed, "Two-thirds of the world accepts reincarnation."

Impressed as I was by the demonstration, I could not but observe, "And two-thirds of the world once thought the earth was flat."

I had seen many regressions and invariably, under hypnosis, the subjects invoked incidents in childhood, which investigated, revealed the accuracy of their subconscious recall. Regressed at random, a sixteen-year-old girl, amazingly recalling the day of her birth, remarked that the hospital room had suddenly gone black. The girl's mother, searching her memory, recollected with a jolt that the lights had indeed gone out right after the child's delivery. A fuse had blown.

It was difficult to say where all this came from, or how evidential it was. Not too much was known about the subconscious, or its link to a universe whose infinite potential we were only vaguely comprehending through our dramatic if blundering excursions into space.

Even as we blundered, we somehow sensed that as the dimension around us became limitless, so did our own horizons expand and soar, with what the great Jesuit paleontologist Pierre Teilhard de Chardin proclaimed "the revelation of the immensity and unity of the world all around us and within us."

It was difficult to define or limit the subconscious, sifting real from unreal. And in trying to appraise this subconscious, the problem was obvious. Just what was true and what wasn't? Was the subconscious force that recalled remote incidents in this lifetime just as valid when it evoked a previous life experience that could not be readily examined?

No matter how recent the past life, memories of witnesses faded, documentary evidence moldered and disappeared, names and places vanished into thin air. In *The Phenomenon of Man,* De Chardin had observed: "Close as they are to us, where are the first Greeks and Romans? Where are the first shuttles, chariots or hearthstones? And where, even after the shortest lapse of time, are the first motorcars, aeroplanes or cinemas? In biology, in civilization, in linguistics, as in all things, time, like a draughtsman with an eraser, rubs out every weak link in the drawing of life."

Was the lack of witnesses, of artifacts, the erosion of time, the supreme consideration? If the subconscious was correct in confirmable areas, why should it become questionable in the twilight zone of a misty previous experience?

If some recall stood up under investigation, did this indicate the remainder was true? Why should the subconscious be better informed, not only about contemporary events, but anything else in time? I would have to know more about the subconscious, more about hypnosis, more about reincarnation even before I could begin to delve realistically into anybody's past life.

The least likely people were interested in reincarnation, and the reasons for this upsurge of interest in a philosophy that dominated the East for centuries were painfully apparent. Never before was the Western world so morally adrift, values so fragile, life so tenuous, man so confused. Sophisticates boasted brightly that "God is dead," intellectuals, pseudo and real, lashed out at materialism, while pushing a dryrot, spiritless materialism geared to the lowest common denominator of achievement grandiosely entitled the Great Society.

Technologically, the West was at zenith. We spoke casually of reaching the moon, exploring Venus, perhaps one day zooming out of our own solar system, but our crime rate was rising incredibly, our relief load was demoralizing, and racial riots, under the posture of civil rights demonstrations, were undermining the very law and order that distinguished us from the jungle.

Many heads were turned hopefully to new horizons, looking for a grand design to tie the loose ends of existence neatly together. In the raptures of poets, the vision of philosophers, even in veiled references in the Bible, some found support for reincarnation and its endlessly unfolding cycle of life.

Reincarnation was nothing to be slighted. Our finest minds had embraced it—Mark Twain, Franklin, Thoreau, Emerson, Bronson Alcott, Walt Whitman. And yet, even the most inspired had little to go on but impressions. Franklin argued that in an orderly nature, nothing was squandered, the human spirit gaining in one experience, could only profit by that experience through being conserved. It was logical, if nothing else.

After one interested himself in a subject, it was odd how pertinent thoughts and events seemed to spontaneously strike one. Every other book I opened seemed to relate to rebirth.

For Plato, Bacon, Goethe, Nietzsche, reincarnation was highly plausible. Plato, the greatest mind of antiquity, conceived that knowledge being a process of recollection was achieved in life stages culminating in the soul's final communion with the nature of God. The philosopher Diogenes was more explicit in discussing the many lives of Pythagoras, a mathematical wonder of the pre-Christian era. "When Hermotimus died, he became Pyrrhus, a fisherman of Velos, and again remembered everything, how he was first Aethalides, then Hermotimus, and then Pyrrhus. But when Pyrrhus died, he became Pythagoras, and still remembered all the facts mentioned."

Where did this memory come from? Why did some apparently have recall, and not others? "I sometimes experience historical revelations, so clear do certain things come back to me," the young Flaubert noted. "Sometimes I think I have lived at different epochs; indeed I have memories of them."

I had no memories myself, and was skeptical of others who did. Almost everybody of this stripe, it seemed to me, particularly in the shadow of death, had a soul need for more than a crematorium or a casket claustrophobically ensconced in six feet of turf. Had not the poet Longfellow trumpeted past the graveyard?—"Dust thou art, to dust returnest, Was not spoken of the soul."

Reincarnation presupposed the existence of an inter-ested God. The human spirit, constantly evolving, kept returning in roles shaped by previous performance, working out its karma, a credit or debit ledger carried over from earlier existence. It was a cheering concept, especially for those who felt that one brief experience ending in oblivion rendered that experience rather pointless. However, only until recent research into the subconscious was there any realistic support for intu-itionists who felt they had lived before.

There were many subconscious channels into the past, under hypnosis, as in *Bridey Murphy;* with the mind-expanding drugs, in psychic trance, sometimes in spontaneous recollections. Thus, many recalled frag-ments of previous existences, speaking languages they knew nothing about consciously and recalling people and events indelibly engraved on their subconscious.

For months on end, I had been exploring the work of Edgar Cayce, who had not only clairvoyantly diagnosed the ailments of people he had never seen, prescribing remarkably confirmed cures, but had made his subcon-scious a fascinating travelogue of past incarnations in Egypt, India, Persia, and Atlantis.

While Cayce remembered best in trance, he did not discount conscious memory in others, as with a thrill of unexplained familiarity they encountered people they had never met before. "How is it," he said, "that some people we meet, we immediately feel as if we had known all our lives, and others we have known for years in this life and still do not feel close to them or understand them? I don't believe anyone can understand this unless there is more than just this life. Nothing lives again un-less it dies, even the grain of wheat in bringing forth that which will propagate itself."

Inspiration flowed inexplicably through the subconscious of the creative. Mozart composed a sonata at four, an opera at seven; Josef Hofmann was a piano virtuoso at three. A Negro boy of eighteen months, of illiterate parents, could repeat perfectly on the piano any music he had heard but once.

What was genius, some said, but a remarkably re-membered development, expressed not in conscious re-call of events but in a particular predisposition, a flair or talent developed in an earlier life? And if not that, what was it?

Cayce suggested that lessons were remembered, im-pressions gained, aptitudes sharpened, even when con-scious memory waned and the life experience was forgotten. How else explain the affinity of so many for lands and cultures so exotically different from their own? Heinrich Schliemann, a German businessman, was drawn inexorably to Greece, unerringly finding the ru-ins of ancient Troy, where generations of professional archeologists had failed. A whole breed of Englishmen were emotionally obsessed with the Mideast. Lawrence of Arabia exerted an uncanny mastery over squabbling factions of fierce nomadic tribes; Sir William Hamilton learned Hebrew at three, and at twelve knew a dozen esoteric tongues—Arabic, Persian, Sanskrit, Hindustani.

Just as certain people were familiar, so were certain places. How explain *déjà vu* that sudden startling con-viction that one had been somewhere before? The poet Shelley, hiking with friends through previously unvisited countryside, suddenly remarked, "Over the hill, there is a windmill." As they reached the hill, and the windmill emerged, he fainted with emotion. Closer at home, the Boston-bred yoga teacher, Marcia Moore, in her only visit to India had been able to describe a strange market place, just before she turned a corner which revealed it as pictured.

Research into the psychic had made me vividly aware of the vast potential of the subconscious. Through its apparently boundless power, psychics could inexplicably visualize the past and future. *The Door to the Future,* published in March 1963, featured a 1956 prediction that a Democrat, to be President in 1960, would be assassinated in office. Other predictions were as remarkable. In New York City, before a skeptical group, sensitive Helen Stalls clapped her hands to her head, crying, "I hear three shots . . . oh, my head hurts so, I can't bear it . . . President Kennedy is going to be assassinated."

Three days later, the President was dead.

In June of 1965, again mustering her subconscious, Miss Stalls observed, "Adlai Stevenson will die abroad, unexpectedly, in a public place within six weeks."

Five weeks later, Adlai Stevenson died in the streets of London of a heart attack.

Often these demonstrations were close to home. In mid-January, 1967, in Manhattan's Fifth Avenue Hotel, a group sat spellbound as psychic Marie Welt, resurrecting the recent past, correctly described a business merger involving Wall Street broker John Rendon, and then foresaw that in two days, against all likelihood, he would receive notice that his teenage son had been accepted into the college of his choice. I would be offered an unlikely newspaper assignment the following Tuesday; would travel to California shortly thereafter, and my book, *Edgar Cayce—The Sleeping Prophet* would reach the best-seller lists in March. All happened as predicted.

More important, how had it happened? Dr. Alexis Carrel, a Nobel Prize winner in science, appraising this power of the subconscious to "know," had no explanation, except to say that when man did find the answer he would have solved the riddle of the universe.

The subconscious traveled with equal facility into the

past and future. Time and space were meaningless. It was a force that was apparently as much a part of natural law as gravity, just as the principles of flying applied long before the Wright Brothers, and electricity before its discoverers: Davy, Faraday and Edison.

Laws governing the universe obviously applied to every aspect of that universe, spelling out the unity between Creator and created that De Chardin spoke of so eloquently. As Fate, it spun out some lives, shortened others. Accepting the psychic, it became evident that man was part of nature's own orderly process, his movements as measured, within their orbit, as any careening planet. Death, fame, birth, tragedy, riches, marriages, divorce, all that man is heir to, had been anticipated through the psychic subconscious. The gifted subconscious of Norfolk sensitive Maude Robinson foresaw, for instance, that within six months an elderly spinster would marry a man she had not yet met, settling down with him in San Francisco. Sixty-seven-year-old Miss Mae Brinkley was furious with herself for being so gullible. "I'll bet," she snapped, "she predicts marriage to every silly old woman."

Months later, a letter arrived from San Francisco for Virginia friends of the former Mae Brinkley—now Mrs. Einar Wald. "Maude," she announced, "is miraculous."

And what was miraculous? That which we did not understand—television, fifty years ago; landings on the moon, twenty years ago; flying saucers, ten years ago; reincarnation today.

The apparently magical subconscious was not the exclusive province of the psychics. It was demonstrable in almost anybody at any time. Radio personality Arthur Godfrey, serving at sea, on a United States destroyer, awoke one night and saw his father—an obvious dramatization of this subconscious—at the foot of his cot. The apparition said it had come to say good-bye. As the figure faded, the startled Godfrey looked at his watch. It was 2 a.m. The next day, a wireless arrived with its message. His father had died. The time? 2 a.m.

Had Godfrey received a telepathic message from his dying father, or had the spirit of the dead man been in communication with him? In either case, the subconscious had been remarkably effective.

Actually, as one thought about it, was reincarnation any more of an enigma than the power to predict, which suggested, as reincarnation did, an orderly pattern in the universe?

One could be proved out. Scientists—Einstein, Carrel, Jung—accepted that a gifted few like Edgar Cayce could travel at will in time and space, with their predictions of war, holocaust, plague remarkably confirmed by events. Reincarnation was another thing. When Cayce discussed pre-Incan civilizations, and these materialized with oceanographic research, was this proof of a previous life in Peru? Was it proof of reincarnation when a woman, mortally afraid of lions in this life, was revealed in a Cayce life reading to have applauded Christians mangled by lions in the Rome of two thousand years ago? At most, these were only signs. Yet, if Cayce was subconsciously right about that susceptible to proof, why should he be wrong about reincarnation? It was all out of the same Cayce bottle.

With this thought, I put the matter aside. Two days later, the report arrived from Canada. It was pungent and to the point, at the same time revealing the writer as an impressionable young man, obviously affected by the charm of his subject.

The girl, now nearly eighteen, was hardly fourteen, editor Dave Manuel wrote, when inadvertently regressed in hypnosis, she had astonishingly begun talking about previous lives, including one in a neighboring Canadian county. She apparently mentioned names, such as a crossroads settlement, which had disappeared from most maps; her own name and that of her husband re-membered by old settlers, and many others whose names lived in old deeds and records. Manuel, hearing of the case, had looked up the family. Their name was MacIver and they lived in Orillia, a small resort town, some eighty miles north of Toronto.

Manuel was accompanied by his wife, Barbara, a knowledgeable graduate of Smith College, and a one-time director of admissions at Finch College. Neither believed in reincarnation, though they obviously found it provocative. With a skepticism that at least rivaled Manuel's, I combed through the report on Joanne MacIver. It was rather complete as regarded the family. Ken MacIver, Joanne's father, grew up in Toronto, where his family had a meat-packing business. He went to a Toronto high school, Jarvis Collegiate, and with World War II joined the Royal Canadian Air Force, hoping to become a pilot. But his eyes weren't good enough, and he was grounded. After the war, he married, and eventu-ally settled in Orillia. There were five children; Joanne was the eldest.

Editor Manuel provided a thumbnail sketch. "Joanne is about as typical a small-town teenager as you are likely to find—healthy, wholesome, happy, good student, out-going, leading cheerleader in her high school. She is also with it [I supposed this meant bright], has the looks to match her personality, and is just beginning to become aware of same."

Dave was impressed by the family's sincerity, but, even so, this only precluded deliberate fraud or hoax. It had little bearing on the validity of the recall. Ever since that first regression, the father had been poring over provincial archives, seeking some tangible trace of Joanne's previous life and death. She had presumably lived as Susan Ganier, near the central Ontario town of Massie, married a tenant farmer named Thomas Marrow, was widowed early, and died late. Not very exciting, but smacking of the prosaic inconsequence of most lives.

The new Joanne MacIver—or was it Ganier?—was dramatically "born" on October 5, 1962. On that Friday evening, as they played cards in the MacIver living room, Joanne and two school friends had suddenly begun discussing hypnosis, a current conversation piece. Joanne tried to hypnotize one of her friends, a young man who maintained he couldn't be hypnotized, and he wasn't.

Knowing that her father had hypnotized people when he was in the Canadian Air Force, she burst into the kitchen, where MacIver was chatting with his wife, Edna, and appealed to him to try. MacIver proceeded to recall his lost art. But try as he might, the rusty amateur could not make the boy go under. Looking up, however, he noticed that Joanne's eyes were closed. She was in trance. She was apparently so sensitive, her subconscious so open, that she had responded to the suggestion given another.

Joanne was then hypnotized, and age-regressed, the first of many such sessions. Dave had listened to a tape of one regression, he and his wife both struck by the electrifying gamut of emotions manifested by a fourteen-year-old. Love, hate, horror, joy, all came through with jolting impact.

The editor groped for an acceptable explanation. "I cast about in all directions. The only thing that I could come up with was that, just as the body of a subject under hypnosis is capable of phenomenal feats of concentrated muscular power and control, so perhaps the mind is capable of infinite imagination. But I had to discard this postulation, because while she certainly could have conjured up the horrors of a pig's slaughter, as she did, no girl fourteen could know the full exultant joys of young married life, or the profound grief of losing a young husband so beloved. All my rational, conscious everyday thought processes told me that what I had just listened to was absolutely authentic, yet inside I felt a tremendous need to reject it somehow. It ran counter to everything I had ever believed."

As yet I knew little about Joanne. What was she like? Despite previous lives under hypnosis, she was only a small-town teenager with no more horizons, I supposed, than any other girl in her milieu. I looked vainly for something objective about her appearance, but the report seemed to convey more about Dave Manuel than the girl. He was entranced by her fathomless blue eyes. "I tried staring into her eyes, they were very far apart, so I had trouble meeting her gaze." His wife was similarly affected. "Barbara tried it, too, and was definitely shook up. Later on, Barbara said it was like taking a whiff of ether—a very picturesque reference to a heady incident. She had the experience of peering into the bottomless blue, as though hypnotized herself."

It had been fun for Joanne, at first. Manuel, checking a tape of one of the regressions, reported, "She usually kept her eyes closed to see more clearly what she was being asked to describe. But she could hear the people in the room with great definition—occasionally she would ask someone to stop breathing so loud—and she could hear the cars going by outside and any noises from the kitchen."

After listening to the tape, the intrigued editor peppered the girl with questions: Was she able to see more of the past life than was reflected in the visualized action of the moment? Was it, in effect, a full range of memory of which she was just describing one specific event?

She replied frankly, no, she could only see one thing at a time, but afterward she could put it in correct sequence, as she did her earliest recollections of childhood.

Joanne's claim of conscious recall was unusual. She was said to be able to look up a hill, and describe what lay beyond, to turn into a road and picture a grove or orchard down the lane, as long as it was in the area visualized in trance. She seemed to be mildly psychic. Sitting in her living room, she had accurately described a television program friends were watching at that moment. Of course, she could have seen the listings or known their habits.

MacIver was rather unusual, too. After the Susan Ganier incident, he had become sufficiently emboldened to take other subjects back to previous lives. There had been a Mrs. Jenkinson, who had lived in a small English town, Huddersfield, in her subconscious visitation, and had mentioned identifiable places in trance. Dennis Campbell, a young serviceman, went back to medieval France and then to Atlantis, and spoke colloquial French under hypnosis.

Atlantis had cooled off Dave Manuel. But he still wondered if the Atlantis myth might not actually be a genetic carryover of lives on another planet. Manuel was apparently falling under MacIver's subtle spell. "Ken was extremely reluctant to talk about any of this," Dave reported, "yet at the same time he seemed compelled by a desire for the spotlight to reveal more than he intended. He also said that New York would be uninhabitable in the year 2000. I pressed him further, but he clammed up."

Had MacIver been influenced by an Edgar Cayce forecast of the century-end destruction of New York, Los

Angeles, and San Francisco, or did he have some inkling of his own?

I was unimpressed by MacIver's posture as a hypnotist or prophet. Far more impressive was a statement by an early settler, octogenarian Arthur Eagles, that as a boy he had known a Susan Marrow, that he had known Susan's family, the Ganiers, and that Susan had died in 1903.

If Eagles was right, then at least there was a Susan Marrow, and the problem was to trace her. On this basis, it seemed worth a trip to Canada. There had been other curious visitors from the States. One eminent psychiatrist, an inveterate researcher of reincarnation, had regressed the girl a few months after sessions with the father.

Manuel, following the tape, was favorably impressed with the psychiatrist's handling of things. "When Joanne, then Susan, was undergoing the agony of her husband's death, he gently suggested it was a week later, then a year, removing her subconscious from the traumatic experience, and all the while emphasizing how happy she felt. When she came to, she was Joanne MacIver."

Contrastingly, after one of MacIver's sessions, Joanne had suffered a distressing experience of conscious recall. Describing out of nowhere an attack by a hired hand, she had unpredictably become panicky and started flailing around wildly on the couch. MacIver, caught off balance by her violent reaction, had abruptly sought to end the session. "He wrenched her out of the trance without first bringing her to time present," Manuel reported. The result was well-nigh disastrous. "She went around in a daze for two weeks," Manuel said, "while her father was incapable of helping her, mainly, I gather, because he didn't even have an idea of what the problem was." The result was that she remained Susan subconsciously for this period. "In the end, Joanne had to hypnotize herself in front of a mirror to straighten out the error." (Now Joanne was doing it!)

Hearing the tape, Manuel's reaction was a lot different than reading a cold transcript. As the girl relived the Susan role, the Manuels empathized with her every inch of the way. "The first thing that jolted us was the part where Susan, as a young child, is watching her father kill a pig. When she shrieked in horror, Barbara and I practically jumped out of our chairs, and later, when she was describing the death of her husband, her grief was so intense that it was almost painful to listen to her sobs become painful wails that subsided into something which I can only describe as keening. On the other hand, when Susan was describing a particularly happy occasion, when her husband Tommy came in from the fields, lifted her up and swung her around, her joy was overwhelming. Listening to it, you couldn't help grinning at her total happiness. When she was asked how she liked newly married life, all she could say was, 'It's nice.' But from the way she drew it out, and the intonations in her voice, she knew what she was talking about. No one, not even the most skillful actress in the world could have faked those emotions. Nor is it conceivable that a teenager exists with the subtlety of imagination to preprogram her answers so thoroughly, even if this was possible under hypnosis."

As I read I couldn't help thinking how naive Manuel must be. Still, aware of her husband's impressionability, one would have thought Barbara would have resisted out of pure feminine contrariness. Nevertheless, I found myself asking like the Manuels, "How does it feel to know you were other people before this? Does the knowledge of prior existence and the memories of it have any effect on your current life?"

The girl had replied calmly—indeed, she seemed to

do everything calmly. "Only when she dwells on it," Manuel translated, "and then she can't be sure how much it influences her. She tries not to think about it."

Even before I finished the report, I knew I would fly up to Canada, if only to see Joanne. At seventeen she was in full bloom, Manuel reported enthusiastically, and if she hadn't lived before, he was positive that it was that generation's loss.

I wondered at Manuel's bland assumption that Susan and Joanne necessarily shared any physical attributes— unless, as Thoreau once pointed out, the sure fingers of time, mind and spirit unerringly left their mark on the physiognomy.

There was obviously a challenge, an undercurrent of excitement in searching for something nobody had really found before. For years, as a newspaper reporter, I had dealt with tangibilities: politics, prostitution, crime, delinquency, homosexuality, drug addiction—and scoffed at the psychic as so much claptrap. Now convinced of the psychic, the so-called sixth sense, by reportorial procedures based on the five senses, I still wondered how objective I could remain through a search for a will-'o-the-wisp such as reincarnation.

Toward the end of May, 1966, I was ready to proceed to Orillia, where the MacIvers were presumably waiting to meet me. I also looked forward to meeting Dave Manuel, who seemed to be searching, like nearly everybody else, for some resolution to the riddle of man's restless quest for himself.

As I debarked at Toronto's Malton airport, I had no trouble picking out Manuel, though I had never seen him before. Even on the apron of the airstrip, he looked like a man on the verge of a great adventure. He was a tall man, with a long, eager stride, and a gleam of expectancy in his eye.

We quickly piled into his car, twisting dexterously through the heavy airport traffic to the open road due north to Orillia. Manuel was young, good-looking, articulate, with an easy manner, reflecting a certain social presence. As we chatted, taking stock of each other, I had a sudden undeniable impression. "You're a Yale man?" I said.

He smiled. "How did you know?"

"Just testing my ESP," I said lightly.

"It's working," he said. I liked that about Dave. Nothing seemed to faze him. He was ready to accept anything or nothing, the mark of the true sophisticate.

The conversation turned naturally to the girl, and the possibility of a hoax. "Believe me," he said, "she's Susan Ganier."

"In what way?" I asked.

He swung in and out of long lines of cars. "Every once in a while, a door opens a bit, and she gets a glimpse of something."

"For instance?"

"She might see a familiar rise, or somebody might say something that jogs a memory."

"Does she remember anybody specific?"

"Not that I know of."

I was sure she enjoyed being a center of attraction.

He shook his head. "I really had to push to get her to talk at all."

I gave him a side glance. "Are you sure you haven't been hypnotized?"

He laughed. "Just wait until those blue eyes fasten on you."

I sank back comfortably. "I can hardly wait."

Manuel smiled good-naturedly. "No sweat, just go at it any way you like."

"What is your feeling about reincarnation?" I asked.

He replied thoughtfully, "There certainly ought to be more to life than chores."

"Then you have a personal interest in this project?"

He chewed on his lip. "I'm just at an age—thirty— when I'd like to know what it's all about. There's an order in the universe or there isn't. If there is an order, we're part of that order, like everything else that lives, breathes, moves or sits." He squinted down the road, skillfully weaving in and out of the fast-flowing traffic. "If there isn't an order, then it's all an accident, and we're accidents, and there's no point to any of it."

Unexpectedly, I had found a philosopher.

Getting back to the project, I wondered why an attempt hadn't been made to hypnotize Joanne for additional information in nearly four years.

"She'd like to forget it. The kids her own age thought her a kook and ragged her mercilessly."

I was mulling this over when the highway markers announced Orillia's approach. Swiftly passing the downtown district to the right, we soon checked into the Sundial Motel, Orillia's finest. We planned to dine, and then, taking our time, mosey over to the MacIvers'. The sun was still gratifyingly warm and the grass beside the pool inviting.

"Before this momentous meeting," I suggested, "how about a little yoga exercise to get the kinks out and brace us for those eyes?"

"I'm game," Dave said, patting his stomach.

As we stretched our muscles, concentrating on yoga's deep breathing, I observed, "As a swimmer, you shouldn't have any trouble with the breathing."

Dave's face broke into a smile. "More ESP?" he said. He had been on the Yale swimming squad, one of the most accomplished in collegiate ranks.

After freshening up, we began a search for a restaurant. Dave headed his car toward downtown Orillia, past rows of solid red brick houses of Victorian vintage. As we rode up one street and down the other, I felt a vague twinge of familiarity and rummaged about in my mind for an image of a comparable hamlet. It was a bit like the small towns upstate New York I knew as a boy, and yet there was a difference. I closed my eyes, concentrating on certain communities, visualizing certain streets and houses. There were similarities, but always that shade of difference.

A special quaintness distinguished Orillia. The name, from the Spanish, meant shore, and Lake Couchiching (Indian for many winds) which rimmed the town, rivaled Lake George's wooded charm. The houses had neighborly porches, and the restfully shaded streets sloped down to the lake. There was a quietude about the town contrasting oddly with my own nervous sense of expectancy.

As I shrugged inwardly, dismissing my feeling, Dave turned his car into Orillia's main street. There on my left, in a glow of sunset, I had a broad sweeping view of a bleak dock and a conglomeration of freight cars on a railroad siding. I felt, unaccountably, a sudden melancholy.

Manuel spoke, but I was not aware of what he was saying. This, jarringly, was my first *déjà vu*, a distortion of memory, the dictionary said, in which a new situation was regarded as having happened before. There was nothing here of the strong assault on the senses, of the eerie familiarity, the morbid fascination which fixed one to a scene over a conflicting compulsion to flee.

I perceived Dave watching me. "What's the matter," he asked, as we pulled up to a Chinese restaurant happily named Shangri-la, "see a ghost?"

"This may sound silly," I said, "but I have the uneasy feeling I've been in this town before."

Dave looked up and down Orillia's Mississaga Street, with its broken clusters of shops and neon signs. "And you still came back?" he asked incredulously.

The proprietor of the Shangri-la seemed little different from proprietors of Chinese restaurants elsewhere. He was slight, affable, almond-eyed, with a bright moon face and jet hair, and spoke the stilted singsong English of Sino-American restaurateurs everywhere.

"Does he look familiar?" Dave asked.

I smiled wryly. "He reminds me of somebody I saw last week."

After a strangely wordless meal, we were off for the MacIvers. Dave threaded his car through heavy weekend traffic to the crest of a hill, where a solid square red brick house confronted us. The name Braemar was etched in the stone over the doorway. Apparently, in Scottish, which the MacIvers were in this life, it meant hilltop.

"Is the house familiar?" Dave grinned.

My attention was caught unexpectedly by an elongated wood-framed figure on the lawn off toward the side of the house. It was either a dismantled flying saucer, a giant wheelbarrow, or the ribbed skeleton of a boat.

"What is it?" I demanded.

Dave laughed. "That's MacIver's folly. Like Robert Fulton, Ken's a boatbuilder. He's been building that one for a year—his own design, all his own work, and who knows, he may get it done some day."

The monster was about thirty feet long, bellying out in the middle. On closer inspection it resembled a giant grasshopper.

We climbed some stone steps, rang a bell, and a man soon framed himself in the doorway. Two towheaded boys, of eight and nine, lurked shyly behind him. He motioned to them. "The Nut brothers, Chest and Wall," he said.

This was Ken MacIver.

He was a ruddy-faced man of less than medium height, with a glint of a gray smile twinkling behind his glasses. "Come in, come in," he said.

We trailed him through a brief hall, into the living room. In a roomful of women and children, my eyes picked out two pretty girls. One had a high marble forehead, a cold pallor, and even features. With her full red lips, upswept gold hair, and bold chin, she was strikingly attractive.

The other girl had the bluest blue eyes I had ever seen. I took her hand. "You are Joanne," I said.

I felt a comfortable glow as the blue eyes peered into mine. "We have been waiting," she said. Her voice was warm and dulcet, her hand seemed to nestle naturally in mine. As I looked into her eyes, I reminded myself that she was only seventeen, yet she could have been any age that was the age of youthful charm and beauty.

It was not her lineaments or features that made her face distinctive, nor the exquisite high color of the gently bred Englishwoman. She had a look, a look that was ageless, endless, bottomless.

For a sweet fleeting moment, the deathless lyrics of the immortal Rossetti swept through my mind:

> *You have been mine before*
> *How long ago I may not know,*
> *But just when at that swallow's soar,*
> *Your neck turned so,*
> *Some veil did fall—I knew it all of yore.*

As I sat down next to her, I was sharply aware that for the second time that day I had experienced an unexpected familiarity, but this time it was strong and sure, reflected in quickened tension and awareness.

I made a conscious effort to direct my attention to the others in the room, bouncing up and down, meeting people: Joanne's mother, three younger brothers and sister Nancy with the sunny smile, a few family friends and the boldfaced blond beauty, whose own overt charms were overshadowed by the younger girl's. I was struck by the resemblance of the other MacIver children, all on the blondish side, to the parents. But nobody resembled Joanne.

My impression of MacIver was quickly formed. He was a naive, guileless man, apparently overwhelmed by the magnitude of the discovery that had dropped into his lap. He openly regarded his daughter with a respect bordering on awe. She was an inexplicable phenomenon, miraculously delivered into his life. His face lighted up whenever he mentioned her name, and he referred to her deferentially, saying always, "If Joanne permits, or Joanne wants—"

There was quite a hubbub in the room. Everybody seemed to be talking at once, only Joanne now remained strangely silent. Finally, she spoke in a throaty whisper, intended only for me.

"Aren't you tired hearing about people who have been reborn?" she asked.

Her lips had parted, revealing an even gleam of porcelain.

"They're not all like you," I said, remembering the rash of silly women who were queens or courtesans in some exotic dream paradise.

I recalled with a start what Edgar Cayce had said about meeting strangers and instantly feeling the familiarity of a previous relationship. Even so, how much of my impression was due to subtle suggestion? Was I being brainwashed by the girl at my side, or by her father, the amateur hypnotist, who sat regarding me with a quizzical smile?

I did feel a bond with her. In this roomful of people, neither of us seemed to belong. There was an aloofness, a detachment, distinguishing her from the others.

She seemed to read my thoughts. "I've never really felt I belonged to this family, though I love them all dearly."

I could not have seen her before. She had been out of Canada only once, traveling with her family, living then in the Canadian Niagara Falls, across the border to Buffalo, New York, for a shopping stint. Any relationship was patently absurd, and yet I had the sudden startling conviction that her innermost thoughts paralleled mine.

"Tell me," I said, "is there anybody in this room you have ever known before?"

She smiled, and her blue eyes wandered around the room, where the company was listening to Ken MacIver describe his surprise at Joanne's remarkable transition to Susan Ganier. She gave her father a fondly tolerant glance.

I repeated my question, watching her closely.

"Why, yes," she said, a blush coming to her face, "as a matter of fact there is."

"And who would that be?"

She seemed mildly embarrassed. "Why, you—you knew that, of course."

I had anticipated her answer. "In this previous life, did you ever live in Orillia?"

She spoke easily. "I lived closer to Owen Sound, some ninety miles west of here. Travel wasn't easy in that day, so I question whether I would have visited there."

I measured her with a doubtful glance. "You actually believe in reincarnation?"

She took no offense. "Long before Dad hypnotized me, I believed I had been before. I just knew things that I hadn't learned in this life."

"What did you know that was significant?"

"I always felt grown-up, never like the other children." She arched an eye toward her father. "I've always felt as though Dad was more the child."

This was certainly not evidential.

She frowned a moment. "I've always had a feeling that I knew what marriage would be like, as though I had been through it even before Dad hypnotized me." She lowered her voice. "I know what I want of marriage now."

"And what is that?" I asked.

"Children. I could never have them before. That's why I came back, to be a mother and to complete a marriage cycle that ended before I had learned the lesson of marriage."

The deep blue eyes looked evenly into mine. My eyes moved first and I could see her father watching me curiously. "You know," he said, "it was predicted that you would come."

"By whom?" I asked wryly.

"Horace, Horace Smith, a friend of mine, he saw it all."

There didn't seem to be anything to say.

MacIver was obsessed with reincarnation. He lived for little else now, taking every free moment from chores as a government auditor to check out his daughter's subconscious experience. He also kept conjuring up anything that had occurred in his own life to fortify his belief. "You know," he said, taking a chair near me, "when I was five years old I had a rather unusual experience, which, as I look back, was my indoctrination to the whole concept of reincarnation."

The year was 1921, he was standing on the dock in New York with his parents ready to embark for Bermuda. "As the line of passengers moved slowly toward the gangplank," he recalled, "a stout, kindly gentleman picked me up in his arms and carried me from the wharf to the ship."

To MacIver's total incomprehension at the time, the stranger announced, "Young lad, I have been saved and born again and you too will have to be saved and born again before you can enter the Kingdom of Heaven. When you are older, you will understand what I mean."

Once planted, the seeds of belief developed in MacIver slowly. As a boy, subsequently, in the woods near his family's summer place, he had had a singular experience while out walking. Suddenly, a wave of nostalgia had surged over him. The aroma of the towering pines, the wild flowers, the dank shaded vegetation, all conspired to assail him with a sense of depressing familiarity. The feeling invoked, rather than the scene itself, lingered long after, strangely stirring his subconscious. "All that I was now experiencing in these woods had happened before, a before that somehow dated far back in the past to another time. I felt a yearning to return to this other era but knew that I couldn't. I wanted to capture this feeling and hold it forever, but it eluded me."

Despite his prosaic occupation or perhaps because of it—MacIver appeared to have a wild poetic streak, and was at the same time uncommonly versatile. Hypnosis, ship designing, writing, aviation, were only a few of the things he dabbled at.

He had gotten into hypnosis early. At Jarvis Collegiate, his Toronto high school, a classmate had called his attention to a do-it-yourself magazine series on the art of parlor hypnosis, guaranteed to make one the cynosure of all eyes.

The friend had thought MacIver would be especially adept.

"Why do you think so?" MacIver had asked.

"Because you look so directly at people and your eyes have such a penetrating look."

Looking at MacIver now, I would not have given him the same kudos. In his khaki shorts, with his slight, yet paunchy figure, he seemed hardly the type to inflict his

will on another. Nevertheless, he had spent many interesting evenings demonstrating hypnosis to friends. But
after the war for many years, until 1962, he had not hypnotized anybody. "My interests changed as I grew older,"
he explained, "and there was no occasion to give another
demonstration."

Long before his experience with Joanne, he had ro-
manticized reincarnation, as I supposed he did everything. He got up and showed me a few lines of verse
written years before, and watched closely, with an
author's ever-present concern for his brainchild as my
eyes ran over it. It told me more about MacIver than it
did reincarnation.

> *My path is linked with yours as one*
> *From experience of the past lived days*
> *Anticipated in a time to come*
> *Our life perfectly blended always.*
> *Join your dreams with mine this hour*
> *That they may together perpetually flower.*

MacIver's eyes were anxiously on mine as I looked up.
"How do you like it?" he asked.

"It's expressive," I said noncommittally.

My answer seemed to please him.

I had no trouble getting at MacIver's version of events.
He seemed agreeable, even eager, to discuss his role in
Joanne's experience. In his anxiety to prove out reincarnation, once she had touched on a previous life, he had
hypnotized his daughter so many times that she winced
at the prospect. Outside witnesses were usually present
at these sessions as he felt this gave it a semblance of the
scientific. He never knew what would come back. In one
of the later sessions, witnessed by a Mr. and Mrs. Arthur
Dick of nearby Bracebridge, Joanne, regressed to Susan
Ganier, at the age of sixteen, had discussed father
Ganier's visits to a neighboring mill. This she described

as McKelver's mill, which excited MacIver no end, as there had been a McGillvary mill in this locale, sometimes called McKelver's, according to old-timer Arthur Eagles, with whom MacIver had discussed various ancient landmarks.

There was confusion at times about specific names, as Joanne's voice often became indistinct as her subconscious stumbled down memory lane. "You must make allowances for the fact that Joanne often slurred the last syllables of a long word," MacIver said, his eyes owlishly fastened on mine.

The reference to Eagles recalled my special interest in the old settler who remembered the Ganiers and Marrows, and I mentioned that I would like to see him before the weekend was over.

MacIver laughed. "If you could manage that, you'd really have a story."

Eagles had died a few months before, at the age of eighty-six.

My face must have shown disappointment, for MacIver said, "He left a deposition, and his niece, Ruby Scott, who lives in Orillia, can vouch for its authenticity. He even remembered some of Susan's friends, and pointed out once where she lived."

As I pondered this new contretemps, the doorbell rang and a young man walked in. He was short and slight, with sharp features, horn-rimmed glasses, and he tugged nervously at a pipe. He was introduced briefly. His name was Tag Watson. He was nineteen, and he was Joanne's beau.

She had stood up when he walked in, and now turned to me apologetically. "I have to get ready now, but we can meet anytime tomorrow."

With a sense of disappointment, I watched the couple climb into a car and drive away.

"They make a handsome pair, don't they?" Dave Manuel said slyly.

With Joanne's departure, the others wandered off and MacIver brought out a pile of papers accumulated in his search for Susan Ganier. From MacIver's rambling conversation, I gathered that Susan Ganier had been "born" about 1835, in St. Vincent Township, in Grey County, some ninety miles away, had married a neighboring farmer, Tommy Marrow, and settled in nearby Sydenham Township, living long beyond her husband into the turn of the century.

Although the period was comparatively recent, the area was so remote, so much a wilderness before the advent of modern communication, that the search for records and landmarks had been frustratingly unrewarding. However, MacIver had not been able to probe a critical thirty-five-square-mile section of St. Vincent, known as the Tank Range, which the Canadian Defense Department had taken over as a proving ground during World War II.

With Dave and myself peering over his shoulder, MacIver spread out a map of St. Vincent, pointing out that the first families had come in 1819. The Crown had given settlers one-hundred-acre grants provided the land was cleared and worked.

Large landowners, not farming themselves, often leased their holdings to tenant farmers in return for land improvements and token payments. The settlers felled their trees in a westerly direction, built their cabins from the logs, and planted their crops between protective rows of timber they had delimbed and left to dry. It was hard living. Despite stoves and fireplaces, cabin temperatures were frequently below zero. Pigs were killed in the fall, salted, and used all winter. Sugar came from the maples. There were no drones.

"They worked or got out," MacIver noted grimly.

Dave laughed. "What, no welfare?"

The forest primeval drew the dour, enduring Scot, naturally aloof and self-reliant, intent on not only a living but a way of life.

Another of MacIver's map showed the original land grants for Sydenham Township. Two or three names stood out prominently. From the extent of their holdings they were obviously absentee owners who had become beneficiaries of the Crown through some substantial service. The name, Alexander Fraser, appeared most frequently, scrawled across a score of lots of varying size. A mile or two south of the Fraser holdings, in St. Vincent, on the dividing town line, another name caught my eye—Archibald Marrow.

It had been scratched over, but was plainly legible.

"Any kin of Tommy Marrow's?" I asked.

MacIver shrugged. "He could have been for all we know."

"Couldn't you trace him?"

MacIver wore an injured air. "It's not as easy as trying to find people in New York," he said.

From his pile of papers, MacIver now produced sheaves of documents, letters, transcripts. He had been very busy for four years, but instead of centering on the Marrows and Ganiers, he had sprawled, literally, all over the map.

"Is there anything at all concrete?" I asked.

He came up with still another map, showing landholdings for more than a century back in St. Vincent. I could make out the names of Hartman and Hagerman in one of the tiny squares, but there was one other name over which these had been scrawled.

He spelled it out rather impatiently. "G-a-n-i-e-r."

With the aid of a magnifying lens, it did appear a possibility.

"How do you know it's Susan Ganier's family?" I asked.

"That's just about where Joanne put her father's house."

I looked at the map again. It was a photostated copy from the file of the Ontario Department of Lands and Forests, the repository of Crown grants from a period before our Civil War. There was no questioning its authenticity.

Distinguishing concession lines, a mile apart, ran north and south, lot numbers east and west. The Ganiers were on the Ninth Line, Lot 37, four or five miles north and east of the Marrow section.

The map was hard to read. It was a negative print, the background in black, the names in white. It would have been much simpler reversed.

"That's easy to do," MacIver said, "if you go on with the search."

In four years, he had apparently not thought of doing this himself.

I turned back to Archibald Marrow.

MacIver's finger ran down St. Vincent's Twelfth Line, stopping at Lot 31. "The entry on the map dates back to 1840, but old Archibald seems to have vanished into thin air. As I mentioned, there's no subsequent record of him, or his relationship to Tommy Marrow, if any." He looked up, his eyes blinking with excitement. "But Marrow is not a common name in these parts. I've found Morrow and Marriots and Maras, but no other Marrows."

My own interest was rising, but names in themselves, without some meaningful sequence of events, were certainly not conclusive.

"Names have been picked out at random from the past through clairvoyance or the action of mind-expanding drugs," I pointed out, recalling the recent case of a well-known physician who had fancied himself a certain

Egyptian pharaoh under LSD, and had then proceeded to a museum and picked out the proper sarcophagus.

Was this evidence that he had lived before as that pharaoh? There was the American businessman, who had visioned himself at a ball at the English House of Parliament two centuries ago, and then discovered that there had been such a function dedicating a restored building after a disastrous London fire.

But such instances, multiplied even a thousand times, proved nothing for reincarnation. Without some evidence of how one life experience flowed naturally out of another, any exploration of reincarnation would be as purposeless as the one-life principle reincarnationists rejected. The life in question would have to be observed in depth, subconsciously and otherwise. The choices made in one life, as Edgar Cayce once suggested, presumably influenced not so much the course of this life but the next. "As ye sow, so shall ye reap," and "He who lives by the sword, shall die by the sword," certainly did not pertain to this life, for, more often than not, the wicked prospered and the names of innocent martyrs were legend. Ruthless conquerors put countless thousands to the sword, lived gloriously, and died in their beds. They would have to find justice elsewhere.

Cayce had his own yardstick for establishing some significant link to reincarnation. "By living the record." For as one lived deeply, growing spiritually, he developed the faculty of remembering. "For when the purposes of an entity are the more in accord with that for which the entity has entered, then the soul-entity may take hold upon that which may bring to its remembrance what it was, where, when, and how. Think thou that the grain of corn has forgotten what manner of expression it has given. Think thou that any of the influences in nature that you see about you—the acorn, the oak, the elm, or the vine, or anything—had forgotten that manner of expression?" Only man forgot—to shield himself from the excessive pain and sorrow and guilt of a previous life, but the lessons were there to be remembered, just as a child often recalled what it had learned without remembering the instructive incident itself.

Still, as a reporter, I felt the need to put the inquiry into a framework compatible with my own background. At this point, it was essential to know how the Susan Ganier story had begun, and how valid its beginning was. As MacIver kept shuffling his maps, I turned to the circumstances of the first hypnosis session.

"Were there any reliable witnesses?" I asked.

He looked startled for a moment. "Why, naturally, my wife Edna and my son Ian."

"They're hardly impartial."

A map slipped through his fingers.

"As I recall it, Barbara White and Paul Torrance, school chums of Joanne's, were visiting with her, when somebody suggested that I hypnotize Paul."

That somebody was Joanne.

At first, MacIver had modestly backed off, but had then permitted himself to be persuaded. He was not averse to a little spotlight.

He had not been able to put Torrance under, but then, as recounted, Joanne had shown herself a good subject by nodding off at the suggestion given another.

"That frequently happens," MacIver said, "in a crowded room, I would never know who would go off."

"Why did you have trouble with Torrance?" I asked.

"You just can't hypnotize anybody against his will."

"How about breaking down the will?"

He shrugged. "I'm only an amateur."

Joanne had stretched out willingly enough for him on the family davenport—a chesterfield.

MacIver quickly put her in trance by getting her to focus on a fixed point. Taking her back in time, he decided to regress her to childhood. "You will be able to recall your seventh birthday party and tell me who was there," he said.

When he got no answer, he tried the sixth birthday. Again, as there was no response, and the children began to smile, MacIver felt a flush of embarrassment. He varied the suggestion. "You're going back, far back in time and space to your fifth birthday party. You will see yourself and remember who was there—back, back, as far back as you can remember."

Joanne's lips began to move, "Reuben . . . Tom . . . Susie." They were totally unfamiliar names. And then MacIver recalled with a start that Joanne had no birthday parties as a child. Wondering where the names had come from, he attempted to bring her to a more recent period of her life, also fresher in his own mind. "You will see yourself at sixteen years of age," he suggested, without troubling to begin anew. "Tell me, what do you see now?"

A smile suddenly transformed Joanne's face, and her voice took on a new lilt. "Reuben is in the orchard with his girl friend, courting. He thinks I can't see him. They are behind a tree." She turned her head from side to side, holding her fingers to her mouth in an attitude of coy surprise. "Oh, they are so funny," she laughed. "He told me they were going for a walk, but I know better. Boys are so silly. I think they see me. I had better be going now."

MacIver, now thoroughly at sea, was too flustered to do more than ask, "What is your name?"

" . . . Susan."

"And your last name?"

"Ganier."

"Where do you live?"

"On the farm."

"What year is it?"

"1848."

"What place and country do you live in?"

"Northern Ontario, Canada."

Joanne's voice was now lighter, each syllable clearly accented, with a musical treble so different from her normal huskiness.

Believing in reincarnation as he did, MacIver suddenly felt with a surge of excitement that he was sitting on a powder keg. "By now," he recalled, "I dared to believe that we might be witnessing a regression into a previous life."

With trembling voice, he had suggested, "You are going back again into the past, you will see yourself in another time and another life." In his naiveté, he had imposed no limitations of time and space. "Can you see yourself," he prodded.

She nodded. "Yes."

"Where are you?"

"On the farm in Quebec."

"Where is it near?"

"Beside a big river."

"What is your name?"

"Suzette."

Again, Joanne's voice had changed. It was not Susan's and it was not her own, for MacIver had pushed her back into still another lifetime.

Not understanding what he was dealing with, he blundered away, demanding of the subconscious, "How did you die?"

The transformation was remarkable. Joanne had been lying quietly, face serene. Her head now jerked up abruptly, and stark terror distorted her face. As though the whole scene lay plainly before her eyes, she cried, "She is playing in the river. Annette, you are going too far . . . come back." Her anguished cry brought chills to those in the room. "She is drowning. There is nobody around. I can't swim. Somebody help me." The last cry was almost a gasp.

Her horror was so real, so all-consuming, that MacIver moved frantically to bring her out of it. Without considering the implications, he snapped out the suggestion that she would awaken feeling refreshed, but would remember everything that she had experienced subconsciously.

She came to, rubbing her eyes and complaining of a bad headache.

But MacIver was still immersed in the session. Eagerly, he asked, "Do you remember anything that happened to you while you were under hypnosis?"

Without meaning to, he had kept her subconscious open with the suggestion that she remember, posthypnotically.

Joanne's blue eyes blanked off into space. She slowly searched her memory. "Annette was my granddaughter. We were on a picnic by the river and the others went away for a while and left me to look after her. She was playing in the water and then waded out beyond her depth. I went in after her, but couldn't swim and we both drowned."

MacIver was aware now that the regression embraced two different lives, provoked by his careless reference to "another time and another life."

"Do you remember about your other life as Susan Ganier?" he asked with fresh enthusiasm.

"Yes, I can remember about the farm. It was very isolated. Reuben was my brother."

"Can you remember where it was located?"

"In northern Ontario. That's all I can remember."

Joanne was yawning now. Her headache had worsened and she felt strangely confused, as though she wasn't quite sure who she was, or where. The people around her had suddenly lost identity; she knew their names, but was fuzzy about her relationship to them. She just wanted to be by herself, close her eyes, and go gratefully off to sleep.

Her father's enthusiasm puzzled her, but she agreed wearily to another session, anything to get upstairs to bed.

Young Torrance and Barbara White, intrigued, promised to be back the following night.

Ken MacIver could think of nothing but the scheduled session. Excitedly, he pictured himself as the first man to prove out one of the great hidden truths—reincarnation.

At promptly nine the next night, the principals took their positions. What transpired was pretty well documented, for MacIver had copious notes of the session, and now referred to them liberally to assure accuracy in the telling.

"There's nothing like being scientific," he said.

I agreed dryly.

Unfortunately—or fortunately—he again made the mistake of fixing no time limit in conducting his regression.

"You will go far back in your memory this time. Where do you see yourself?"

"In France."

"Where do you stay?"

"In my uncle's castle, it is big and up on the hill."

"What is your name?"

"Michael. Castle so big ... *mère* ... I hate *mère*." The French for mother had slipped in.

The subject's change in sex, so startling to me, went unremarked by MacIver.

Still only dimly aware of what he was dealing with, he sailed ahead, "You will now go ahead in time. It is twenty years later. How old are you?"

"Twenty-five years old."

"What are you doing?"

"Riding a horse and living in the castle."

"Who is your husband?" he asked, disregarding the gender clue, given him earlier.

"Hoosband, hoosband," she expostulated indignantly, "I haven't any hoosband. I am a man. I have no wife. I have one good friend." She spoke now with a strong accent.

As MacIver fumbled through his notes, trying to arrange them in sequence, Dave and I exchanged rueful glances. His questioning exasperatingly ignored such pertinent details as time, locale, lineage. It got no better as he went along.

"What are you doing now?" MacIver had then asked.

"I am riding a horse with Paul, my only friend."

"Is there anyone else with you?"

"No one else. I have an ugly face, nobody likes me."

"How did you die?"

This time, Joanne reacted calmly to the death question.

"My mother had my head cut off. Mother hated me, and she had me executed."

MacIver, remembering Joanne's earlier trauma over Suzette's drowning, quickly skirted this area.

As he pored over his notes, I took the opportunity to interrupt. "Wasn't it odd the way she skipped from one life to another?"

MacIver jauntily lit a cigarette. "If she had one life, she had many."

He returned to his notes. "Ah, here it is. This was the strangest yet."

Again he had got more than he bargained for with an imprecise suggestion. "You will now go back even farther in time. What do you see?"

"Many people dead from the fever. The ants ate them up."

MacIver then asked, "What is your name?"

The answer, phonetically, was O-I.

"How old are you?"

"Thirty-two."

I waited patiently for more about ants.

"What do you eat?"

"Bananas."

"What country do you live in?"

"Africa."

Dave Manuel's ears pricked up. "Many African tribes," he observed, "think of their homelands broadly in terms of Africa."

"Do you live in a house?" MacIver next asked.

"No, in a hut."

"What is it made of?"

"Bamboo from the forest."

"How many children have you?"

"Six."

"Are you a woman?"

"Yes."

"What year is it?"

"I don't know."

"What color is your skin?"

"Black like the night."

At long last, MacIver asked, "What happened with the ants?"

The answer was dramatically unforeseen. "The ants came and ate the people up. They ate the elephants, they ate everything."

"What did you do?"

"I ran away from the ants. I ran fast."

"Did you take the children with you?"

"No, the children were sick."

Manuel and I again traded glances. O-I had left her children to the ants. A heartless, indifferent, or terrified mother, she had put her own skin ahead of her children's.

"What happened when you came back?"

"The children were gone."

The ants had done their work well.

MacIver, still experimenting, still holding the spotlight, took Joanne subconsciously forward another two hundred years in time, into still another life.

Now her name was Marguerite, and she was in the act of dancing, when Joanne's subconscious tuned her in.

"Is anyone with you?" MacIver had asked.

"I am dancing with myself."

He didn't know what to make of that, and again quickly moved her forward. The year was 1792, it was spring, and she was on a farm. She was Suzette again, and MacIver, now that he had placed the life cycle, wanted no more of Suzette's traumatic reactions. Swiftly, proud of his new power, he again took her back in time.

Now she lived in Virginia, the year was 1701, and she was a fugitive slave. She had fled her home plantation with an infant child who perished on the way and thus became an innocent victim of her mother's flight to freedom in the North.

Again, the life experience had apparently built up a karmic debit pattern around children.

"She didn't have much luck as a mother," MacIver said, blinking brightly through his glasses.

Dave laughed. "That's the understatement of the day."

The sprawling nature of the questioning had me in constant confusion. "Why didn't you concentrate on one lifetime?" I asked.

MacIver assumed a pained expression. "I did," he said defensively, "I just didn't want to keep anything from you, so you could judge the merits of the regression for yourself."

The collegian in Dave Manuel asserted itself. "Give me the facts, man, the facts."

"How about the Susan experience?" I said. "That's most recent, most checkable, and that's what you have most of."

MacIver's voice rose irritably. "All right, just tell me what you're interested in."

He consulted his notes closely now. "Ah," he said, "here's Susan."

He had opened up this line of inquiry with refreshing explicitness.

"You will again see yourself as Susan, what is your last name?"

"Ganier."

"When did you die?"

"In 1903, in the winter. It was very cold."

"What is the name of the nearest town?"

"Massey."

MacIver had spelled it Massey, not knowing then of a nearer Massie, little more than a crossroads now, though a hundred years before it was a thriving settlement with mills, church, general store, post office, and horseshoe nail factory.

Massie was perhaps fifteen or twenty miles south of the "Ganier" place in St. Vincent, but still closer than Owen Sound, an alternative market town in north Grey County.

"They could have lived there for a while and moved," MacIver offered with his usual aplomb.

"As long as you're speculating," I said, "you could put them at the North Pole."

He flushed slightly, and turned back to his notes. Asked about her early life, Susan had said, "I didn't go to school. We were too poor. I had to stay home and help on the farm."

MacIver jumped around again. "Did you get married?"

"Yes."

She named her husband—Tommy Marrow.

The wedding was performed by a preacher named McEachern, and a reception and dance with hard cider for refreshment followed. MacIver, still groping about for verifiable names, asked if Tommy ever went to Massey.

"Yes," she replied proudly. "Tommy bought me a new dress. Oh, it is a lovely dress. Red, I like it very much."

She wasn't quite sure where he had got the dress.

MacIver then took her forward in time. "You will see yourself when you are older in this life. Tell me what you are doing."

"I am combing Reuben's little daughter's hair." She sighed. "Oh, why can't I have any children?"

MacIver pressed on, "Did you have any children at all?"

She shook her head sadly. "We couldn't have any children."

MacIver's next question evoked an emotional storm of cataclysmic proportions.

He explained, half-apologetically, "I had no way of knowing how the question would affect her. All I asked was, 'Can you tell me about any neighbors?'"

It seemed an innocuous enough question. But Joanne had leaped up on the chesterfield, her eyes wide, and staring glassily into space. She then scooped up a cushion, brandished it like a shield across her stomach, and screamed, "Go away, Yancey. Don't you touch me. Don't come near me."

The change in her was startling. Her eyes had become

mere slits, she was ashen-faced and her breath came in gasps. Her lips were bared back over her teeth and she seemed ready to do battle for her life.

MacIver was too shocked to react promptly, but his wife jumped at him to take Joanne out of trance. Though panicking, he didn't want it to appear that he had lost control. With a show of calm, he quickly brought her out of it. But again, he failed to remove posthypnotic recall.

As the others, including Barbara White and young Torrance compared reactions, Joanne strolled about the MacIver house in a daze. That night, she tossed and turned, mumbling incoherently, bothered with nightmares for the first time in her life.

This confusion stayed with her for more than a week. She seemed to float in and out of a room, pale and pensive like a schoolgirl Hamlet who had seen a ghost. She didn't speak unless spoken to, then replied automatically, and perfunctorily moved on. Even her features had subtly changed.

"Her eyes," MacIver recalled, "seemed slanted downward like an Oriental's, and her cheeks pushed out."

She might have altered her cheeks with her tongue, but how could she have changed her eyes? It seemed incredible.

MacIver regarded us in that earnest way of his. "I am not exaggerating," he said. "I hardly recognized her myself."

In this period she actually fancied herself Susan Ganier. She had a curious feeling of moving in two worlds; recognizing that Ken was her father, yet seeing still another father, a farmer, whom she helped in the fields, and a mother, Catherine, to whom she felt closer than to her own mother. She had nostalgic recollections of cows and pigs and apple trees, of harvests and sleigh rides—nothing she had ever experienced as Joanne MacIver.

Names and faces streamed through her defenseless subconscious—Tommy Marrow, Yancey, Reuben, and others. She felt an assault on her emotional structure, without quite comprehending the extent of it or the source; at times there was a poignant feminine yearning, again an upsurge of hate and fear, or of love, and an overall sense of loss and emptiness.

"She was like a zombie," MacIver recalled.

On a Sunday, October 14, eight days after the traumatic session, the MacIvers sat down with Joanne and expressed their concern.

She seemed to know exactly what they were talking about. "Don't worry," she said, "I know what to do."

It sounded rather fantastic, as had about everything else I had heard, but MacIver was ready to swear by it. "Immediately after our conversation with her," he said, "she went up to her bedroom, sat at a dresser, closed her eyes, and 'knew' that when she opened them she would be Joanne again."

Dave looked like he was on the ropes. "And it worked?" he said, gulping.

MacIver nodded solemnly.

"Where did her powers come from?" I asked.

He shrugged. "She's always been psychic. Once she stopped before a neighbor's house, and said with a sad face, 'Dad, Mrs. McSweeney is not going to live out the month.'"

"I guess that was the end of poor Mrs. McSweeney."

MacIver regarded me suspiciously. "That's right," he said, "how did you know?"

"I'm psychic," I said.

Joanne appeared to be a glutton for punishment. She had no sooner recovered from one subconscious convulsion, than she was exposed to another. The very night she had pulled herself together, MacIver's friends, Mr.

and Mrs. Arthur Dick, were down from Bracebridge, about thirty-five miles north of Orillia, and MacIver asked Joanne if she would again be hypnotized, as there were so many areas still to be explored.

She agreed, on his promise to proceed cautiously.

Once the visitors had settled comfortably in the living room, Joanne took her position on the chesterfield, and the session began. MacIver was now primarily concerned with locating Susan Ganier's home base. Having finally learned the importance of being precise, he carefully placed Joanne in the past before shooting his questions at her. With some attempt at explicitness, he asked where her father took his grain to be milled. The answer was indistinct, sounding like "Mr. McKelver," and was so recorded in the notes Mrs. MacIver was taking in shorthand.

An obvious similarity of names struck me. "Maybe she was trying to say her own name, MacIver," I said.

MacIver looked appalled. "It sounded nothing like that when she said it. She slurred over the last syllable, and there was obviously more."

As most people are, Susan Ganier was vague about directions. She lived north of Massie, of that she was sure, but she couldn't recall how long the trip to the mill took, or the roads. "He comes back the same day," she said.

There were curious idiosyncrasies of speech. She traveled with her father to Massie, not by horse-and-buggy, but by "buggy and the horses."

"That," she explained, "is the way Daddy said it. He was French, and that's how he said it when he spoke English."

The older the subject in the regression, the more there was to remember and talk about. So MacIver quickly took Susan beyond her marriage, when she presumably had a life of her own with a husband. They didn't visit much, she recollected, but went to an occasional dance at a neighbor's. They drove there in a buggy.

"Can you tell me where Tom got the buggy?" he asked.

"He bought it when he went to buy the pigs at Massie."

MacIver moved easily from livestock to marriage. "Can you tell me where you bought the wedding dress?"

"We didn't buy it. Mother fixed an old dress over for me."

"Did Tom ever take you to Massie?"

"Once."

Instead of asking the occasion, MacIver asked, "What way do you live from Massie?"

"I think north of Massie."

"Do you ever go to a store?" he asked.

"We don't go to stores too often."

"Do you remember the man who owns the store?"

"Sometimes it was one man, sometimes another."

MacIver again skipped about.

"Tell me about the house you lived in when you married Tom?"

"It was a pretty house. There were two small bedrooms that I thought would be for my children. There was a little kitchen and a sitting room."

"I'll bet you were young when you married."

Joanne replied with an expression she had certainly never heard in her conscious life, nor had MacIver, for that matter.

"I was like Daddy said, the foal who was ready to ride."

In his preoccupation with locating the Ganier farmstead, MacIver now resorted to a ruse to extract the desired information. "I would very much like to come and visit you," he said in a soothing voice. "How would I go about it?"

In trance, she tugged reflectively at her lip.

"Well, go to Massie and go north from Massie, and just

ask for Ganier and everybody will know where to go to
see me."

That may have been the way Susan Ganier would have
answered the question, but it certainly wasn't helpful.

MacIver rephrased a question he had asked but a few
minutes before. "Joanne, can you tell me the names of
the storekeepers at Massie? You can remember . . . just
take your time."

Where he had previously drawn a blank, he now got
some response. Joanne's lips quivered, and then halt-
ingly—"MacGregor and Mmmmm . . . Milligan, MacGregor
and Milligan." Since she coupled the names, MacIver felt
they applied to one store. (Once, as Susan Marrow, she
had mentioned another storekeeper as Ames or Amos.)

MacIver now concentrated on her childhood. Life was
not very exciting for young Susan. She occasionally attended the Methodist church, a half-mile or so down the
road, and school sporadically before dropping out because of chores. There were few gala days in the frozen
wild. Christmas was meager in fare if not spirit. There
was not even a Christmas tree, though the woods were
full of pine.

"Did you get anything at all for Christmas?" MacIver
asked.

She mulled it over a while, and then her face precipitately brightened. "I had an orange. It was a good orange,
and I had some candysticks and applesauce."

Hardly a Yuletide banquet, but her lips smacked in
happy reminiscence.

There was a bit more, nearly all trivia. There were so
many things MacIver could have asked but hadn't. One
missed question after another struck me: Who were her
friends, as Susan Ganier or Marrow? What were the
prices of staple commodities; flour, sugar, meat? Who
were Tommy Marrow's parents? How did Susan carry on

after Marrow's premature death? Why hadn't she married again, and why were there no children?

I could think of a score or more questions, which if not proving out reincarnation might at least disprove it.

I looked up to catch Ken MacIver's anxious eye.

"What do you think so far?" he asked.

"There could have been more questioning at this stage," I said.

"There was," he said, "but Edna's shorthand didn't get it all. You might talk to the Dicks. I had a definite feeling that Art Dick was impressed."

MacIver's hypnosis was strictly old hat. He had put Joanne in trance by getting her to concentrate, and his posthypnotic suggestions had lacked force, even when he did finally resort to them. A professional might have gotten much more.

He felt he had learned something from watching the psychiatrist in action. He had merely spoken casually in putting Joanne under. Impressed by his academic mystique, MacIver wanted to play back the tape made of that regression.

But at this point, Dave and I were more curious about Arthur Eagles and his corroborating testimony, our most tangible link to reality.

"Where did you find him?" Dave asked.

MacIver fairly beamed. "That was quite a coincidence," he said, "running into Old Eagles."

Eagles' discovery was pure chance. With Dr. F. Crawford Jones, a psychiatrist interested in his project, MacIver was returning from a disappointing trip to the Massey farther north, mistakenly assumed to be the Massey mentioned by Joanne. The discrepancies were obvious. Susan had cavorted among the apple orchards, and there were no orchards there. The terrain was also different, but, above all, there were no white children at this

Massey when Susan was still a child. This Massey was definitely out.

MacIver thought the other Massie might be worth a try. Dr. Jones was game, and they stumbled into a random farmhouse in Sydenham Township late that night. To justify his appearance at an unholy hour on a blustery wintry night, MacIver advised a surprised farmer he was engaged in genealogical research—the truth, after a fashion. The farmer, happy to have somebody to talk to, told of an old settler, in his eighties, who lived on the Eleventh Concession Line, a mile and a half north of main highway 26, and who might be helpful.

This settler was Arthur Eagles. A widower, he had lived in the township all his life, as had his father Charles before him. Besides a family sawmill, the Eagles family operated an ambulatory threshing outfit before the turn of the century, and Arthur knew the countryside as few others knew it.

MacIver, with Jones, set out at once for Eagles' farm, at nearby Woodford. However, it was the middle of the rugged Canadian winter and the snow was house-high off the main roads. His car had no chance of getting through the long narrow lane to the Eagles' house. Disappointed, he and Dr. Jones headed back for Orillia. But once home, chewing over this newest lead, he sat down and called Eagles on the telephone. The old man's voice was clear and responsive.

Did he know a Ganier?

Yes, he had known a family by that name.

Marrow?

A Susan Ganier had married a Thomas Marrow—that he was sure of. He had never known Marrow, but remembered his father talking about him.

MacIver was delighted. "You can imagine how I felt," he said, "when Eagles told me that he recalled Susan

Marrow as a widow, living alone in a rundown house."

MacIver peppered the old man with questions.

"One at a time, please," Eagles had pleaded.

"Do you remember when Susan died?"

"Oh, about 1903," Eagles replied.

For a man in his mid-eighties, Eagles had an astonishing memory. He remembered neighbors Brown and Norris and even Yancey. "Yancey," he recalled, "lived at a place called The Mountain."

Under MacIver's prodding, he recalled other pertinent names. "Mrs. Speedie, the postmistress at Annan, was a good friend of Susan's."

"Can you recall a McKelver who had a mill?"

"McKelver's mill," Eagles replied, "was in what is now the Tank Range back of the Twin churches. I think it was also called McGillvary's."

Only reluctantly putting down the phone, MacIver made a date to see Eagles in the spring, when the first thaw set in and roads were again open. All winter he looked forward to that meeting.

On April 6, with an Orillian businessman, Paul Uhlig, who served as a witness, he drove back over Route 26, turning off at the Eleventh Concession for the Eagles place. Arthur Eagles greeted them at the door. His face was weather-beaten; his general health excellent, and he was in good spirits despite a recent auto accident. He briefly discussed his family. His grandfather, Samuel Eagles, was one of the earliest settlers. The family had been quite prosperous, running a large sawmill near Vail's Point, at the top of the township line dividing St. Vincent from Sydenham.

The father, Charles Eagles, had been a benevolent sort, reveling in good works. And so the son had thought nothing of his father calling for the widow in his buggy— a democrat—and taking her shopping in Owen Sound.

It was about the only time she ever got out.

That last winter, his father, thinking Susan might be cut off without provisions by an unusually heavy snowfall, had asked his son to dig his way in and see if she needed help. But he never made it.

To back up what he had just told them, Old Man Eagles cheerfully gave his visitors a supporting statement. Signed by him, it was witnessed by Uhlig and MacIver.

Eagles' hand wavered, but the information certainly didn't. It was most emphatic.

"I knew Susan Marrow," the affidavit began, "when I was between the ages of fourteen and twenty-one years of age. Her husband, Tommy, died about the time I was three years old, from what my parents told me. The Ganiers were friends of Jack Stitt, an acquaintance of mine. I often saw them in his company and believe they farmed near Strathavon—in Sydenham Township—Grey County."

Eagles retained a vivid impression of the widow in her latter years:

"Susan Marrow was average height, around five foot four inches tall and was well built, and really an average good-looking woman with a weight of around one hundred and fifty pounds when she was around sixty years of age. I do not believe that she was much older than in her sixties when she died." He put her farm near Annan, in Sydenham Township, not far from the St. Vincent line. He was also familiar with the mill owner, McKelver. "I believe that my father bought a sawmill from a man named Peter McKelver, which was his right surname, but who was also called McGillvary by some people."

Strathavon was in Holland Township, just south of Sydenham, and only a mile or so from Massie. Familiarity with this community suddenly made sense.

MacIver carefully folded away Eagles' statement. "It occurred to me that the Ganiers may have moved off their original land, living near Massie and Sydenham at one time or another. After all, I've done plenty of moving in my time."

As MacIver raced back over the years, I found myself thinking how difficult it would be to check records or landmarks in the incredibly bleak wilderness that was Upper Canada a hundred and more years ago.

Eagles was the only witness, and it would have been only human to twist whatever he had said into a convenient conclusion.

MacIver blinked in surprise. "What do you mean?"

"You may have suggested certain names, and the old man's desire to feel important may have done the rest."

MacIver drew himself up stiffly. "Other people were there whenever I spoke to Eagles, and for that matter, he once sent me a note initiating the subject himself." Shuffling through his papers, he dug out a letter. It was signed by Arthur Eagles. "I do remember Susan Marrow," Eagles had reiterated in a legible scrawl.

MacIver was constantly on the go, livening up the search by taking Joanne with him whenever she was free of school. He had come to anticipate the weekends, when they could scour the countryside together, tracking down old graves and ancient settlers. It was a welcome respite from the monotony of government accounting work.

One week after the Eagles meeting, MacIver took Joanne over the ground where she had once presumably lived. Chinks in her subconscious, imperfectly closed, seemed to touch off recurring flashes of memory.

Naturally, they drove to Massie first, and MacIver kept asking whether the country seemed familiar. Joanne had never been in the area before, though it was only sixty-five or seventy miles from Orillia, but she kept staring entranced out the car window. "The apple orchards remind me of the orchard on the Ganier farm," she said.

It seemed to me, as MacIver related it, that one apple orchard looked very much like another.

MacIver shook his head. "That's like saying one Chinaman looks like another. It was the feeling of familiarity that was important."

I sniffed. "She found what she was looking for."

Imperturbably, MacIver got on with his story. Soon, they reached Massie's four corners and got out of the car, inspecting the old mill, still in operation, and a small store. With a handful of scattered houses, this was all that remained of a once thriving village.

They were standing around near the mill, when Joanne turned and pointed up the hill. "That is the way to the Ganier farm," she said firmly. "The scenery is changed. It's not quite as I remembered—something is missing—but I know it's the way."

Where it was narrow dirt road a hundred years before, it was now paved two-lane highway.

"You realize, of course," I said, with a glance at Manuel, "that none of this is evidence."

MacIver threw up his hands. "Evidence, evidence, what is evidence?"

"Evidence," said Dave patiently, "is something tangible that is subject to confirmation."

"Well, this is all subject to confirmation."

"By whom," I said, "Joanne?"

"Well, Joanne wouldn't lie," he said testily.

"Not knowingly," I said, "but she may believe something so strongly that it takes shape as reality in her mind."

He was unconvinced. "That would still be the case if she had lived before."

With MacIver confusing impression with evidence, the discussion inevitably bogged down, and he turned back to his story as though there had been no interruption.

As they continued north, MacIver constantly prodding her, the road became increasingly familiar. "I remember driving up it in a wagon," Joanne finally frowned.

MacIver was now beside himself with excitement. He kept asking Joanne to indicate landmarks, such as rises and hollows before they got to them, and she kept responding successfully.

Deliberately now, his wheels flying, he passed close to the village of Annan, in the area where Eagles had placed Susan Marrow. Following Eagles' directions, he passed through Silcote, a settlement even bleaker now than Massie, and turned east, coming smack up against the Tank Range.

Stymied by a wire barrier and NO TRESPASSING signs, MacIver twisted around and headed for the Eagles farm a few miles away. From the time he met Eagles, he had been wanting to confront him with Joanne. He had briefly explained his interest in reincarnation, but Eagles' practical mind had brushed it aside. However, as old as he was, the octogenarian did have a lively appreciation of the fully blossomed girl who now stood smiling before him.

"Do you see any resemblance," MacIver asked, "between Joanne and Susan Marrow as you knew her?"

Eagles looked Joanne over carefully. "There's a sort of resemblance," he said doubtfully. "Both have the same build and Joanne is good looking the same as Susan Marrow."

I had been thinking that Eagles at best could only be comparing an aging Susan with a young Joanne when Dave interrupted, logically, "Why should there be any

resemblance at all when it is only the spirit that is reborn?"

MacIver smiled tolerantly. "People's personalities are
reflected subtly in the way they look. This is obviously
true where you feel you have known somebody before,
even when you can't put your finger on the points of familiarity."

And this expression of personality would develop in
one life and perhaps evidence itself early in the next
life—so MacIver felt.

MacIver considered this Eagles interview a great suc-
cess, particularly when Eagles recalled that Tommy
Marrow's death had been cloaked in an aura of mystery.
"They said it was an accident," Eagles wagged, "but my
father always felt there was something strange about it."
That was all he could remember.

Homeward bound, Joanne suggested they return to
Silcote, and turn east again. As they approached the
town line, she suddenly cried out, "Slow down and go up
this road. I know it well. This road also goes over to the
Ganier farm." They drove north up a narrow dirt road,
and reaching the top of a rise found themselves on a plateau overlooking the countryside. Joanne pointed toward the Tank Range below, and a road branching east
into the heart of it. "The farm is two miles up that road,"
she said confidently. But there was no way of entering
the range, and so reluctantly they turned back, Joanne
looking back wistfully over her shoulder.

The range seemed a likely search area. "Ganier family
graves may be in there, as well as the farmstead and the
orchard she knew as a little girl," MacIver said. "And, of
course, Archibald Marrow's place is just within the wire
barrier, at a crossroads called Morley."

"Can we get in there?" I asked.

"You shouldn't have any trouble," MacIver said, "but

I'd soft-pedal the reincarnation. They might think you were soft in the head."

For practical purposes, the Ganier phase of the investigation didn't concern me as much as the Marrow. I had already been told there were no provincial death records prior to 1879, and certainly no birth records. There was obviously more chance of checking out subsequent vital statistics, Susan's death for instance, if this meant anything.

For even granting Joanne's accuracy, another alternative than reincarnation suggested itself. As it had to me earlier, it now occurred to Dave Manuel that Joanne, gifted perhaps with a strong psychic sense, may have picked up random experiences of others through pure extrasensory perception.

MacIver shook his head doubtfully. "If it was ESP, her life experiences might have merged or overlapped. As it was, they were all at distinctly different times."

"Have you noticed any significant carryover behavior traits?" I asked.

MacIver took off his glasses, and rubbed his eyes, "As a matter of fact, when Joanne was quite young she had a horror of the water, the only one in the family at all like that."

Dave looked puzzled. "Where did that come from?"

MacIver laughed, rolling his head. "Suzette, Suzette, remember her drowning?"

"She certainly didn't have any luck with her trance children," I observed.

"That's another thing," MacIver said.

"Meaning what?"

He suddenly turned vague. "Oh, Joanne will tell you. It's rather personal."

We spent more time over maps, and then Dave, reflecting my own confusion, suggested we listen to the psychiatrist's tape which had impressed him with its stark reality.

MacIver thoroughly enjoyed bringing out the tape recorder, winding and rewinding the endless spools. Somehow, the mechanical device seemed to lend substance to the project. As I already had received the gist of the session from Dave, I was primarily interested in Joanne's reactions—voice, manner, attitude, any delicate nuance revealing of her subconscious personality. And so we settled back to a comfortable half-hour, joined by a few of the company who had straggled back to the living room.

The psychiatrist pretty much went over the ground MacIver had. But there were interesting additions, and he was considerably smoother.

Once Joanne was in trance, the time period was quickly and precisely established. In 1843, the scene opened on the Ganier farm, the ten-year-old Susan playing in the fields.

"And what else do you do when you are not playing?" she was asked.

"Oh, I am cleaning out the barn because the cows mess it up. They're dirty animals . . . and they make me clean it out once a week and I hate it."

"Who makes you clean it out?"

"My father," disgustedly, "but Reuben never has to do it."

"Oh, he doesn't?"

"No, Reuben helps Dad with the plow instead and I'd much rather do that."

They talked about food, Joanne mentioning they had pie often because of their orchard.

"What kind of an orchard do you have?"

"An apple orchard . . . it's beside the house, and we have good apples, and we have good pies, and we're going to have one tonight."

"What else are you going to have for supper?"

"Bread and pickles. Maybe it's cucumber, and we're having milk from the cows, and, oh, we're going to have pig, too."

"Pig?"

"Uh-huh, the one that Daddy killed last fall."

Joanne's voice was perceptibly different, soft and childlike, almost purring.

But it was to be suddenly transformed.

"How did he kill the pig?"

"With a knife . . . ooo." Her voice started to rise.

"You saw him?"

"Ooo . . . ooo . . . Daddy, don't." The rising crescendo had become a shriek of pure, unmitigated horror, crashing unmusically against our ears . . . "ooh . . . ooh . . . oh . . . ah." I could almost visualize the blood streaming out of the stuck pig.

"All right," the psychiatrist suggested calmly, "we will just forget about that now, shall we?"

"Oh . . . ah . . . ah," sighing.

He took her forward a year, and a happy smile came over her face. Her father had just given her a new calf. "I'm taking it for a walk, and it's got a rope around its neck. He's not like the other big cows."

"Does he have a name that you have given him?"

"Oh, I haven't named him yet. I have to think it over, but he's pretty."

"What names are you thinking about?"

"Jesse."

Looking up, I saw the smiles of amusement.

"Jesse? Where did you get that name?"

"I don't know, it's just when I look at him, it seems to suit him; maybe he could be called Jesse." She wasn't quite sure. "But I don't think I like that name for a calf . . . maybe Spotty, because he's got black spots." Her voice was dreamy. "He's pretty, the prettiest cow I ever saw."

"And does he belong to you?"

"Just until he gets big and then he's Daddy's."

"What do you do on Sundays?"

She hesitated, as though trying to synchronize her subconscious. "Oh, sometimes . . . usually we sit around the table and Daddy reads . . . no . . . he doesn't."

"What does he read?"

"Oh, the Bible. It's nice to know the Bible."

"And do you belong to church?"

"Well, we don't really belong to a church, but sometimes we go, but not too often."

"And when you go to church, what church do you go to?"

"The Methodist church down the road."

"And does it have a minister there regularly?"

"Just sometime, but we don't go there too often."

"How far down the road is the Methodist church?"

The information was often inconsequential and contradictory. Yet I soon understood what had impressed Dave. It was the depth of emotion. She would have had to be a Bernhardt to fake it. The day after she married Tommy her voice rang with joy. "Here he comes," she cried, "he's coming in from the barn and I'm on the porch. Oh, he picked me up and swung me around. Oh, I am so happy, I am so happy. Tommy says he's happy, too. That's why he swung me around."

I felt like an intruder.

Painfully, she spoke of her mother's death. "Daddy found her on the couch, and he thought she was asleep, but she wasn't asleep, she was dead." She fought to hold back her sobs.

Joanne—Susan—had trouble spelling not only Ganier but Susan. She was obviously illiterate.

She was not strong on names. Her brother was Reuben,

his wife Rachel, Old Man MacGregor, and Urket or Urkett, or Urkurt were neighbors. Few other names meant anything to her.

Yet one name was always sure to arouse her. This was Yancey's. She bridled when questioned about him, and a guard instantly went up.

"Do you have a neighbor Yancey?"

"He's not a neighbor."

"Now, who is he?"

"He's a man who worked for Tommy once."

"All right, what's his last name?"

"It's just Yancey."

"Just Yancey."

"Yes."

"He doesn't have a last name?"

"I don't know. They just call him Yancey."

"Did he stop working for Tommy?"

"Yes."

"Well, what happened?"

She paused. "I don't think I had better tell you."

"You can go ahead and tell me, if you want to."

"Don't want to." She was adamant.

The questioning shifted to the Marrow farmstead. "Are there any hills or mountains, or anything like that?"

"Just sort of rolly and good soil, some apple trees."

"How far are you from the water?"

"Not too far, about four miles, maybe four miles."

Susan was a true provincial. She knew that Montreal was in Quebec—her father's family was from there—but hadn't heard of Toronto until she was fully grown. It seemed almost incredible, except that Toronto's original name, York, may have survived in the backwoods country.

The session wasn't terribly convincing. Only two new names had come out—MacGregor and Urkett. Reuben and Rachel were a familiar combination, vaguely recalling some musty rhyme. And there was a puzzling contradiction. Joanne had first said MacIver was Mason Ganier, Susan's father, but later denied his previous paternity.

MacIver himself had wondered, guiltily, if he had pushed this relationship on Joanne. And if he had imposed one suggestion, couldn't he have others?

The psychiatrist had suggested quizzing Joanne, hypnotically, on the likely source of her subconscious information. Both she and MacIver readily agreed.

Joanne answered the first few questions easily, giving her MacIver name, her birthdate, October 22, 1948, her age fourteen, and the current date, June 17, 1963.

She was taken back, still as Joanne MacIver, to age thirteen, before the original sessions with her father.

"Have you ever heard the name Ganier?" she was now asked.

"No."

"Have you heard the name Susan?"

"Heard it in books."

"Tell me the name of a book in which you heard the name Susan?"

"There was a doll named Susan in a book, but it was a rag doll."

"What happened to that doll?"

"I think a dog bit the head off it and it got lost in the bushes."

"Did that doll have a husband?"

"It might have had a clown for a husband or a boy friend."

"What was the name of the boy friend?"

"Andy, I think."

At least, it wasn't Tommy.

The questioning turned to Reuben and Rachel.

"All right, now, have you ever heard the name Rachel?"

"Yes, in a song."

"You will be able to remember the song and repeat it for me?"

"'Reuben, Reuben, I've been thinking what a great world this would be.

"'If the men were all transported far beyond the Northern Sea.

"'Oh, my goodness, gracious, Rachel, what a queer world this would be.

"'If the men were all transported far beyond the Northern Sea.'"

The psychiatrist asked, "You like that song?"

"Not particularly."

"Where did you learn that song?"

"Public school."

"Now, Joanne, have you ever heard the name Mac-Gregor?"

"Yes."

"Where did you hear the name?"

"In the story, *Peter Rabbit.*"

"And what did Mr. MacGregor do?"

"He had a farm and Peter stole the lettuce and carrots."

"Have you heard the name Ames?"

A flat, "No."

"Did you ever hear the name Mason? Name in a book?"

"No, isn't a mason someone who works with bricks or cement?"

Asked whether she knew anybody named Tommy, she named three, one an eight-year-old boy.

"Have you heard the name Marrow?"

"No, the marrow in your bone, maybe?"

She knew two Catherines, schoolgirls, but no Yancey or McKelver.

The psychiatrist next brought her forward a bit in time
to October 30, 1962, three weeks after she had first been
hypnotized.

"Have you ever heard of Susan Ganier?"

She now answered, "Yes."

"Where does that name come from?"

"Apples."

"What about apples?"

"The farm."

"What sort of farm?"

"An ordinary farm."

"Have you seen the name on a farm?"

"I just remember about the farm and the apples."

"Where did you see that farm?"

"Before this life."

The father's assault on the girl's subconscious had either brought a dormant life experience to the fore at this
time, or the seeds of a purely subconscious experience
had been newly planted.

The testing continued: "Now, I want you to go back in
your memory, long before the present. I am going to
count from one to five, and you are going to be Susan
Ganier. It is going to be the day after your marriage, as
Susan Ganier. One . . . two . . . three . . . four . . . five. What's
your name?"

"Susan Ganier . . . I forgot . . . I got married yesterday. I
am Susan Marrow."

"What are you doing now?"

She had opened her eyes, sitting up suddenly. Her eyes
were glazed, and she didn't seem to recognize anybody,
including her father.

"How do you feel now?"

She replied uncertainly. "I don't seem to know who I
am. I don't seem like Joanne, or Susan, or anybody. I'm
not even like myself. In fact, I don't even seem to be here

at all." She glanced around the room with a troubled eye, and this wisely ended the session, the psychiatrist taking her back to the present.

His inquiry did not turn out as MacIver had hoped. He stayed for a weekend, chatting with a few people, including Arthur Eagles, whom he thought an impressionable witness. He was not impressed by the regression. Under hypnosis, he said, the subject was often apt to confuse incidents from the present experience with recollections of a prior life.

Three years after this latest session, there were still many gaps in the Susan Ganier story, which might be cleared by further questioning under hypnosis. I mentioned the possibility of Joanne's being regressed by an expert hypnotist, one not presently acquainted with the MacIvers or myself.

MacIver looked troubled. "I promised her I would never hypnotize her again; and that went for everybody." He blinked unhappily. "Of course, if you could convince her . . . " His voice trailed off helplessly.

"How can I when you can't?"

He looked at me oddly. "You might have more influence than you think."

I shrugged off this remark as another of MacIver's little mysteries.

Earlier, in my discussion with Joanne, I had sensed her boredom with her double-life role, but certainly she could not go around talking about being reincarnated without expecting attention.

"She should be used to the spotlight by this time," I said.

"You never get used to being scoffed at," MacIver said warmly.

I saw no logic in her not being hypnotized again at this point. The sessions would be as private as she wanted them, and nothing revealed that she objected to as painfully personal. This struck both Manuel and myself as eminently fair.

MacIver was still unhappy. "It's up to her," he said irresolutely.

Why was he now so protective, when his earlier efforts had blithely exposed her to embarrassment?

"I had no way of knowing then what would happen," he said. "I was just trying to generate enough attention to enlist the help of anybody who may have known of the Ganiers or Marrows."

Joanne was no stranger to publicity. She had already had moments of "glory." Three years before, there had been stories of her experience in the Toronto star and other metropolitan newspapers, and she had briefly starred on television.

How had all this come about?

MacIver rather lamely explained. Not getting anywhere with his search, he had inserted an ad in the Personal column of the Toronto *Star* on February 15, 1963. Sheepishly, he showed me a tear sheet from the classified section. I read with some astonishment:

"Anyone interested in assisting research of a case surpassing Bridey Murphy in importance and proven locally in Ontario. Contact M. Ganier, General Delivery, Orillia."

MacIver had the grace to blush. Yet, his ad was no more intriguing than its neighbors. For instance:

"Lynn R: Nothing too extravagant, let me fetch a piece of the moon. Nev."

Or:

"Your voice and smile an asset. A better success with it. Your wish always."

As I pored over the "Agony" column, Dave Manuel asked, "So then what happened?"

MacIver replied briskly. "I heard from a private detective who was looking for a fee; two or three people who believed in reincarnation and wanted to do something about it, and a television show. The TV people pretended a purely personal interest at first, but then when they discovered ours was a serious project, they asked Joanne to go on their show in Toronto."

TV commentator Pierre Berton, an obvious skeptic, had treated Joanne's claims tongue-in-cheek, but interest in Joanne's experience was so strong that the show was subsequently rerun.

MacIver next turned for research help to the Theosophical Society in Canada, which held as self-evident truth that man developed through the lessons carried from one life to another. They weren't interested. "They believed in reincarnation anyway," MacIver said, "and so had nothing to prove."

Nevertheless, the Theosophical Society brought the case to the attention of Allen Spraggett, the Toronto *Star's* religion editor, and Spraggett was sufficiently intrigued to investigate.

MacIver, already irked by snide reactions to the telecast, agreed to a story only if Joanne's anonymity was preserved, but withdrew this objection on the newspaper's insistence that the article would be meaningless without her name.

Spraggett dispassionately cited the features which seemed to distinguish the MacIver claims from most parlor regressions:

"There was a village named Massie located in Holland Township near Owen Sound.

"The name is still used by residents of the area, although it does not appear on most maps. Today, the spot is just a crossroads. But a century ago it boasted a horseshoe nail factory and two hundred inhabitants.

"Arthur Eagles of Woodford—an octogenarian who

has lived in the area all his life—signed an affidavit attesting that he knew a Susan Marrow, the widow of Thomas Marrow. He said that as a young man he used to drive her to Owen Sound in the buggy to shop.

"Vail's Point, mentioned by Susan Ganier, does exist.

"Named after a very early settler, it is the apex of a promontory which juts out into Georgian Bay between Owen Sound and Meaford.

"Susan Ganier mentioned a good friend of hers, a Mrs. Speedie, who was postmistress in the neighboring village of Annan. Mrs. Speedie's tombstones can be seen in Annan today. She died in 1909."

Spraggett had been impressed by the psychiatrist's session. "Listening to the tape," he wrote, "one is struck by the two things: the thoroughness of the psychiatrist's cross-examination, and the insistence with which the hypnotized Joanne stuck to her story."

He had talked to the psychiatrist, who had been convinced there was no fraud. "I am sure that there is no trickery involved. Joanne and her father are sincere, well-adjusted people." He found the evidence tantalizing but fragmentary, after a weekend of research.

Spraggett's story ran on page one, on February 6, 1965. With it was a companion piece, reporting the bizarrely psychic experiences of two ultrasensitive reporters: Henry Thoreau and Charles Dickens. Thoreau's experience was uncritically subjective. "I have a distinct recollection of having been with Jesus Christ. I must have been one of His disciples."

Dickens' experience was more like my own. "Charles Dickens tells of stumbling onto a scene which he had never visited before which—strangely—he remembered. 'If I had been murdered there in some former life I could not have seemed to remember the place more thoroughly or with more emphatic chilling of the blood.'"

Joanne had a brief run. Two days after the *Star's* article, the Toronto *Telegram* dryly front-paged:

"Orillia's Joanne MacIver, whose father led her back to an earlier life during a hypnotic trance, isn't satisfied with a double identity. Her claim that she lived and died in the 19th Century as Susan Marrow, widow, was followed by details of even earlier appearances: On a St. Lawrence River farm in 1792; in Virginia, in 1701, when she fled to Canada to escape slavery with her baby, and in Africa in 784."

"They didn't take the affair very seriously," I remarked.

MacIver shrugged. "Joanne hasn't had an easy time. She's even been attacked on the radio. That's one of the reasons she's not terribly interested in going ahead."

That brought up a point. "Then who is interested?"

MacIver shifted around in his chair, confronting us with a gleam in his eye. "Wouldn't it be wonderful," he enthused, "if we could prove out reincarnation right here in Orillia."

I saw MacIver's position clearly now for perhaps the first time. Joanne's experience had given him new horizons which he could hardly have hoped for otherwise at this stage of life. He had been hopelessly bogged down in a deadly nine to five routine, one dull day stretching predictably after another, and then, boom—through his daughter—he had suddenly become a man of affairs. All along the road of life there had been frustration. In the Air Force, he had wanted to fly, and had been grounded instead. In marriage, he had sought romance and travel, and Edna had preferred to sit in Orillia and produce children. He dreamed of adventure and she of selling real estate. Even his boat, sprawled inconclusively on his lawn, had sprung out of the new zeal brought on by his overnight plunge into the heady waters of reincarnation. Suddenly, he had become a figure to whom writers and scientists gave their reasoned attention. Librarians and archivists consulted with him gravely, neighbors pointed him out. He was a celebrity, the "father of the girl who had lived before."

He not only interested people but influenced them, involving the most unlikely individuals in his search. Young Torrance's father, a physician, was one of the few immune to the MacIver magic. "Poppycock," was his comment, "pure poppycock."

MacIver's feathers were not ruffled. He merely went on bringing new people into an inquiry that seemed to go off in all directions at once. It would be arduous going over MacIver's tracks, not to mention seeking new clues. But needing to start somewhere, I decided to check the Eagles deposition with his niece, Ruby Scott, this document being as specific as anything I had seen yet.

As Mrs. Scott lived in town, this could be readily arranged.

MacIver nodded equably. "Yes, she's very interested in the project," he said. "We can call on her anytime."

"I think I'll drop over with Dave Manuel," I said.

His face dropped. "Don't you want me to introduce you?"

"I can manage," I said.

"As you say," he pouted, "but I thought we were in this together."

Always diplomatic, Dave cut in hastily, "We have all the confidence in the world in you, Ken, but you surely see the need for an independent investigation."

MacIver swallowed hard, but in a few moments was in good spirits. "Mrs. Scott is very much interested in Joanne," he said jauntily, "very much interested."

Mrs. Scott was a gentle woman, with a heavily seamed face and careworn features. Her mother had been Arthur Eagles' sister, and she remembered him well. She was familiar with the deposition, and could vouch for the signature. With quiet pride, she pointed out that her uncle was widely known and respected throughout the Sydenham-St. Vincent area. "If he said he remembered Susan Marrow," she smiled, "then he remembered Susan Marrow. He had a mind like a steel trap."

Nearing seventy herself, she recalled the Twin Churches which Joanne had mentioned in one session. "They were on the township dividing line," she said, "down from Vail's Point, where the Eagles family had their sawmill."

She had lived in the Sydenham area as a child, and recalled how even then, before the automobile and the popularity of the telephone, communication was difficult. The winters were incredibly harsh and long; huge banks of snow were often piled to the tops of the telegraph poles. "We had only a few weeks of good weather in those days," she reflected, "but the winters have become increasingly milder in recent years."

"Can you remember any very old people besides your uncle in that area?" I asked.

She shook her head. "I haven't lived there for a good many years, but even so, nearly all of my uncle's contemporaries have long passed on." She thought a moment. "You are going to have a time finding anybody to check anything with from before the turn of the century."

I had already suspected this, but felt there must be two or three octogenarians around if I looked hard enough.

Mrs. Scott had only a passing acquaintance with the MacIvers. She had been pleasantly impressed by Joanne, and by MacIver, for that matter. They were the kind of people she had known all her life; plain, unpretentious, and unpresuming. She had no reason not to trust them.

We got around to Joanne's previous-life experience.

Mrs. Scott looked back at me with eyes that had seen a good deal of living. "It wouldn't surprise me. The Mac-

Ivers seem like honest people." Her thoughtful eyes held mine. "It does seem as though there must be a reason for it. Doesn't the Book say that little children shall lead us?"

While undecided on reincarnation, she still felt there was more to life than the five senses. "I don't laugh at anything that reveals the Lord's interest in us," she said quietly.

I left a little easier than I had arrived. Eagles had signed the statement, and he was essentially of sound mind. That, as Dave agreed, was a start.

I turned now to the session in which Joanne first became Susan Ganier. Paul Torrance, now twenty, was in Toronto that weekend working, but eighteen-year-old Barbara White, the second witness, was employed in a local restaurant, and brightly available.

We sat down together in a shaded glade in the White backyard, around a picnic table, while a big angry-looking dog strained at his leash. Barbara was a pleasant-faced girl, with an intelligent glint in her eye.

She had no difficulty recalling the two sessions. "How could I forget them?" She smiled.

She had been quite friendly with Joanne, a classmate, but they had drifted apart, as school chums often do, and she saw her seldom of late, though they lived in the same block. "I like her all right," she shrugged, "we just don't have much in common any more."

I digressed momentarily. "Was Joanne popular in school?"

Barbara's mouth turned down. "Many of the boys liked her; I don't think she cared much what the girls thought."

"She's quite attractive," I said.

"Oh, yes, the boys liked her."

I studied the girl across from me for a long moment. "You think she was overly aggressive, don't you?"

She looked away, without saying anything.

"You know," she said finally, changing the subject, "there was a complete change in Joanne's personality under hypnosis. I never saw anything like it. Nobody could have made that up, not even the greatest actor. She really had to feel what she was going through, and she made you feel it. It was truly shocking when she saw that pig stuck, and then when she thought she was being attacked—if you could have heard her scream—I never saw anything like it before, she actually bared her teeth . . . "

They had been playing cards when the conversation got on to hypnosis, and Paul said that nobody could hypnotize him. When Joanne proudly mentioned that her father had once done hypnosis for entertainment, the children eagerly picked up the suggestion that he try his skill.

Paul Torrance had made notes of one session, and together we ran through them as Barbara kept nodding. "That's very much the way I remember it."

"Was there any possibility," I asked, "that the session was deliberately set up?"

She looked puzzled. "Joanne's father didn't even know what we had been talking about. He was in another room. And it all happened quite spontaneously. Actually, he was even more surprised than we were when Joanne went all the way back into another life, and he didn't seem to know what to do about it."

There had been nothing prearranged about her visit. "We just dropped around after dinner, as we often did. Paul lived across the street, and I in a neighboring house down the way."

Now that she had four years to think about it, had the experience affected her thinking in any way?

She laughed pleasantly. "I hadn't thought anything about reincarnation before, but it occurred to me at the time that Joanne must certainly have lived before, since she was apparently reliving her lives right in front of us. As I reasoned it then, the experience had to come out of somewhere."

But away from the dramatic impact of the moment, looking back on it calmly, she had not been able to reconcile rebirth with her own conventional religious beliefs. She was no longer sure what Joanne's experience signified.

"Still," she said, "looking at her, as she went through it, you had to believe that it was coming out of her own experience."

"Why couldn't it all have been pure fantasy?"

She shook her head. "The things she went through, together with her reactions, were more realistic than anything happening in a class or on a date. It sent the chills up your spine."

"You have no doubt then that it was completely unrehearsed?"

She gave me a clear look. "There is no question of that, not the slightest."

It had been a rather pleasant interview and there was no doubting Barbara's impartiality. As she saw it, the first session was sparked, not by Joanne or MacIver, but by Paul Torrance's skepticism.

That night Dave asked how things were shaping up.

"In what life?"

"The one that's beginning tomorrow," he said.

"It'll keep till then," I said.

"How about those blue eyes?" he smiled slyly.

"We'll know more about them tomorrow."

I closed my eyes gratefully, but tired as I was I couldn't get off to sleep, my thoughts revolving oddly enough not around Joanne's subconscious experience but my own.

Was my *déjà vu* the result of an overfired imagination.

Had my preoccupation with reincarnation activated my subconscious in some inexplicable way? If it was purely a clairvoyant impression, perhaps a dream hazily remembered, why had I felt so strong a sense of oppression? My thoughts galloped on, unreined. If I, or some disembodied part of me, some unquenchable atom of indestructible energy, had roamed through this community a hundred years or more ago, in what form had this adventure occurred? How exciting to have been Samuel de Champlain, the French explorer who camped on Lake Couchiching three hundred and fifty years before, or heroic General Steele, whose statue decorated the lawn of the public library, or even a gallant Huron chief who desperately gave ground to the encroaching whites.

I had steeped myself in Orillia's past, until I was as well informed as any hometown booster. Orillia was the Sunshine Town, the Mariposa of essayist Stephen Leacock, even in death Orillia's leading celebrity. Its long history antedated the white man. The earliest known settlers were the Hurons. The Iroquois drove out the Hurons, and the Ojibways and Chippewas later moved in. In 1831, the English restricted the Indians to reservations, and in 1838, gave whites settlement privileges, moving the Indians out again.

Orillia was the last link in the Underground Railroad, over which fugitive slaves were ferried from the States, automatically free the moment they touched Canadian soil. Many blacks stayed on, forming a community at nearby Oro, where their church still stood. But most eventually rebelled at the climate and drifted away.

Orillia prided itself on its lack of change. Yellowed photographs of the downtown area, showing Mississaga, the main street, before the turn of the century, could have been snapped only the day before except for a few renovated storefronts and the absence of overhead wires. Most residents were old stock English, Scottish, Irish, in the durable mold of their forebears. They looked like them, dressed like them, and sighed wistfully for the old ways, the old disciplines, and teachers who believed in not spoiling a child by sparing the rod:

> *Barbara Ross, she went to church*
> *And prayed to the Lord on Sunday.*
> *She prayed to the Lord to give her strength.*
> *To whip the boys on Monday.*

Barbara Ross was my last waking thought. The next thing I knew, the sun streaming through a fold in the drapes told me it was morning. I moved out onto the balcony for a breath of Canadian air. It was a little snappy, but the sky was clear, the sun friendly, and beautiful Couchiching lay before me, its glasslike surface mirroring the blue sky overhead. I stood for a moment, admiring the view, watching the trees stir with the breeze, when again, without warning, a strong feeling of nostalgia stole over me. My eyes swept the lake, the sense of familiarity growing, as I wondered without conviction whether my imagination was playing me tricks. I retired to my room, strangely depressed.

At breakfast, I carefully forbore mention of my new bout with *déjà vu.* We had a quiet meal, Dave apparently reacting to my own mood. The silence was broken, as we climbed into his car and headed for the MacIver home. "Will she stand for being hypnotized again?" Dave asked.

I shrugged. "Only her subconscious can fill the many gaps that now exist."

At Braemar, Joanne was waiting. She looked very much the teenager in blouse and mini-like skirt, and yet there was a contrasting assurance that bespoke a calm maturity.

At this time, I met Horace Smith, a local businessman, who, according to MacIver, had predicted my arrival.

Smith was a heavy-shouldered man of fifty or so, who spoke with a decided burr. He fancied himself as being psychically endowed. Initiated by MacIver into the mystic art of dowsing, he frequently moved across Mississaga Street, smiling contentedly as his steel coathanger, twisted into twin forks, nodded dramatically over the underground sewer pipes.

Smith's dark face lit up as Joanne and I discussed the best place for a quiet tête-à-tête. "Why not drive around?" he said. "There's nothing more private."

Joanne agreeing, we drove aimlessly through the streets, my mind framing questions while my eyes roamed restlessly for familiar landmarks. Joanne sat silently, looking beautiful without trying.

"How," I began, "did it feel to be hypnotized?"

She frowned, without looking at me. "It varied with what came out."

In trance she was not completely unawares. "I could hear my father's voice," she said softly, "and all other people's voices, too, even when they whispered. I could hear the sounds of cars in the street outside, and I felt warm and comfortable and relaxed. Then, after a while, there was a roaring in my ears, like an express train. I could feel myself falling. There didn't seem to be any bottom to it—just down, down, down, like dropping gently through a bed of feathers that wouldn't quite hold me. I was fading away. I couldn't see anything, just a shadowy grayness and a feeling of nothingness."

As usual, she had expressed herself remarkably well.

This reaction had occurred even as the trance was being induced. With the actual regression, the sensation of falling, and the noise, abruptly ceased. "Then," she recalled quietly, "a scene appeared, a farm scene, very clear in all its colors, just as in real life. It was quite natural, and my reactions were the same as though I was fully awake."

Joanne's conscious awareness of her surroundings diminished as the subconscious took over. When her father finally awakened her, not cutting off her memory, she felt strangely confused, blindly resisting a return to the conscious. "Somehow, I didn't want to be awakened. It was so much easier to go back and see the farm and watch the pleasant things that I remembered." Her blue eyes took on a faraway look I was to know so well. "It's odd," she said, "but when I came to, I was not myself. I was that other person for a time, and it took an effort of will to come back to my real self."

"And what is your real self?" I asked.

She looked out the window. "I'm not so sure any more."

I laughed. "Aren't you being a bit theatrical?"

She moved her shoulders ever so slightly. "I just can't help what people think." Her eyes fixed on mine. "I just don't know how much of what I am now is influenced by the desires and frustrations of a previous life."

"Do you really believe that?"

"Do you believe what you are?"

"That's not quite the same," I said. "You can't expect anybody to believe you lived before by just saying so."

"There's much more to it than that, particularly in the way a reborn life expresses what is brought over from the past." She looked at me reflectively. "Why do we feel that we knew each other before?"

"That happens to many people," I said.

She regarded me scornfully. "Of course it does, for the same reason."

"It could be *déjà vu*," I said. "I've had an experience of that already."

She looked puzzled. "What's that?"

As I explained, she laughed ironically. "How can you accept that, and not reincarnation?"

"*Déjà vu* establishes itself in its occurrence."

"And so does reincarnation—it just doesn't fit into any intellectually acceptable pattern."

Again I remarked that she spoke with a fluency well beyond her age and background.

"I've always been old," she commented, without appearing complimented. "I was old when I married Tommy, and I was old when he died, old and incomplete."

I knew what she was thinking of. Childlessness and premature widowhood had been Susan's karma. One could only speculate what Joanne would make of it.

I fell into the easy smugness of older people. "Just make sure that your transplanted desire for children doesn't run off with you."

Twin dimples came to her cheeks. "I'll marry," she said placidly, "whoever I am meant to marry." She pondered a while, then gave me a sidelong glance. "Are you driving to Massie before going back?"

"No, should I?"

"You might find it interesting."

"I can do that if and when I return." I regarded her out of the corner of my eye. "If we get on with it," I said, "you would have to be hypnotized again."

She shook her head. "I've been hypnotized enough."

"New leads might develop from additional questioning."

Her voice was edgy. "I'd like to please Dad, but I really am tired of it."

"Don't you like the center of the stage?"

She grimaced. "It was fun at first, but people began thinking I was some kind of nut or worse."

"But aren't you interested in knowing more about Susan Ganier?"

"I know who I was."

I laughed. "Isn't it more important to know who you are?"

"The only life you can express," she agreed, "is the one you live now."

I was again struck by her inexplicable maturity.

"There are times," she went on, "when I feel far more knowledgeable than my father, but I respect his views."

A warning seemed indicated at this point. "If you go ahead," I said, "your whole life may be drastically changed. You may become a celebrity of sorts and Orillia may become too small to hold you."

I looked at her appreciatively. She had a peaches-and-cream complexion, a high domed forehead, long auburn hair, a determined chin and mouth, a good straight nose, and, of course, blue eyes. All in all, it added up to something special.

"I've considered all that," she said calmly, "but when I meet the right man and marry, that will put a clamp on it."

I had never heard this expression before. "You could still have a career."

Her lips tightened. "I'm here to marry and have children. I couldn't have children the last time."

I fell in with her mood. "You weren't very nice to your children, from what I heard."

Her eyebrows raised questioningly.

I recalled the African life, in which a helpless brood of six had been left to the ants.

"That wasn't very nice, was it?" she agreed, with a laugh.

"I suppose hypnosis, evoking what it did, was a rather trying experience."

"In more ways than one," she affirmed. "To begin with, after the first session, I found it hard to fathom a previous life. But everyone else in the room was very enthused, and started speculating about it." She looked up apologetically. "That is not saying they believed in reincarnation, but they were interested in seeing me rehypnotized, to find out the validity of it all. Frankly, I was quite skeptical. I found it hard to understand, and thoughts of my having made the whole thing up entered my mind. But something deep inside of me resisted this explanation and I had the feeling that this thing was true. So my curiosity and their enthusiasm had me agreeing to another session."

Among her peers, Joanne was barely tolerated. Occasionally, a classmate would point mockingly to his head as she walked by. But it wasn't until the Pierre Berton television show that she found herself a controversial figure. She was cruelly lampooned behind her back and to her face. Her first high school year was a trial. In student clusters in the corridors, her approach was a signal for the whispering to start. Or bolder students would cat-call, "Hey, baby, how go all the lives?"

Teachers were cool, considering her a spotlight-seeker. Her relatives were publicly embarrassed and suggested her parents talk some sense into her, not realizing that her father virtually shared this previous life of hers.

"You name it, and people called me it," Joanne observed mildly. "Queer, crazy, insane, a liar, a publicity hound, a money-seeker."

The last caught my attention.

"And how were you to make money?"

She laughed disdainfully. "I got hardly anything out of the television."

She fell to musing. "I don't regret any of it now. It made me mature in a hurry, as I had to learn to evaluate things. By this time I accepted reincarnation as a plausible way of life, and this helped me tolerate criticism. If I had reacted angrily or questioned my own motivations, the reincarnation theory would have suffered, since I was now identified with it."

She treated herself to a little inspirational verse whenever the going got sticky:

> *Dare to be a Daniel*
> *Dare to stand alone*
> *Dare to have a purpose firm*
> *And dare to make it known.*

I laughed. Had she actually felt herself in the lion's den? There was a glint of steel in her eyes.

"It made me realize how small-minded small-town people can be. They wouldn't even listen to the truth, but rejected it without a hearing. Regular churchgoers were the loudest objectors and said the nastiest things."

"You got a hearing on TV," I put in.

She snorted. "Mr. Berton was not interested in my experience as evidence of reincarnation. He just thought it would make a good laugh for his show. Before taping time, he hurriedly skimmed through my father's notes, and to this day I don't think he understands what the whole thing was about."

This seemed a possible injustice.

"Not really," she said, "obviously from what he said, he thought we were after publicity and gain." She looked at me squarely. "I can vouch for one thing. I wasn't interested in either."

"What were you interested in?"

She thought a moment, frowning. "I was carried along at first with the idea of being the one to establish something positive and uplifting to the world. I didn't know what else had been said or done in this field, so it was all new and wonderful to me."

"But surely you had heard of reincarnation?"

"My father occasionally mentioned reincarnation before I was hypnotized, but I had not thought about it.

Now the whole idea plopped right into my lap."

Had it affected her everyday thinking?

Her eyes lit up like a sunny day. "I don't think I ever thought deeply before. Now I began thinking hard about what life was about."

At seventeen, this was an undertaking.

She began pondering life's vagaries. Some people, however undeserving, seemed to monopolize life's rewards; others, honest and God-fearing, suffered only hardship and grief. If God was all-loving, forgiving, supremely impartial, then why were people created unequally to begin with? Why did some have all the success and good fortune, others nothing?

Contemplating the various aspects of reincarnation, she realized it could be applied instructively to explain injustices and inequities, and this, she felt, was to be her contribution to a confused world.

"Reincarnation could be compared to attending school. Each life is a grade. If one learns his lessons well, he is promoted to a higher grade. But if he doesn't understand, he must repeat his year."

It was a pretty good analogy.

She elaborated. "Reincarnation works this way, generally. If a person makes mistakes, fails to realize he has made them, and refuses to better himself, in his next life he must be made to realize his faults."

She seemed to have it all figured out.

She smiled. "I personify what we're talking about."

"How do you see it applying specifically?" I asked.

"If a person is mean or deceitful, in his next life someone may be like that to him. As you sow, so shall you reap, doesn't apply to this life, as we can see. A rich man, for instance, is either being rewarded or tested—to see how he treats this blessing."

"Suppose a person had all he wanted of life, and

didn't want to come back?"

Man proposeth, God disposeth—it was as simple as all that.

She propounded a Hindu view, "When a person has perfected himself after many lives, his cycle of reincarnation will end in communion with God."

Smilingly, she anticipated my next question.

"I have quite a few lives to go," she said, "before perfection."

I chose to take her remark seriously. "There haven't been many perfect lives since Christ."

"Perfect in the sense of correcting shortcomings," she amended. "There have been many like that."

At times it was difficult to realize that she was in many respects a perfectly normal, average teenager, who had represented her high school in a provincial track meet only the day before.

I couldn't resist. "How did you do in the 220-yard dash?"

"Not very well," she replied seriously. "I got off to a bad start, and besides I hadn't been training as I should."

"You may suffer for that in the next life."

She grimaced. "I wouldn't worry about that if I were you."

As she sat, musing, I felt an impulse to reach over reassuringly, reminded of Browning's ode to a maiden fair:

> *Just because I was thrice as old,*
> *And our paths in the world diverged so wide,*
> *Each was nought to each, must I be told?*
> *We were fellow mortals, nought beside.*
> *I claim you still for my own love's sake,*
> *Delayed it may be for more lives yet.*

My reverie was rudely interrupted. "I have to get back," Joanne said. "Tag will be waiting."

I pointed the car homeward.

"Will you consent to be hypnotized?" I asked.

She hesitated.

"There are so many avenues yet to explore," I said, "but don't if you have the slightest misgiving."

Her mouth set in a thin line. "All right, if it's what Dad wants."

"What do you want—that's what counts?"

"I'd like people to think seriously about reincarnation. It could give them new understanding of God and of their place in His universe."

"And it has done that for you?"

"I'm vastly more sure of myself since I know what I'm here for and where I'm going. It has given me a certain peace and more tolerant outlook, though I'm still often taken for a crazy, mixed-up teenager."

What had the English apostle of reincarnation, the Reverend Leslie Weatherhead, said? "In the same family some children seem to have a strange wisdom, to be 'old souls,' to have a maturity beyond their years . . . whereas some adults behave like silly children."

MacIver was nervously awaiting us, and so was Tag.

"Well?" MacIver said.

I was perfectly matter-of-fact. "Joanne has put the hypnosis up to you."

"Who would you get?" he asked.

"Somebody recognized, who has never met any of us."

"Fine," he said, "if it's all right with Joanne."

Events had moved differently than I could have anticipated, and I now had to consider how objective I could be when my own feelings were involved.

"I will have to talk over the project in New York," I told MacIver.

His face fell, but Joanne was supremely indifferent. The last I saw her, before heading back, she was skipping out the door, arm in arm with a pipe-chewing Tag.

In three or four hours, as a cab carried me from La Guardia Field to midtown Manhattan, I marveled at the transition from the simple rusticity of Upper Canada to the nerve center of all the ceaseless striving that made this the biggest anthill of all. The change was at least as great as Joanne had made in two lifetimes.

In New York, I conferred with many hypnotists psychiatrists, psychologists, internists, laymen. I wanted a skilled, independent operator, motivated principally by curiosity or adventure. He would be his own man.

Also, to be sure, I thought often of Joanne, without any conclusion forming in my mind. Meanwhile, considering my next move, I did some homework. As the world center of reincarnation, where the diseased and downtrodden stoically accepted their karma, India was naturally a leader in exploring the justifying concept of rebirth.

Professor Hamendra Banerjee, a parapsychologist of the University of Rajasthan, Jaipur, had spent years "seeking a scientific explanation of those rare cases in which people have shown an astounding ability to recall details of past lives." One of his two hundred cases concerned a ten-year-old girl whose father was a school inspector in Chatarpur, central India. "From early life," Reuters news service reported, "Swarna Lata claimed that her real home was at Katni, a town several miles away, and that she had two sons. She described the house with remarkable accuracy, as it had been eighteen years previously."

Curiously, a housewife, Bindia Devi, had died of a heart attack just eighteen years earlier in the house described by Swarna Lata. She left two sons.

Banerjee, surprisingly, didn't attribute this apparent subconscious recall to reincarnation but to extracerebral memory—extrasensory perception. For him, reincarnation presupposed a spiritual translation of one life to another, and there had been no spiritual experience here.

His research took him abroad to other countries. In England, he investigated the "reborn" twins, Jennifer and Gillian Pollack. Soon after the girls' birth in 1958, Mr. and Mrs. John Pollack of Whitley Bay, Northumberland, felt the children were reincarnations of two other daughters, Joanna, eleven, and Jacqueline, six, run down by a car seventeen months before.

Twin Gillian, the Pollacks said, had striking memory hangovers. Though the fatal accident was never discussed around her, she described Jacqueline's injuries in detail—and correctly picked out Joanna's toys in the attic. Jennifer seemed to have even greater recall. Seeing a doll that had been put away after the two deaths, she cried, "That's my Mary," the name given by the children. One day, Pollack had put on an old smock, in disuse since Mrs. Pollack wore it to school the morning the two girls were killed. Jennifer asked, "Why are you wearing Mummy's coat, the one she used to wear at school?"

There was a puzzling carryover physically. Jennifer, the younger twin by four minutes, had an unusual white scar slanting down her forehead above the right eye. Jacqueline, the younger sister, to whom she was relating, had an identical scar, result of a fall when three years old. Also, Jennifer had a distinctive birthmark above her left hip, and so had Jacqueline. The family considered these "signs."

The father was thoroughly convinced. "I am a convert to Roman Catholicism," he said, "and as such I am told I cannot believe in reincarnation because the Church forbids it. But I can no longer accept this in view of what both my wife and I have witnessed and heard through the twins."

Skeptics were quick to pick holes. They noted that Pollack first began to think of the girls being reborn when his wife became pregnant. He insisted she was having twins when the doctor could detect only one heartbeat. But a week later Pollack was proven right.

Obviously, reincarnated, the twins doubly mitigated a parental sense of loss. The Pollacks no longer visit their children's graves. "We feel," Pollack said, "that they are back with us in the form of twins."

This account was by no means extraordinary. As I sat down one day with my disbelieving editor, he recalled the experience of an American recently met in Bermuda.

They had been thrown together at a small party. My editor had been chatting with novelist F. Van Wyck Mason and an American naval captain, when they were joined by A. C. Campbell, a retired insurance executive, and his wife. The conversation was the usual cocktail hour fare, until the American Campbell, known as a hardheaded businessman, announced he would soon be traveling to Sicily to visit his birthplace.

Politely, somebody asked, "When was that?"

"Early in the eighteenth century," Campbell solemnly replied.

The party suddenly became quiet. "You could have heard an olive drop," my editor recalled.

As all eyes turned on him, Campbell explained, without a trace of self-consciousness, "Ever since I was a boy I have known I lived before in Sicily and Italy. Visiting the mainland, I have been irresistibly drawn toward cities and sites that were familiar though I never saw them in this century." He was able to visualize streets, buildings, and shorelines, and tell his wife about them beforehand.

My editor, weaned on the Bridey Murphy story, was naturally intrigued. "Did your remembrance come under trance?" he asked.

Campbell shook his head. "There is really nothing

mysterious about my experience, nothing occult. It is just something I've always known, just as I know I am here in Bermuda."

Reincarnation as a philosophy had no significance for him. His was a purely personal experience, so strong, that as a man of practical affairs, he was impelled to act on it. Having always visualized a villa in Sicily as his birthplace, he drew up a description from memory, and engaged private investigators to locate the original.

They had no luck. But this did not faze him. Obviously, like so many others, the house had been torn down long before.

But Campbell had remembered other buildings and sites, and his sleuths were now on their trail.

The story had certain implications, but my editor, like myself, was not intellectually disposed toward reincarnation.

"What made this practical man so sure he had lived before?" I wondered.

My editor frowned. "It was probably a simple case of *déjà vu.*"

"Is it possible," I asked, "that some are given a glimpse of the past, as others sometimes see the future?"

He shrugged. "For what reason?"

It was a good question, which I pondered even as I researched the potentialities of hypnosis. Through a respected and progressive physician, I had met hypnotist Joseph Lampl, founder of the Academy of Applied Mental Sciences in New York. Lampl lectured, practiced hypnotherapy, and taught hypnosis to serious practitioners like the physician who had sent me on to him.

He was a born skeptic. "Reincarnation?" he exclaimed. "I've never seen any proof of it." He laughed sardonically. "Anybody you regress comes up with a previous life; I'm only surprised if their recall doesn't check out."

"How do you account for such accurate recall?" I asked.

His lean, saturnine face darkened into a scowl. "It could be extrasensory perception. Expanded through hypnosis or drugs like LSD, the mind often seems to have boundless powers."

"What mind?" I asked.

He looked puzzled.

"Conscious or subconscious?"

"It's not that simple. I've been hypnotizing people for twenty years, and the more I do, the more I feel there's merely an expansion of consciousness."

"How can consciousness suddenly become aware of something that wasn't there before?"

"Conscious and subconscious are merely convenient labels. We associate supermemory, clairvoyant impressions, dreams, with the subconscious, deductive reasoning with the conscious. But they may overlap with the subconscious seeping its impressions to the conscious, without individual awareness of the events forming these impressions."

It sounded rather complex to me.

"Not really," he said. "Most of us have conscious impressions of people. We may like or dislike a certain politician without remembering exactly why. The specific incident that formed our impression is forgotten, but the impression remains."

In a way, he made a case for the vaguely familiar recollections cited as evidence of reincarnation, the unexplained aptitudes of a Mozart or Josef Hofmann, the exalting sense of inner direction that held some to a course fraught with obstacles.

However, like Virginia Tighe of Bridey Murphy fame, Joe thought racial memory—not reincarnation—responsible for past-life impressions hazily distilled from a smoky past. "Some scientists," he observed, "believe that people are born with certain patterns engraved on their brains, which may be the source of racial memory, or"—he grinned—"reincarnation."

"This theory," I pointed out, "could account for a Bridey Murphy, whose recollections were of an Ireland where her ancestors had actually lived. But it doesn't explain individuals who recall lands—and languages—where their forebears never were."

Joe wasn't impressed. "The fact that people speak strange languages unconsciously that they never knew consciously may arise from some factor we don't even know about. Whatever is dredged out of the subconscious must form some pattern with life itself to mean anything. If anybody comes back, they come back for a reason—and it's not your reason necessarily."

He had seen the subconscious opened under LSD as well as hypnosis. In one notable case, a young woman had the same startling experience under both LSD and hypnosis. She was strangled to death.

In her LSD trip, she suffered the sensation of being choked by a man whose face was vaguely hidden from her. She had the distinct impression that the assailant was actually a young man she was dating. Panicky, she broke off with him, then, hoping to salvage the relationship, she turned to a hypnotist who regressed her before birth. She was on a desert with a swarthy young man. They had wandered for days on the hot sand, and were slowly expiring of thirst. He spoke to her tenderly, in a language later identified as Arabic, and then, hazily, as she lay in the sand, too weak to move, she realized why he was tearfully bending over her. He was about to strangle her. But this, she realized now, was an act of love. He was sparing her a far more horrible lingering death.

When she came out of it, she was no longer troubled. She saw it clearly now. The LSD experience, instead of

foreshadowing her death, had raised the lid on a previous life. "It was my past I had glimpsed, not my future, so
there was nothing to worry about."

While she had regained confidence through the revelation of her subconscious, Joe Lampl was considerably
less impressed. "As I said before," he stressed, "none of
this, whether spontaneously, under hypnosis, or LSD,
has any significance unless it forms a consequential pattern with the life of the individual."

Banerjee had made a similar point, equating reincarnation with the translation of a spiritual experience, but
the meaning of this was unclear.

"The life they are living now," Joe explained patiently,
"must flow out of whatever has gone before, shaping the
choices they have to make. Otherwise, there isn't any
point to any of it, and the whole recall could be purely
clairvoyant."

Coldly, he assessed the young woman's experience.
"There's a certain ostensible confirmation, because of
the similarity of the death recall, but it still could be racial or genetic memory—a flash from the past—or, some
phenomenon we don't even know about." He smiled
thinly. "Her thinking she lived before doesn't make it
so"—he eyed me quizzically—"any more than with the
girl in Canada."

The idea grew on me that Joe was the hypnotist I
wanted in Orillia with me. He was not the man to be
bowled over by an intriguing story—or face.

"How would you like to hypnotize this Canadian girl?"
I asked.

He laughed mirthlessly. "And make her live again? Why
not?"

I appealed to his vanity. "I want somebody completely
independent, completely disinterested materially,
somebody who is his own man. Would you be curious

enough to tackle the project on your own time, in your own way?"

A smile spread slowly over his Machiavellian-like face. "Why not? I've worked for nothing before. Besides, I'd like to meet this fabulous wonder with the blue eyes and the great hypnotist, her father."

"Would you anticipate difficulties in view of her feelings about being hypnotized?"

"Anybody with a knowledge of the technique can hypnotize another person. The girl is apparently a good subject. But the susceptible are just as strong-willed as those who resist hypnosis. The only difference is they are not continually blocking, not as apprehensive as to what may be revealed once the conscious barriers are removed."

And so I had found a partner in my venture, if and when the final search for Susan Ganier began.

As the days wore into weeks, without any decision on my part, I became increasingly introspective about my own experience in Orillia. I didn't accept reincarnation, and nothing I had observed or been told did more than intrigue me. However, I was sufficiently sophisticated to understand that my own limitation was no basis for rejecting what I didn't know about. In an infinite universe of billions of stars and planets, anything the Creator chose to do was possible. Man, as St. Thomas Aquinas had pointed out, had no surprises for God.

Meanwhile, I was being prodded by my editor in New York and by Dave Manuel in Canada. Dave apparently felt that an expository presentation of reincarnation could point up the value of combining certain aspects of Eastern and Western thought. "If the consummate earthly goal of Eastern man is to achieve sublime contemplation and oral perfection," Dave wrote, "then it would appear that the equivalent goal of Western man must be creation, be it artistic, structural, industrial or philanthropical."

Now what did this have to do with reincarnation?

"Through meditation, Eastern man removes the lid on his subconscious and psychic power, and belief in reincarnation inevitably follows. So Western man, convinced of reincarnation, would inevitably embrace meditation as part of his way of life."

The young editor seemed alert to the spiritual lag threatening our technologically advanced social structure—the revolt of the student generation against traditional moral values, the reckless misuse of drugs in a restive search for purpose in a purposeless world, the lack of public outrage at outrageous public servants, the creeping rise of statism with its corrupting promises of security from cradle to grave. Man was living uneasily in a world he was no longer sure of. "Western technology," Manuel observed, "has rendered obsolete the Judeo-Christian teachings that stood us in good stead for so long. So, in a sense, God is dead, and Western man, deprived of any spiritual buttressing, is dangerously adrift. We are at an ominous turning point; man's technology has outstripped evolution's natural safeguards and threatens to outrun his capacity to direct his own destiny. We are riding in a rapidly accelerating limousine, with no one at the wheel."

Just as Christianity had adapted to evolution, it could adjust to life on other planets, different life than ours, spirit life perhaps, but still in God's image, for God was Creator and Creation, and everything was in His image. And surely it was all planned, all destined in an endless unfolding that made reincarnation plausible. For if life was not planned, it was accidental, and we ourselves were accidents, flung accidentally onto a speck of whirling matter that was itself an accident. Nothing then made sense. There was no development, no orderly continuity, no reason for being, except to vegetate and die. But this nobody could truly believe, regardless of the outcries from angry lips, and still go on hopefully. For there *was* noticeable progress, with man keenly conscious of his own evolvement. With the uneasy feeling that our comfortable world was slipping away had also emerged a new awareness of man's boundless potential. As De Chardin indicated, we were teetering on the brink of great new discoveries:

"Our earth of factory chimneys and offices, seething with work and business, our earth with a hundred new radiations—this great organism lives, in final analysis, only because of, and for the sake of, a new soul. Beneath a change of age, lies a change of thought. Where are we to look at it, where are we to situate this renovating and subtle alteration which, without appreciably changing our bodies, had made new creatures of us? In one place and one only—in a new intuition involving a total change in the physiognomy of the universe in which we move—in other words, in an awakening."

The Search

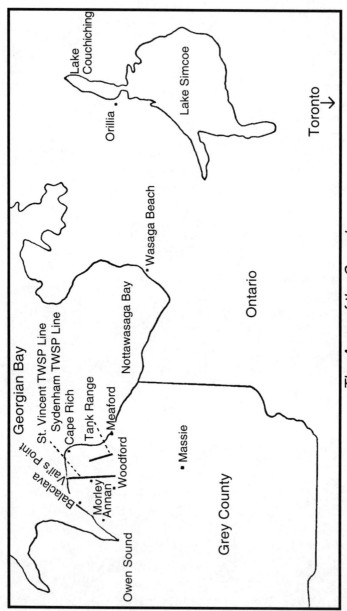

The Area of the Search

CURIOSITY INEVITABLY DREW ME back to Orillia. Yet I was not ready to take the plunge all at once, needing a sounding board to resolve my own doubts and misgivings.

My old friend and confidant, the ever practical surgeon, was waiting at the Ohio airport. "Glad you stopped off," Crowley said, giving me a searching look.

We rode silently for fifteen minutes, neither intruding on the other, until he finally pulled up before a nursing home.

"Just this one call," he said.

We were greeted cheerfully by a middle-aged woman who ushered us into a small room, where four old women were lying inertly in bed. At our entrance, their heads went up, and they held out pathetically bony arms, heavily corded with blue. "Doctor, Doctor," was all they could say.

All were over ninety, with no specific ailments that were treatable. They were just worn out, and had to be helped to eat, sleep, and relieve themselves. They had no privacy, no dignity, no awareness. They were shells of whatever they had once been.

The doctor made a perfunctory examination, and uttered a few encouraging sounds. His charges, hardly understanding, were already gaping vacantly at the ceiling as he turned away.

The whole scene had disturbed me more than I cared to admit. Back in the car, I registered an uneasy commiseration for those who had apparently lived too long for their own good.

Crowley laughed ironically. "Subconsciously, you're wondering whether this is all you have to look forward to yourself."

"And is this all?"

"Not really, it doesn't make sense, even though longevity is the great American dream." He squinted through the windshield into the sun. "Would you say, looking at these old people, that you were observing the culmination of anything that mattered, if that was the all of it?"

"They had some function, I suppose."

"So do the birds and the bees, but man is of God, and this awareness sets him apart."

His eyes clouded over with visions of a thousand cancers removed in the marble of great hospitals and of myriad limbs amputated in the muck of a dozen dirty battlefields. "Every once in a while on the operating table," he sighed, "you know there is somebody at your elbow, and that somebody is God."

My mind turned back to the old people who had long ago ceased to function for themselves.

"Do they know why they are here?"

He shrugged. "Not necessarily; it all depends on their level of development, and what they have done with their lives."

"And so they were here to learn, and then die, without

profiting by what they had learned?"

He laughed grimly. "Not quite, though it may have worked out that way."

"Why do you think we're here; you or I, any of us?" I persisted.

"To remember, for by remembering, we develop." He frowned. "Of course, we don't always remember what we remember."

It sounded like a bad joke. "Not remembering, how do we remember?"

"Intuition, instinct, the animals have it, why shouldn't man?" He pushed back from the wheel reflectively. "Sometimes we remember in different ways. Surgically, I may do the right thing, not quite knowing why. Or a page of history suddenly forms battle lines before my very eyes."

The Civil War, surprisingly, had preoccupied him from boyhood. "I lived"—he scowled—"and died in that war, there is no doubt of that in my mind."

I could hardly believe my ears. I had known Crowley intimately for years, without once hearing him make reference to reincarnation. My own thinking had apparently drawn him out.

Remembrance had come to him on the bloody battlefields of Anzio and Salerno, when suddenly, bending over a mangled form in the mud and slime of Italy, he knew—knew—why he had been so long obsessed with the Civil War. As he stood now, so had he stood at Antietam, Vicksburg, the Wilderness. He could almost smell the blood and stench of those blighted battlefields.

As I marveled to myself how little we really know anybody, he said gravely, "I have lived before, and I shall live again—like the old people you saw—but there is no reason why my next life should be any more meaningful or joyous than this one." He smiled dourly. "I'm a hard learner."

We rocked along for a while, and then with the briefest of smiles he asked, "Haven't you ever felt especially involved in some period, in some distant land?"

As a boy I had read everything I could on the French Revolution and the Rome of the Republic, fascinated by the heroic flavor of the times. But that certainly was all there was to it.

He nodded absently.

He knew about my quest, of course, but not about the drama of my first meeting with the girl, and the *déjà vu* that had made Orillia seem as cozy as my backyard, though a bit more eerie.

His face now broke into a craggy smile. "If it's a valid experience, there may be as much purpose for you to be there, as for her to remember. But you won't know unless you get on with it."

That night, after dinner, I not only pondered the girl with the blue eyes but Crowley. Not many in his stereotyped profession would have been so introspective or outspoken. But his remembrance had still been triggered by the traumatic impact of the battlefield, not by the medically mundane.

Musing on Crowley's battle experience, I could recall another soldier for whom the tragedy of war had been a succession of familiar memories. He would have been the last in the American command to be accused of fantasy, yet there was hardly a battlefield, or terrain, in two great wars that General George S. Patton did not visualize before he actually saw it. In his own mind, down the centuries, he had been a living "reincarnation of a fighting man." With vivid detail, he described battle sieges and campaigns of old. "He saw himself," noted Ladislas Farago *(Patton: Ordeal and Triumph)*, "in the phalanx meeting Cyrus the Persian; with Alexander the Great at the walls of Tyre; on Crecy's field in the Hundred Years'

War; as a general with Murat 'when one laughed at death and numbers trusting in the Emperor's star.'"

The "reincarnated" Patton was amused when his commanding officer, the Englishman Sir Harold Alexander, said admiringly after a stirring World War II success in North Africa, "You know, George, you would have made a great marshal for Napoleon if you lived in the eighteenth century."

"But I did," Patton said, smiling to make light of it.

He had striking flashes of memory in widely diverse battle arenas. The first, as noted by Farago, was in France in 1918 while training an American tank corps. "He was sent on a secret mission to a place he had never been before," Farago reported. Picked up by a staff car, he was not told where he was going. Nevertheless, approaching the crest of a hill in the darkness, Patton said to his driver, "This camp we're going to, isn't it just over the hill to the right?"

"No, sir, our camp is farther ahead. But there is an old Roman camp over there to the right."

That night, at the rendezvous, Patton, still living with his memories, turned to an officer and pointed out a window. "Your theater is over there straight ahead, isn't it?"

The officer shook his head. "We have no theater here."

The next morning, in daylight, Patton found his theater—a Roman amphitheater—about three hundred yards away.

His experience in Sicily, conquered by him in 1943, was even more dramatic. Taken on a guided tour by Signora Marconi, the curator of antiquities, to the ancient sites, he not only anticipated what she was about to say but corrected her on obscure details. In one instance, at Agrigento, Farago noted, the American general even amended her scholarly version of the Carthaginian land-

ing at the port, and meticulously described the bitterly
resisted advance on the capital city of Syracuse, which
he had known nothing about, logically.

The Signora's eyes widened. "Have you been here before, General?" she asked.

In Sicily for the first time in his life, Patton replied
carelessly, "I suppose so."

Like Patton's, Crowley's recall had been stated without
pretension, and with no concern for its acceptance. Indeed, the scientifically oriented Crowley questioned
whether conclusive evidence was possible—or necessary. "It might be too painful to remember."

As I left for Canada, he shook my hand and bid me
well. "Blue eyes," he observed, "can be distracting."

Driving from Ohio, I slipped quietly into Orillia,
checked into a hotel, and spent the next morning exploring the town. The Canadians in the street were like the
people I grew up with in upstate New York, and I saw
nothing odd about their nodding to me. Three or four
even stopped to chat, and then, lo and behold, I heard
my name being called.

Turning, I made out the owlish countenance of Tag
Watson, Joanne MacIver's pipe-smoking friend.

"Joanne," he said, "has been expecting you."

MacIver, himself, was out of town for a few days.

I got Joanne on the phone. Her voice was light and
musical. As the day had turned hot and sultry, I suggested she join me poolside at the hotel.

In an hour or so she turned up. Her eyes were even
more radiant than I remembered them and her teeth
gleamed evenly. She changed swiftly into her swimsuit,
a bikini, and plunged gratefully into the pool.

"Susan Ganier never looked like that," I observed.

With a quick smile, she sat down beside me, chewing
speculatively on a blade of grass.

"You know," she said, frowning, "when I was Susan, plowing the fields, I loved the feel of the warm earth on my bare feet."

"You didn't plow in a bikini?"

She gave a trill-like laugh. "I must have had a sensuous nature even then."

"How do you know?"

"Whatever I remembered under hypnosis, I have a vague recollection of consciously."

I told her what I expected of her. "I would like to engage you in the search for yourself, to stir perhaps some conscious recall that can be subsequently explored."

"Then you won't hypnotize me again?"

"That comes later."

She gave me a clear, penetrating glance, "How involved will you get?"

"Not at all personally."

"Oh, I see, this involves only me."

"My role is obviously that of an observer."

She smiled thinly. "It must be wonderful to determine one's own role."

Disregarding the sarcasm, I remarked again on the aplomb of one so young.

"I'm as old as my memory," she said crisply, "and as young as my body." She looked away. "Is there anything else to discuss?"

I mentioned my interest in Old Man Eagles, the sessions with Barbara White and Paul Torrance, and the impressions of others who sat in on the sessions.

She smiled. "Dad has practically the whole town interested in his search."

"Why is that?" I asked.

She shrugged. "On the frontier people rely more on intuition than the intellectual limitations imposed in schools."

Again I was struck by the astonishing range of her mind.

I mentioned I would be busy for a few days hunting up witnesses and finding a place to live.

"Where will you live?"

"Lake Couchiching."

Her eyes danced. "That's spooky," she said with a tiny shiver. "There's a sea serpent there."

"Have you seen it?"

She laughed. "It's more fun not seeing it."

"Like imagining you've lived before."

She turned her eyes challengingly on mine. "St. Paul saw nothing until his eyes were opened."

And then she was gone, her bikini safely tucked in her purse, and a mocking smile on her lips.

Through the local Chamber, I soon found a house on the lake, the owners living by coincidence next door to the MacIvers.

In no time, I was ready to begin. Paul Torrance conveniently lived across from the MacIvers. He was an athletic young man, apparently sure of himself, who wasted little time thinking about reincarnation. He made a few inconsequential changes in the notes of the first session, nodding confirmingly when he was quoted as scoffing at the start: "It's all baloney; nobody can hypnotize me."

And there was little question as to what he still thought about it all. But skeptical as he was, he had no doubt of the spontaneity of that first session, or of Joanne's sincerity. "They believe it, all right," he said, with a thin smile.

Although Eagles was dead, he was currently about the best witness I had. It was a question of how well his affidavit would stand up. His testimony was of major import in putting Susan Marrow not only where Joanne indicated she lived—but on this earth at all. He had been a very old man, and like many oldsters he wandered. I had gone through his deposition and subsequent correspondence with a reportorial regret that I had not been around while he was available for questioning.

Still, in 1903, when Susan presumably died, Eagles was in his early twenties, and old enough to have remembered clearly. He had good references from contemporaries, and from people he had spoken to about Susan and Tommy. Only one investigator, the psychiatrist, had decided after a flying visit that Eagles was a questionable source.

There were several points to consider. Had Eagles been unduly influenced, his recollections of the Marrows prodded by an overzealous MacIver? Overnight, he had become a center of attention, and may have innocently sought to maintain this role. Consequently, I was particularly interested in the first meeting with MacIver, in which he recalled the Marrows, and the circumstances surrounding the subsequent deposition.

In both cases, there were independent witnesses. Paul Uhlig, an acquaintance of MacIver's, had become involved in the search when MacIver mentioned it in Uhlig's shop one day. At forty, Uhlig had lived long enough to ponder man's destiny in the brief span allotted him. "If this was all there was," Uhlig said, "life seemed hardly worth the struggle. By the time you've learned something, you're ready to go." In a world perhaps billions of years old, it seemed incongruous that the spirit should be irretrievably lost, when nothing else was.

Having a questing mind, Uhlig had jumped at the chance to accompany MacIver on one of his trips to the Eagles farm. "I didn't want MacIver handing him a lot of leading questions and I made him agree that we would not mention the Marrow name first; it would have to come from Eagles."

They made the trip to the farm at Woodford in October, 1963. For MacIver it had become a fascinating game, but it was serious business for Uhlig. "I made MacIver live up to our agreement," Uhlig recalled. "Eagles spoke about people he had known sixty years ago and more, and then voluntarily brought up the Widow Marrow. That is how he referred to her, throughout. He had never known Tommy, but he remembered hearing his father talk of a Tommy Marrow being hurt in an accident. He wandered a bit, as old people will, but he always picked up the thread of the narrative.

"Apparently, his father had felt sorry for the widow and occasionally they had driven her to Owen Sound, when Eagles was only a small boy. There, she had done some shopping while Arthur's father performed his errands."

Uhlig had asked Eagles what he thought about reincarnation, and received a blank look. "It was too much for the old man to grasp," Uhlig recalled, "but without being pumped at all, Eagles remembered that in the latter years the widow had lived in a shack near the town line." The roads were poor, and she was difficult to reach, except in the brief summer period. "In the winter of 1903, one of the worst," Uhlig remembered, "Eagles' father had become concerned about the widow, and had sent his son after her. But Eagles couldn't cut through the snow-locked wilderness and in the spring they heard she was dead."

Eagles had seemed a remarkably cooperative witness.

"Wasn't he at all surprised at being asked to make out a deposition?" I asked.

Uhlig smiled. "Old people," he philosophized, "have run out of surprises and they are happy to be noticed."

"Perhaps," I suggested, "he went along with the Marrow story so he would continue to be noticed."

Uhlig shook his head. "There was no question that the

Susan Marrow who Eagles knew was very real to him. He even described what she looked like."

Others were equally impressed by Eagles. Bob Fournier, a twenty-two-year-old veteran of the Canadian Air Force, twice visited the old man. Fournier, a MacIver neighbor, had first seen Eagles in the fall of 1963, and again a year later. On that first visit, Eagles had led them up a dirt road near Silcote, and pointed into the Tank Range, saying, "The Widow Marrow lived in an old cabin over there toward the end of her life." He even recalled what she was like, saying, "She was quiet and never made a fuss."

The old man's sureness had impressed Fournier. "I saw nothing surprising about Eagles recalling his past. What more did he have to do but sit around and chew over the years? He worked some, from farm to farm, but wasn't anywhere nearly as active as when he traveled around cutting hay, getting to know just about everybody."

There was no effort by Eagles to please his visitors. Indeed, Uhlig had been impressed by the old man's restraint. "He didn't pretend to know the widow well, or know much about her. From what he said, it was obvious they weren't friends. She was living alone, and apparently didn't want to be bothered, and nobody bothered her."

In the year between visits, Fournier saw signs of Eagles' failing. He was no longer as spry as he had been, but his mind was still keen and his memory alert. They had got on to hypnosis, and Eagles, with a chuckle, had recalled where a man had seduced a woman under hypnosis, only to have the husband shoot and kill them. Fournier had found the account accurate.

MacIver had kept asking Eagles about other names. "As I recall," Fournier said, "he even asked whether the Ganiers could have Anglicized their name."

Eagles thought it might have become Gay-nor, or even Gainer.

"Didn't he think it odd that MacIver kept returning with the same questions?" I asked.

"They were introduced differently," Fournier said. "Besides, the old man liked company."

"Maybe he was trying to keep the company coming back?"

"Once he had confirmed everything, why should we come back?"

"Had Eagles, old as he was, taken it on himself to point out the widow's abode?"

Fournier thought a moment. "Ken MacIver asked if he could show us where the Marrow farm was. He said it was close to the Tank Range, a mile or so north of Morley, and that he would be glad to point out the spot."

This would be the farm she had shared with Tommy, moving out before Eagles was even born.

Fournier explained with a shrug, "They passed it on the way to town, and could have naturally mentioned it."

I kept questioning Eagles' sharpness. "Did he recognize you?"

Fournier smiled pleasantly. "Not the first time, or you might be inquiring about me."

Where did Fournier stand on reincarnation?

He hesitated. "There are times when it seems almost too rational; it explains everything, and that's just too pat."

MacIver had got Fournier interested in hypnosis four years before, eliminating an inordinate adolescent shyness with the power of suggestion.

I regarded the young man curiously. "Do you think hypnosis actually induces truer responses?"

Fournier laughed. "Once Ken hypnotized me, telling me I would feel as light as a feather for two weeks."

And?

"For the next two weeks I was floating through the air."

"Suppose he hypnotized Joanne, telling her she was Susan Ganier?"

"Even if he had, it would have been meaningless without Susan Ganier having some life of her own." He thought a moment. "And, of course, she would have remembered perfectly then."

Had MacIver had his way, he might have hypnotized Joanne every other day, looking for new leads. On the strength of Joanne's—Susan's—statement that it was a day's travel or more to Massie, MacIver had traveled some two hundred miles north to the mining country around Massey, trying to find the landmarks she mentioned—the apple orchards, the rolling hills, the plateau, even the twin churches.

It would have seemed far simpler to have first investigated the Massie in neighboring Grey County.

"Didn't MacIver stop to think that no horse and buggy could make two hundred miles in one day?" I asked.

Fournier laughed. "That's Ken for you; he gets enthused, and just takes off. He's not one for planning."

Three years had passed since engineer Art Dick and his wife had witnessed the session fixing the distance to Massie, but I was hopeful Dick's recall would be as fresh as other witnesses. Dick lived in Bracebridge, a small community north of Orillia, in a comfortable trailer. He was a slim man of fifty-eight, with no definite views on reincarnation, but having known Joanne since a child, he was curious about her experience.

"Why," I asked, "did MacIver overlook the nearer Massie and journey to the Massey far north of it?"

Art Dick laughed good-naturedly and lit up a cigarette. "Blame that on me," he said. "I had traveled all through central and northern Ontario, as a sales engineer, and had only heard of one Massey in all those years, and that near Sudbury."

Blue smoke trickled slowly out of a corner of his mouth. "The girl had mentioned that Massie was near Owen Sound, but I told MacIver it must be northwest of Sudbury. I knew of no Massie near Owen Sound, and I knew the area."

Dick had been struck as others by the girl's quaint expressions, "I was like Daddy said, the foal who was ready to ride."

Twice she referred to "the buggy and the horse," instead of the colloquial horse and buggy, explaining, "That's the way Daddy said it. He was French, and that's how he said it in the English he wanted everyone to speak."

She had reacted strongly to some questions, making no secret of her dislike for Rachel, brother Reuben's wife. "I thought she was a hussy, and just went after Reuben to have a husband."

Asked about neighbors, she did vaguely recall a Dutch family buying property down the road, and her father helping them to build their barn. "It's a funny name . . . I think it is Dutch. They are Dutch people."

Just thinking about Old Man MacGregor made her laugh. He worked in a store, as Dick recalled, and was quite the country cutup.

After some hesitation, another name slipped out. It had a familiar ring—Yancey. But Dick was intrigued by her sudden clamming up when asked to give Yancey's full name. "I won't tell you," she said tautly.

MacIver, questioning her, asked casually, "Did something happen?"

A look of distaste came over her face, and she shook her head vigorously. For a while it looked as though the session was over, but MacIver got her talking again.

Out of the continued questioning came a hint of a typical Christmas in the wilderness of snow. As previously recorded, there was no Christmas tree, and Susan's proudest acquisition was an orange, together with a made-over dress. "Mother fixed up an old dress and I wore it so I would look nice for Tom."

The orange was a rare prize. "It was small and green," she recalled. "The skin was hard, and dried up, but it tasted good. It was my first orange."

Progressed out of girlhood, her face became wreathed in a happy smile. Dick recalled the subtle change in her voice as her lips framed the name Tommy Marrow.

"Make no mistake," Dick said reminiscently, "she was an entirely different person than the Joanne I knew before. Her voice changed, in registering emotion, and was nothing like Joanne's. When she caught Reuben and Rachel in the orchard, her voice tripped with happy laughter as she said, 'I know what they were doing,' only to change dramatically when Reuben chased her and she screamed in mock terror." He could almost hear her now: "They were behind the apple tree [giggling] but it was awfully funny. I think I will tell Mommy, but I think Mommy already knows. Oh, they see me [great consternation]. What shall I do? Hi, Rachel, I was just going to get the cow. [Now an aside.] Reuben knows I was only telling a lie. Oh, maybe he is going to get a stick and spank me [great alarm]. He is! He's chasing me. Don't hit me, Reuben. I didn't mean to spy on you. [To herself now.] I'll tell him that if he hits me that I will tell Daddy. Oh, Reuben—brothers are so stupid."

Art Dick closed his eyes as though better to visualize the panorama of another life and time. "No person in this world," he finally said, "was that clever an actress. I was convinced, as I sat there, that something was taking place I had never witnessed before."

Intrigued, he put a few questions himself.

"Where are you getting your ideas?" he asked.

She shook her head. "I don't know . . . I keep thinking."

"How do you feel?"

"Tired . . . I don't think I'm going to let Dad hypnotize me any more."

And so the session had ended, impressing not only Dick but his wife. There was no doubt in Mrs. Dick's mind of the authenticity of the experience, whatever it signified.

"If Joanne was making it up, she must be another Sarah Bernhardt. She was either telling us what really happened to her, or getting it from memory of something she was told, but it had to come from somewhere. She just couldn't have made it up."

There were a couple of plus marks. Obviously, from what I was told, MacIver had not conveniently dug up one Massie when the first fell through. The names Joanne had mentioned, MacGregor, Yancey, Reuben, represented definite personalities. "You just felt," Dick said, "that she was talking about people she knew very well."

As the tea and biscuits were brought out, I recalled an earlier reference by Dick to an experience of his own.

"Oh, that," he said, stretching his legs out luxuriously and tapping a cigarette. "I was about twenty-two or twenty-three then—it was late in October of 1931, and I had made arrangements with a chum to join me for a week's camping." They had met in Muskoka, sixteen miles northeast of Huntsville in Ontario. "That first morning, my friend and I decided to take separate courses to track partridge, meeting back at the camp for lunch. About a third of a mile from camp, I found an old road running up a long slope in the direction of the Big East River. Another half-mile or so of stiff walking brought me to a clearing which had obviously once been farmland. There was a gentle incline ahead, and on the crest a great slab of rock. Looking ahead, it all suddenly seemed familiar and I knew"—his eyes met mine—"I knew that if I ran up the slope there would be a commanding view of the Big East River, with the river bed taking a sharp bend to the right. And I knew there on the far side of the riverbank I would see a hand-hewn log cabin."

He succumbed to an overpowering urge to run up the slope, and clamber over the rock, gazing spellbound into the valley below. Everything he had pictured lay spread out before him. "I looked down on the river, seeing the bend and the crumbling ruins of what in the distant past had been a cabin." The roof and upper walls had yielded to time, but the hand-hewn foundation still remained.

Dick had been overcome with emotion. "Successively, I felt joy and love, sadness and regret. I felt somehow that my life had been involved with the log cabin. And now I have a compelling desire to retire to this area, building a log cabin, and tapping a waterfall for electric power."

Was this *déjà vu,* pure and simple, or was it more? Dick himself posed the inevitable questions: Was there renewed life after death? If so, did a person occasionally carry traces of memory over from one life to another? Could this reservoir of subconscious recall be tapped with any degree of accuracy?

It had been an interesting evening.

Regardless of whether Joanne had ever been Susan Marrow, it was easy to understand how little communication there had been. The winters were unbelievably hard and bleak, marooning settlers behind snowdrifts up to fifty feet. The pioneers, mostly of tight-lipped British stock, stayed to themselves. Farmers two or three miles distant didn't know their neighbors or their names.

They were too busy trying to survive. Sickness was common, doctors inaccessible or nonexistent, and whole districts decimated in a single winter.

One of the first settlers, John Vail, staked out his farm in 1825, and gave the promontory on Georgian Bay the name Vail's Point. It was still wilderness thirty-five years later. An old resident, whose family worked the Tank Range area at a time the Marrows were presumably there, recalled, "The first time my father returned to Orangeville, he walked. The second time he had oxen that had to be driven singly on the narrow trail which was only a blaze through the woods. My mother drove one of the oxen attached to a small sleigh. The third time Father and Mother made the journey, they traveled on horseback."

The Hunts might well have been neighbors of the Ganiers, sharing the same experiences. "Mr. Hunt," reported local historian E. L. Marsh, "located on the Ninth Concession of St. Vincent, which was still a forest, built a log house and made a clearing about it. One season the potato crop failed, and the wheat was nearly all rusted, so that the little good grain they had must be kept for seed. For food they had only corn and turnips, and not enough of even these for the winter supply."

Survival hung on a razor's edge. One day Charles Hunt overheard his mother saying again and again to his father, "What shall we do?"

There was no food in the house.

"The Lord will provide," he said quietly.

Just then there was a knock at the door. It was an old friend, returning a loan the family had never expected. "The next morning the boy set out with his father to buy flour for winter food for the family."

In 1858, five or six years before Tommy Marrow's reported death, there was a general crop failure, and flour and grain were distributed to the needy. They worked it off. There was no welfare.

Buried away, inhabitants often lost sight of the day or week, and even the year. In 1843, when Susan Marrow was presumably ten or eleven, a pious pioneer was attracted one Sunday by the sound of axes chipping into wood. Spotting an old man and a boy at work, he angrily demanded if this was the way they observed the Lord's Day. The old man replied mildly, "We ain't got no almanac here and we can't tell when Sunday comes."

Churches were few and far between, and ministers were hard to come by. "We beg leave to state," the early Scots noted, "that it will be necessary in making application for a minister [Presbyterian] that he be able to preach in Gaelic as well as in English, as many of the settlers from the Highlands do not understand English well."

Services were usually held in homes and schoolhouses. Few could afford sending their children any distance to schools. There were chores to be done.

The first Methodist service was held in Meaford, St. Vincent Township, in 1840, but there was no church with a minister for years after that. In Susan's area, there were Methodist services but apparently no churches until shortly after her marriage, so she would have married in any available hall.

Even then, there was interest in the psychic, dowsers being the surest way of locating water. "The accuracy of the divining rod in finding water was proved over and over again," historian Marsh reported. "Indeed, it was an indispensable method before the days of boring down through the earth and rock. Carrying a forked branch of witch hazel or willow grasped firmly in the hands and pointing outwards, the water-witch or wizard walked slowly over the ground. If water were present, the point of the stick would turn down towards the ground in spite of all efforts to hold it firmly. Early wells in the County [Grey] discovered in this way produced a never-failing water supply."

The government made a special effort to settle the land. In 1848, newspaper advertisements in Montreal, then the government seat, hailed the County of Grey as a veritable Garden of Eden. Settlers were offered fifty acres as a Crown grant, fifty more at fifty cents an acre. All they had to do was make improvements, or get tenants to do so.

Through the eyes of his own father, a 'Forty-niner, historian Marsh gave a pretty good picture of what happened to a typical pioneer family. It took four days to move the family the few miles from Sydenham to their new home in the bush. Meanwhile, a bear had visited their shack, and finished off their sugar and pork. The floor of their home was the earth, leveled with picks, and there were no windows, as the house had not yet been chinked with mud or moss.

A small schoolhouse came along three years later, open only during summers, and teachers made their own arrangements for remuneration.

Not everybody stayed. Indeed, it almost seemed at times as if nobody stayed. "The Edward Millers left in 1854 for greener pastures."

While all this local history was a necessary backdrop for the search, it was certainly dull and tedious work. I was longing to get out into the country and get the feel of things for myself. Meanwhile, MacIver, back in town, was counseling me at every turn. "It's not going to be easy," he said with his customary air of authority. "I've been thoroughly discouraged myself many times."

I expressed my interest in tracking down the Marrows and Ganiers.

He shook his head. "I think Ganier must have changed his name; it seems to have disappeared into thin air, unless it's on a grave in the Tank Range."

"We can look for Ganier, Gaynor, or Gainer," I said.

There were obvious leads. What had happened to Archibald Marrow? What directories, gazetteers, or files held a clue to Mason Ganier, Tommy Marrow, and Susan; their births, marriage, deaths? The vital records were scattered about; in Ottawa, the national capital; Toronto, provincial headquarters; Owen Sound, the county seat, and Meaford in St. Vincent.

My first quest for records took me to Toronto, and the Department of Public Records and Archives in Queens Park, where I was soon up to my elbows in stacks of musty files. Many of the papers were stained and brittle with time, and revealed better than any chronicle the way the land was acquired. An application to the Crown land agent, November 1853, was signed with an X, by one Thomas Barman. "Herewith," it went, "you will receive the sum of five pounds as a deposit on account, in the first concession of the township of Sydenham, which I hereby apply for permission to occupy and cultivate with a view to purchasing in conformity with the notice issued from the Crown land department."

It soon became apparent that X was the major purchaser. Could Tommy Marrow write, and for that matter had he owned the land or been merely a tenant farmer? Again, what connection, if any, was there between him and Archibald Marrow?

I pored over the precious files under the watchful eye of an attractive librarian. She smiled sympathetically. "The records are painfully incomplete. My ancestors pioneered up that way, and there weren't even any real roads until 1866; the settlers usually arrived by boat."

The records revealed the informality of pioneering in

the bush. Early settlers squatted where they liked, improving the property even without the scrap of a legal claim. In 1850, Octavious Knight notified the Crown land agent: "If the south half of lot No. 15 in the first concession of the town of Sydenham is still vacant, I should feel obliged by the putting down my name for the purchase of it when the opportunity offers as I have lately erected a house thereon and hope within a short time to commence other improvements."

One name kept popping up. Alexander Fraser was an absentee landlord, with several lots on Sydenham's First Concession Line; namely, Nos. 33, 34, 35. He had others somewhat removed. In 1843, when Susan would have been a child, Fraser was trying to sell off land through agent J. B. Spragge of Kingston, Ontario, with a prospective buyer to "purchase the same from Mr. Fraser, paying one-fourth of the purchase money down and the residue in four equal annual installments."

Occasionally, I saw a familiar name. In 1843, Samuel Eagles, grandfather of Arthur Eagles, received a Crown warrant, and there were Millens, Atkinsons, MacGregors, but no grants for Marrows and Ganiers, before I turned to the earliest directories for Grey County. Again, a handful of familiar names: Charles Eagles, Arthur's father; John McMillan in Morley, Margaret and William Speedie, at Annan, and MacGregor. Here, too, the records were obviously sparse. Even the dead, certified by headstone, often went unlisted.

The librarian was still sympathetic. "They weren't fussy about registering anything in those days," she said.

In *Smith's Gazetteer* for 1888, I found M. Speedie, General Store, indicating that the Widow Speedie, the Widow Marrow's presumed contemporary, had taken over her husband's emporium. In Massie, I turned up a Robert MacGregor, a blacksmith, not a storekeeper.

Lovell's business directory, describing Massie as a post office station, turned up a Joshua Milligan, a onetime storekeeper, serving as postmaster. The flour mill was operated by a William Brown.

Relevantly or not, a MacGregor and Milligan were now established at Massie, both in trade, but apparently independent of each other.

The directories obviously were limited to the accessible. "You might check the census returns on microfilm," the librarian said. "They're hard on the eyes, but more complete than the directories."

She was right about one thing—the eyes.

I saw Morrows but no Marrow, Graniers but no Ganiers. Actually, a flutter came to my stomach as the film for 1851 wheeled to Catherine Granier, and stopped. Except for the first "r," perhaps slurred under hypnosis, the name was Susan's mother's. And there was a Tommy, next to hers, but a brother, not a son-in-law. But this Catherine Granier was too young, it developed, to be Catherine Ganier.

As the hours passed, a new librarian came on and I found my popularity waning. Holding a land map spelling out Archibald Marrow, I asked for the Marrow grant.

The librarian regarded me coldly.

"What year would that be?"

"About 1840."

Painfully, she explained that after the federalization of Canada in 1867, all Crown deeds were transferred to Ottawa.

I traced out the Marrow name on the map. "Would you look," I asked, "for an official report of inspection on this particular lot on the Twelfth Concession Line of St. Vincent Township?"

She eyed me with frosty disapproval. "I stated that we have no Crown papers for that period."

"I did notice others in the files," I said mildly.

She shrugged coldly, and moved off to some mysterious inner chamber.

In a few moments she was back, carrying a flimsy file, which she put down without a word.

Shuffling through some musty papers, I soon found a report from the Honorable R. B. Sullivan, commissioner for Crown lands, and the name Archibald Marrow.

A land inspection, made a short time after Marrow had acquired his one hundred acres, resulted in a one-word report: "Vacant."

Archibald Marrow had never done anything with his grant. His failure to stay on the land weakened any belief that he might have fathered Tommy Marrow, aged ten or eleven at this time. However, even the negative report, as the only indication of the grant itself, pointed up the serious omissions in the records. Obviously, people engaged in a struggle to endure had little thought of anything but that struggle.

In the morning, not very optimistically, I dropped into the provincial registry office in Toronto's Lombard Street to check the beginning, middle and end—birth, marriage and death—of Susan and Tommy.

With almost perverse delight, the girl at the desk announced, "We have no vital statistics before 1869."

That struck me as a bit odd.

"They just weren't very good about sending in records," she said indifferently. "But they might be registered locally."

With Susan dying in 1903, I put down two dollars for a search for a death record, and was told I would be duly informed. By this time, I had a feeling that any records surviving from the previous century must have a charmed life.

Inside of me, gradually, was building up the wish to

browse over Susan's past, explore the areas where she lived and died, prowl the old cemeteries, chat with old-timers, and absorb the subtle aroma of her time and place.

MacIver was delighted with my decision. He approached the foray into North Grey as he would a holiday. "We'll leave early," he said, "lunch on the way." His eyes gleamed happily as we discussed the agenda: Talking to oldsters in Meaford, checking the cemetery at Annan where Margaret Speedie and her husband were reportedly buried, checking the records in a nearby lodge—Orange Hall—where Susan and Tommy may have married. While permission to tour the Tank Range had not yet come, I still wanted a look at the roads bordering the range, take a run through Massie, and get a glimpse of Georgian Bay, where Joanne said she could remember rowing as the child Susan.

As we took to the road on a gloriously sunny day, Joanne was in a festive mood, gaily humming the lilting melody, "We're off to Dublin in the green . . . "

"Wouldn't it be wonderful," she said, "if we were just having a lark, without a thought of anything?"

Her blue eyes were sparkling, and her cheeks blooming. I had never seen her so radiant. But it was the day, not the occasion.

"Don't you like the idea of looking for yourself?" I asked.

She shook her head. "What are you going to find—nothing, I'm sure, that will convince you." She looked over fondly at her father, preoccupied with the driving. "The problem is that I accept reincarnation, and you don't."

"I suppose you're looking for Tommy Marrow at every crossroads?"

"Not at all," she replied coolly. "I don't think it works quite that way."

"Not even a reasonable facsimile?"

She regarded me with a jaundiced eye. "Do you believe in anything?"

I laughed. "Believe half of what you see, and nothing you hear."

She sniffed. "Do you believe in God?"

"I can see what He does."

"Only what He permits you to see," she said scornfully.

Under MacIver's deft driving, the miles to Meaford had skipped by without settling anything but a place to lunch on Meaford's main street.

As the others toyed with coffee and dessert, I slipped across the street to a hardware store, where I understood a remarkable nonagenarian, Joseph Walker, was employed. I picked out a spare, ruddy-faced, bespectacled figure with a genial smile, and asked, "Could you tell me where I can find Mr. Walker—he's a man ninety years old."

My eyes kept searching around the store, which was neat and commodious, for an obvious nonagenarian.

"I'm Joe Walker," the man smiled. "And I'm ninety-one."

"You're Joe Walker?" It seemed incredible; he looked no more than sixty or sixty-five.

A customer dropped a coin, and Joe Walker bent down from the waist and scooped it off the floor.

"How do you do it?" I asked.

"Just keeping busy," he said, with a twinkle in his eyes. He waved an arm around the store. "I sold this place and thought I'd retire, but the new owners wanted me to stay on because I knew the stock, and I've been here ever since."

Here was a man, it seemed to me, who would remember anybody he had ever known.

"Never knew a Marrow," he said, "Gainers maybe, but no Ganiers."

"Do you remember a widow in the Morley area, who might have been considered eccentric?"

His face puckered in concentration. "I just don't recall anybody like that. But, of course, there were a lot of people I didn't know. That's a dozen miles, and that was some distance then."

"How about Arthur Eagles, did you know him?"

He laughed. "Everybody knew Arthur Eagles. His family had a mill, and he got around quite a bit."

"Was he considered reliable?"

"Oh, yes, Arthur was a highly intelligent man." He thought a moment. "But I didn't see him the last few years, not after his automobile accident."

"Did his mind fail?"

"Nothing like that, just hard for him to get around."

Old Man Walker was still musing as I joined Joanne and her father in the car, and headed for Annan, to witness the grave of the woman whom Joanne had called Susan's friend.

Annan was a tiny, tree-shaded community, so peaceful that its main street was hardly distinguishable from its cemetery. We saw nobody in its streets or the graveyard, which was peopled by Stewarts, Ramsays, Stephensons, Scots, all, and a Reilly, of the Ould Sod. I was at Joanne's heels, when she stopped speculatively before a red granite headstone studying the inscription. I soon discovered why.

IN MEMORY OF WILLIAM SPEEDIE,
DIED MARCH 1, 1885, AGED 79
A NATIVE OF PERTSHIRE, SCOTLAND

Oh sacred grave, what precious dust
Is here committed to thy trust.
But oh the soul has fled on high
To bloom forever in the sky.

Also next to it:

> ALSO HIS WIFE, MARGARET EADIE,
> DIED JUNE 27, 1909, AGED 86 YEARS
> A NATIVE OF PERTSHIRE, SCOTLAND

Joanne stood silently a few moments, then moved on to another stone. With a smile, she pointed to the valedictory:

> JAMES F. BLUE, WHO DEPARTED THIS LIFE
> DECEMBER 27, 1856, 28 YEARS OF SINS
> *Missed are the dead who died in the Lord.*

And how revealing it might be if the dead could talk.

"It's too bad," I said, "that Margaret Speedie can't communicate from the grave. I might be convinced."

"And how would she do that?" Joanne asked.

"With information only she could have known."

"How could you prove it if only she knew it?"

"There might be a record of it somewhere," I said.

She smiled. "Then someone else would have to know."

I regarded her with some exasperation. "What are you trying to show?"

"How difficult it is to establish reincarnation by general rules of evidence."

"Then how would you prove it?"

She broke into a hearty laugh. "By talking to somebody like me."

Behind me MacIver made an effort to restrain himself. "That Joanne," he chuckled, "you got to believe it."

From the cemetery, due east, it was but a few minutes to the edge of the Tank Range and the Orange Hall. There had also been a Grange Hall in the area, but MacIver was not sure of its location. Orange Hall looked dark and forbidding.

"If Susan and Tommy were married in that hall," MacIver said, "the records should be there."

The custodian of the hall, Russell Hill, was on his lawn, chatting with friends, when we drew up to his farm-house. He was a square-faced, powerfully built man, with a distant eye.

"Good day," I said.

"Maybe," he said dourly.

I nodded toward the hall.

"Any chance of getting in there?"

"What for?"

"I'm checking a family who lived around here a hundred years ago."

He shook his head. "The records were moved out years ago, to other lodges."

My face must have reflected my disappointment. "I wanted to check on a marriage."

"Only Orangemen lodge functions took place in the hall."

"There would have been no wedding then?"

He shook his head. "Not in the hall."

"Who were the Orangemen? I asked.

For a moment I thought there would be no reply. "They were Irish, Protestant Irish, originally, and they just banded together."

Significantly, perhaps, they took their name from William of Orange, the Protestant prince who displaced a Catholic on the English throne.

It had been another dead end.

"Hill could be wrong," MacIver observed in the car, "or maybe they were married in the Grange Hall."

He looked at me inquiringly. "What next?"

"How about heading for Balaclava, and John Lourie, the farmer who knew Arthur Eagles so well?"

Tennyson had made the name Balaclava famous in his

"Charge of the Light Brigade," a heroic chapter in the Crimean War, but MacIver wasn't sure of its derivation. "All I know was that it was a Scottish settlement."

Lourie was obviously not expecting anyone. He came to the door in his stockinged feet, and ushered us into a cluttered living room.

I briefly mentioned the Ganiers and Marrows.

Lourie frowned. The names were vaguely familiar, but he couldn't place them. He was an old man, but still years younger than Eagles.

"Do you know Joe Walker?" I asked.

"Never heard the name before."

I explained that Walker had a hardware store only a few miles away.

"We mind our business in these parts," he said.

When I mentioned Eagles, Lourie's eyes floated toward the ceiling. "A good many people didn't like Arthur."

My interest quickened. "Why was that?"

"Arthur Eagles never forgot anything. And there are some things people like forgotten."

"What would you think of any affidavit he had signed?"

"That Arthur had signed?" Lourie slapped his knee hard. "I'd close my eyes, and sign it after him, that's what."

He was not old enough to remember a Susan Marrow dying in 1903. But he knew somebody who was.

"Have you talked to Mrs. Arthur McDonald?"

I had not heard the name before.

"She's ninety and she lives with my brother Duncan and his wife at Bognor." He cackled, "She's Duncan's mother-in-law."

He took us to the car. "No sir," he said, "Arthur Eagles never forgot anything."

In the car, MacIver looked vindicated.

"Interesting," I said, "but hardly evidential."

"What is evidential?"

"The same kind of evidence you would turn up for an accident, crime, or normal birth."

On a county map, I picked out the pinpoint, Massie, a few miles south of Bognor. "We may as well make that one, too."

MacIver gave me a curious glance. "There isn't much there."

"Perhaps I'll see what Susan Ganier saw at Massie."

"Massie was a metropolis then; two hundred inhabitants, a thriving mill, stores, and now it's only four corners."

Joanne broke in, "It's on the way, and the creek behind the mill is so pretty."

MacIver's little compact shot forward, and we zoomed up and down back roads like a roller coaster, until we reached the farmhouse where Mrs. McDonald lived. As luck would have it, she was out for the day. Going on, we would have missed Massie, had the MacIvers not known it was there. It was that nebulous.

Getting out of the car, Joanne wandered down the road to a nondescript mill, and we trailed after her. A husky man was standing outside the mill, looking at it as though he owned it. He did.

Gordon Lang knew little about the mill's history, but volunteered that a Mrs. McPherson had thoroughly researched the town's past.

"Why," I asked, "would anybody do a history of Massie?"

"Something to do with a school anniversary," he said.

Joanne had sauntered beyond the mill to the creek, and was examining names scratched into a stone wall near a small dam.

"If you come up with 'Susan loves Tommy,' with an arrow through a heart, I'll jump into the reservoir," I announced.

She laughed infectiously. "I should have sneaked up last night with a chisel."

With a smile, she picked out the letters M-A carved into the wall; the rest was broken off.

"It could have been Marvin, Mason, Martin," I said, "besides this cement wall doesn't look a hundred years old."

She traced her finger over the two letters wistfully, as MacIver finally drew up. "Under hypnosis," he said, "Joanne once said that her father, Mason, and her mother met at Massie."

"I didn't see that in the notes."

"Not everything got taken down."

"Somebody," I rejoined, "could have been scratching in the most logical name of all."

"What would that be?"

"Massie."

Joanne was watching me, and I could sense her disappointment. Why I didn't know, but I suggested one more stop.

Jean McPherson was a handsome, sophisticated woman, with a fresh complexion and an active mind. We listened admiringly, as she rattled off names and dates. The flour mill, operated by Alexander Massie, more than a hundred years before, had been one of Canada's oldest and best, serving a wide radius. It first changed hands in 1862, and was operated successively by Massie, Small, Brown, Lickford. A sawmill was added in 1859.

"How about MacGregor and Milligan?" I asked.

She shook her head. "Josh Milligan ran a store about that time. Robert MacGregor, a blacksmith, came later."

Marrow and Ganier rang no bell. "There was a Morrow family," she said, "but they moved on to Owen Sound."

The day, except for familiarizing me with the local topography, appeared a complete washout.

But MacIver did not agree. "How about Milligan's store?"

"There was no MacGregor and Milligan."

"There was a MacGregor, and he might have worked one store or another. We just assumed their togetherness."

MacIver's personality increasingly engaged my attention. He lived for one thing: the establishment of Joanne's previous life. In the shadow of old age without attaining his smallest goals, he was obviously resigned to gaining recognition through his daughter. He had not only tried, unsuccessfully, to establish himself as her Ganier father, but had, successfully, drawn a good part of the community into his search: the veteran Fournier, shopkeeper Uhlig, psychiatrist "Casey" Jones, merchant Horace Smith, even Bob Marshall, a staid official of the Ontario Provincial Department of Municipalities.

His appeal to Marshall was typical MacIver. Hearing that Marshall toured the hinterland, inspecting assessments, MacIver had asked him to check any names—in tax books or cemeteries—similar to those turned up by Joanne.

Marshall himself had little to report, nor did he think he would stumble onto anything. "Those old headstones and grave markers had a way of disappearing," he grinned. "I remember once calling on a Farmer Murphy in Grey County who had just paved the floor of his barn with stones from old cemeteries."

Wouldn't the outraged ghosts of the dead rise up one day to haunt Farmer Murphy?

Marshall laughed wryly. "I don't know about that. The barn burned down three weeks after he built it."

Undecided on reincarnation, he still wondered about the source of fragmentary recollections, bordering on *déjà vu*, because of rather remarkable experiences of his own. Some fifteen years before, touring the Balaclava area with a local assessor, he came on a narrow gravel road winding up a rise. Peering up the hill, he said, "There's a two-story log cabin about a mile ahead on the left."

The assessor smiled. "There's no house up there, or we'd have a record of it."

Never in the area before, Marshall could only shrug. However, as the two men drove along, there on the left, as Marshall had indicated, were the ruins of a log cabin— with one story. But on closer inspection, finding a staircase, it became obvious the house was originally two-storied, an oddity in that section.

That wasn't all, for as the assessor gingerly circled the structure Marshall called out, "There should be a well back of the cabin, just to the left."

There was a pause, and then a puzzled voice, "How did you know?"

It was not his first such experience. In World War II, Marshall had been ordered from his RCAF base at London airport to a coastal base in the south. He set out by car with a comrade. After some hours on the road, with headlights taboo because of a blackout, his companion suggested they pull up to the side of the road.

Marshall stared into the darkness. "Three miles ahead, we'll come to an inn, and we can spend the night there."

His companion snorted. "Don't spook me."

In a few minutes, they spied the shadowy outline of an ancient English inn. And there they spent the night.

I wondered if Marshall had been in that part of England before.

"Not any more than Balaclava. Both areas were new to me."

Then how had he remembered?

"I'm sure I don't know."

I put the next question casually. "Had you known these places in a previous life perhaps?"

The bureaucrat smiled politely. "I only know what I remembered. Anything else would be pure speculation."

Through it all, MacIver maintained his usual ebullience. Whatever the disappointment, he was never discouraged. "It's just a question of luck," he said, "and so far we haven't had any." For some reason, he felt that the proscribed grounds of the Tank Range would turn up the Ganier graves, and the farmsteads, churches, and orchards Joanne had talked about in trance.

MacIver excitedly pored over a map of the range, a square shoulder of land in the northeast corner of St. Vincent Township, jutting into Georgian Bay. He had marked the name Ganier on the Ninth Concession Line, and a mile below had written in the name of a Henry Brown, an actual homesteader, and another mile and a half, directly south, still another Brown. There was a Brown, Benjamin, a mile east of Henry Brown, and a William Brown, two miles west of Henry. Just north of the old Archibald Marrow lot were Charles and Thomas Brown. The place was crawling with Browns.

MacIver beamed from behind his glasses. "You must remember," he said, "that Reuben, Susan's brother, married a Brown, Rachel."

"He didn't marry them all, did he?"

MacIver conceded vaguely, "Brown was a very common name."

MacIver had marked in a church, about a quarter of a mile south of his Ganier farmstead.

"Now where did that come from?"

"From Joanne," he replied easily. "She said the church was down the road." He pointed to another church site, a mile or so up from the Archibald Marrow plot, toward

Vail's Point, on Georgian Bay. "This, presumably, is the Methodist church Susan went to after she married Tommy."

"Where do you figure Tommy was buried?"

"Tommy was buried on his farm, the Ganiers in the churchyard near their home on the Ninth Line—that's straight from Joanne."

If so much of what he was looking for was in the Tank Range, why hadn't he been through it before?

"I have been through parts," he said, "but never the guided tour—that can only come from the major in charge, when they're not firing those big shells."

"When is target practice?"

He reflected a moment. "Tuesdays, I believe."

"That leaves six days."

He betrayed some impatience. "You just can't wander aimlessly over the place, it's full of unexploded duds, and besides they wouldn't let you even if you were that fool hardy."

The officer in charge, recently succeeding a Major Perkins, was a Major John Malone.

"I don't know about him," MacIver said with his customary air of intrigue.

"We only want to look at some old houses and graves," I pointed out.

MacIver guffawed. "The houses are old ruins; what time didn't do, shells and tanks finished off."

On one Tank Range map MacIver had noted with an arrow: "Notice all the large apple orchards. Finest apples grown in Canada are here. Joanne recalls the fine apple orchard of Ganier."

I measured the map distance from the arrow to the Ganier farmstead. It must have been a mile away. "That doesn't put them on the Ganier site."

"The only remaining orchards are on the Tank Range

periphery, but it was essentially the same apple country."

The meeting with Major Malone, to prepare the way for our excursion, had been arranged through Ken Wells, a Canadian newspaperman and radio commentator, who had written a best-seller, *The Owl Pen,* about making money out of honey.

The Major was tall, lean, and tough, and nicknamed Spike. He spoke with a brogue, but the softness ended there. He had trained at Sandhurst, the English West Point, after distinguishing himself on the battlefield in World War II. "After every ranking officer in his tank brigade had been killed," an admirer recalled, "Sergeant Malone took over the brigade and showed rare command qualities."

He had now been Army for thirty years, and his service had taken him all over the world, including the Orient. He had been on the international truce team supervising the French exodus from Indochina after Dienbienphu in 1954, and two years later he was in the Gaza strip, refereeing the uneasy armistice that followed the Anglo-French-Israeli invasion of Nasser's Egypt. Quite a figure, the Major.

MacIver still thought it unwise to mention the underlying reason for the search. "They'll think I'm some kind of nut," he said, "and it may also make them feel a little silly."

After I had reluctantly agreed, Wells told the Major of my interest in old families who had once lived on the Tank Range site, and the Major had quickly agreed to pilot me wherever I wanted to go. "It shouldn't take long to go over the cemeteries and ruins," he said.

Such disarming generosity again impelled me to disclose the real purpose of the search, but MacIver again demurred.

As it was, the conversation verged from the French-Indochina War to the current conflict.

"What are our chances in Vietnam?" I asked.

The Major's blue eyes clouded over. "My sympathies are naturally with the kids off the farms of Alabama and the streets of New York who are showing what great fighting men they are. But if the French couldn't do it after ninety-seven years, what chance does anybody have?"

He brought out photographs of two separate troop defiles on opposite sides of heavily tangled underbrush. They were only a few feet apart, and yet one column was completely unaware of the other.

"The Viet Cong can conceal an army in the trees and brush forming a perfect ambush," he said, "and it's impossible to flush them out with the weapons now in use. You're fighting their war on their terms; it can go on interminably." He had no solution. "Obviously, as Canadians whose fortunes are tied to our big neighbor, we wish the U.S. success. But . . ." He smiled bleakly.

He stood up and extended his hand. "We'll be glad to assist your research, any day but Tuesday." His craggy features relaxed. "There'd be shells around our ears that day."

I agreed to give twenty-four hours' notice, picking a day convenient to Joanne, and Casey Jones, who was interested in various aspects of the search. For a psychiatrist he was a gregarious sort, with a remarkably open mind. As I got to know Casey, I discovered he had his own special reasons for the search. By ordinary standards, he was a notable success, at the top of his profession, heading the largest Canadian school for the retarded. Practically half of Orillia worked for him. He lived in a lovely home, raising four precocious teenagers, and enjoying it. Yet, something deep down was troubling him. He was recently divorced, and suffering from a chronic illness, but I sensed it was something else—something broader, something at the very nub of life.

At Ontario Hospital School, he was every day reminded of life's inequities as he clinically supervised mental derelicts of all ages and descriptions. Why were these cursed from birth as idiots, Mongoloids, morons, and others, often of the same family, thrust into lives marked for health and happiness?

It was a question which another Cayce—Edgar Cayce—had defined with his philosophy of reincarnation. Cayce had felt that major human events within one life were largely predetermined: birth, work, death—but by reactions to events, by the choices he made, man shaped the karma—the debit or credit ledger—shaping his next life.

Everything about us was planned—the seasons, the movements of the planets, the endless cycle of animal and plant life. The leaves budded, bloomed, then withered and fell. Did the leaf, tumbling, know it would renew itself in another season, taking pretty much the same shape as the old leaf. Or was it an entirely new leaf?

"Whatever drops out of life is somewhere," said the philosopher Emperor Marcus Aurelius, "for the world loses nothing. If it stays here, it also changes here, and is dissolved with its proper parts, which are elements of the universe and of yourself."

Casey Jones was sufficiently sophisticated to understand how little man knew of the universe and his place in it. "At one time we thought we were the only planet with life, now we realize we are a rather unimportant speck in a universe of billions of planets."

He regarded me with a dry smile. "With infinity a definite possibility, how can we rule out any plausibility?"

Was there life on other planets?

He shrugged. "The most serious scientists consider this almost a certainty today. The only question seems the form this life may take. Through vanity perhaps, or lack of imagination, we have the idea this extraterrestrial life should resemble earth life. But it could be something completely different, without physical form."

Life without material substance was certainly an energy force, intangible, invisible, but expressing itself in dynamic terms—perhaps a spirit form. But whose spirit? The spirit of the dead, of the yet to be born, or of those who somehow inhabited the timeless spacelessness experienced in our own forays into space?

"Do you believe in spirits?" I asked.

"I've never met any."

"What else would reincarnation indicate?"

He nodded. "That's right, but plausible or not, it remains to be proven." He paused. "An orderly cycle of life might explain some obvious injustices: children born with physical and mental handicaps, the innocent suffering, the wicked prospering, wars, disease, death."

In a spirit of adventure, Casey had accompanied MacIver on his first excursion to Massey, and subsequently visited Eagles with him. He was obviously intrigued by the search at this stage, and rather pleased to be included in the expedition into the Tank Range.

Joanne, too, seemed pleased at Casey's being along as we headed out one morning for the range. "He's solid," she said, in the teenage vernacular.

Casey showed just how solid he was. "How does the Major feel about the search?" he asked, as he deftly wheeled in and out of traffic.

"He thinks it's some sort of genealogical search—which, in a way, it is."

"Aren't you going to tell him?"

"It might only embarrass him."

Casey's ruddy face turned reflective. "That should be his decision."

Traveling west on main highway 26, hugging the shoreline of Georgian Bay (somehow Nottawasaga Bay at this point), we cut through the heart of Ontario's picturesque resort country. After Wasaga Beach, a honky-tonk playland, we swiftly approached the Blue Mountains, a blur of color whose smooth slopes ran almost down to the road. Joanne, an inveterate skier, exclaimed enthusiastically, "What great sport, they come from all over the country for it."

It seemed a wonderfully romantic winter paradise.

Joanne sniffed. "You can't prove it by me."

Eyes aglow, she pointed to the ski runs and tows, and the chalets nestling snugly below. "Why worry about romance, when there's a chance to ski?" We didn't know how curiously prophetic her words were then.

One moment she was a paragon of wisdom, another an unsophisticated adolescent, rather backward as adolescents went these days.

The search itself still left her cold.

Casey chuckled quietly. "She's had four years of it, and she's sick of it."

"The Tank Range should be a new experience," I said hopefully.

"Yes," she agreed perfunctorily, her eyes floating back to the slopes of the Blue Mountain.

"During the winter," she said, "it's beautiful, the glint of the sun on the hard snow, the skiers flashing down the hill."

As an expert skier, Joanne was one of the youngest in the Canadian Ski Patrol, a lifesaving group.

"I wonder," I said, "if Susan Ganier was a skier?"

She snorted. "Snowshoes would have been more like it."

We were now rolling through the town of Meaford, and the Tank Range entrance was only a few miles off. At the marker, Armoured Fighting Vehicle Range, Casey took a sharp right and headed for a gatehouse.

Joanne was practically hanging out the window. "You know," she said, "this road is terribly familiar."

"You were around here a couple of weeks ago," I pointed out.

She grimaced. "You see, that house there—" she pointed to an old stone building, with the solid foundation of a Shaker barn—"that house—or one like it—was the Norris house."

I consulted a map MacIver had given me. The names Angus and Alexander Norris had been inked in, with the year of domicile, 1855.

"Your father has it here," I said, unimpressed.

"I gave it to him," she said.

"I thought Eagles had mentioned the name Norris."

She nodded. "But I picked out the spot on the map and there it is, just as I saw it."

"That's great proof," I said wryly.

"I am just telling you what I recall."

At the gatehouse, a guard took our names, and then murmured politely, "The Major's expecting you at Administration."

Casey parked his station wagon next to a giant tank

The Major soon burst into the scene. He shook hands with Casey and gave Joanne a surprised glance. He obviously had not expected a girl.

"I'll take you around myself," he said. "There's a few duds around and," he grinned, "we wouldn't want anything happening to them."

He ordered a jeep. "It makes for a bumpy ride, but we won't get stuck in some rut."

Joanne and I climbed on back, Casey next to the Major who wore a beret at a rakish angle.

The Major turned to Joanne. "Your name is MacIver?"

Joanne nodded demurely.

"A good Scottish name," he said

"Have you ever heard the name Ganier?" I asked.

He turned his head, a blank look on his face. "There's a Horace Gandier hereabout, is it the same?"

I shook my head.

He brought out a relief map of the range, and crisply reviewed the mission. "You want to see cemeteries, an abandoned house or two, and check over the general terrain." He frowned. "I only know of one cemetery."

Joanne spoke up. "There should be another, by the Twin Churches."

The Major shook his head. "I know this range pretty well, and that's the only cemetery." The Twin Churches were also news to him.

Joanne showed no sign of retreating. "One of the cemeteries is on the township line."

The Major cocked a quizzical eye at the map.

"It's not marked here," he said.

"How accurate is the map?" I asked.

"Accurate in every respect," he said. "Now who would be in that cemetery?"

"Somebody very close to Joanne," I said. "Actually, it's her background we're interested in."

His ears pricked up.

"Well, we'll drive over the place, including the township line, and you will be able to see for yourself." He smiled. "I'll take you to the cemetery I know about first."

We were soon lurching along a narrow dirt road, passing old ruins of houses with an occasional wall standing, and gutted tanks with gaping holes in them. "Those new shells go through a tank," the Major beamed, "as though they were butter."

The jeep suddenly braked to a stop. The Major jumped out, and waved a khaki arm toward an area to the right, incongruously set off from the tangled brush by a white picket fence.

"I don't know what you'll find here," the Major said doubtfully, "people keep chipping off parts of the stones as souvenirs." He surveyed the small graveyard dispassionately. "When Defense moved the last homesteaders off this property, it agreed to maintain the graves." He hitched his shoulders. "But some fifteen headstones have disappeared in the last few years alone."

Some of the stones had sunk even with the turf, others stood at a tilt, but all told the inevitable story:

> *Each in his narrow cell forever laid,*
> *The rude forefathers of the hamlet sleep.*

I quickly passed through the rows of graves: Mac-Larens, Carsons, Andersons, Holingheads, but no Ganiers or Marrows. Joanne studied an epitaph faded by time:

> *Boast not thyself of tomorrow, for thou*
> *knowest not what a day may bring forth.*

Then this sobering reflection:

> *Few are thy days and full of woe,*
> *Oh, man of woman born.*

"It is remarkable," I observed, "how philosophical the living are about the dead."

She turned away. "There's got to be another cemetery," she said, with a frown.

"There's one farther along," the Major said, "but with only one grave, a girl's."

"There's another one," she insisted, "on the other side of the range, around Morley, by the Twin Churches."

The Major eyed her speculatively. "I've had two tours of duty on this range, and as I said, I've never heard of another graveyard or the Twin Churches."

As the Major climbed back into the jeep, I whispered in Casey's ear, "How can I tell him we're looking for the grave of a girl riding in his jeep?"

Casey chuckled quietly.

The Major's soft brogue broke in. "We'll take a run up the Seventh Line to Cape Rich, then cut over to the lake, then down the Ninth Line, and over Lower Spring Road to Morley. That takes in most of the range area."

As we bumped along, brushing aside low-hanging branches, bevies of wild life—beavers, an occasional otter, and deer—scurried before us, and mallards, partridge, and quail flew overhead.

The Major cast about a practiced eye. "Funny about these animals, they stay out of range the day we shoot, and then, like clockwork, when it's safe, they come out from cover."

Casey laughed. "Odd that a target range should be a haven for wild life."

Behind every little rustle of foliage, I had the uncanny feeling of being watched, occasionally glimpsing the white tail of a startled doe. "A true hunter's paradise," I observed.

The Major nodded. "Hunting's forbidden, of course. But sometimes we go after a rabid fox, or"—he winked roguishly—"the game gets so thick we have to launch a defensive attack."

Approaching the promontory of Cape Rich, we clambered down a jagged slope onto a pebbly beach of Georgian Bay. The waves broke against giant stones, deposited ages ago by the glacier, and the surf lapped at our feet. The horizon sank away without hint of land, and we might have been facing out on the ocean instead of an inland bay.

Joanne rustled about at my elbow. "Does this do anything for you?" I asked.

She wrinkled her nose. "One body of water looks very much like another."

"How about roads and houses and landscapes?"

"That's different—feelings go with them."

I laughed. "I have feelings about Couchiching."

She tested the wet sand with her toe. "You might have had a meaningful experience there."

"I doubt it."

She turned away abruptly, rejoining Casey and the Major.

"I don't want any of you straying off," the Major cautioned, "touching off those duds."

"Do shells generally wind up in the bay?" I asked.

He chuckled. "Only when we overshoot. By and large, they land on an old tank or ruin."

Continuing our hegira, we wound around the gleaming surface of Mountain Lake, known locally as Little Lake. "In this virtually primitive spot, unspoiled by man," the Major observed, "the fish swimming around in that clear, sparkling water have an incurable blight." They were strangely spotted.

"How did that happen?"

He shrugged. "It could be the law of retribution—maybe they had things too good."

Joanne seemed to be stirring restlessly. As we passed a cluster of apple trees, she eyed the fruit speculatively, and then as we proceeded down the Ninth Line toward a collection of ruins, she half-stood up and blurted, "I've been over this road before."

The Major gave her a mystified glance, then waved toward a pair of dirt tracks slanting off to the right "That's the road to Morley."

Joanne nodded. "I know."

In a few moments, we were in the midst of ruins. "Can we get out and walk around?" Joanne asked.

The jeep came to an abrupt halt.

Nearby was a hillock, the Mountain, which gave the lake its name, and the Mountain was where Arthur Eagles had recalled a Yancey living. The Ganier tract was roughly where Joanne was now studying the ground, occasionally turning up a tuft of grass or a stone. But the earth had been churned up by tanks and there was not even the semblance of a ruin there.

"There's no cemetery here," the Major said, "nor any churchyard."

Joanne looked up the road. "The church was up there a bit." Her voice betrayed a curious wistfulness, and her eyes stared off into space. She was up in the clouds somewhere, visualizing the old homestead as though it were spread out before her. "The Ganier place," she recalled mistily, "had log walls, a small living room, two bedrooms, with a kitchen on the north side, and a fireplace in the corner." She moved about dreamily. "Rachel Brown lived close by on the opposite side of the road."

The Major was obviously bewildered. "We're interested in a family named Marrow, over by Morley," I hastily interjected, pointing to a barely legible Archibald Marrow on the land map.

The Major glanced up. "Now what relation was he?"

"I'm not sure," I said, settling back into the jeep.

After passing a firing area, nostalgically labeled Caen, Dieppe, Ortona, we turned into a rutted dirt road which went directly to Morley.

At Morley, we came to the township line, St. Vincent ending on one side of the road, and Sydenham Township beginning on the other. Now about three miles south of the bay and Vail's Point, we turned north, past a marker, Morley Firing Point, and rode for a half-mile or so without seeing another cemetery.

Joanne kept craning her neck. "It would be by the Twin Churches," she said.

I looked at her curiously. She seemed unusually animated. "You're getting interested?"

"I just have a feeling," she said softly.

On Concession Line Nine of St. Vincent, we had seen nothing but old ruins, nothing that resembled Joanne's description of the Ganier place, since there was nothing standing, and now she was insisting on additional landmarks there were no evidences of.

"Never heard of a cemetery in this area," the Major repeated with a wag of his head.

"Let's turn back to the crossroads," I suggested, "and go south from there; she might see something that would ring a bell."

The Major momentarily took his eye off the road, jogging his head back a bit. "I don't want to seem overly inquisitive," he drawled, "but exactly what kind of search would this be?"

Casey nudged me. The time had come to confide in the gallant Major.

"Have you ever heard of reincarnation?" I asked, without preamble.

The twin cords in the Major's neck suddenly stood out, forming what some call the elevens (11s). He showed no other response.

"Did I shock you?" I asked.

He shook his head. "I'm thinking."

"About what?"

"Who would be reincarnated now, the young lady?"

"She had a vision of a sort that she lived before."

He smiled. "She looks a little young for that."

"Her name was Ganier then, and she was married to a

Tommy Marrow—anyway, that's the story."

Somehow, bouncing down a dirt road in a jeep, it all seemed terribly absurd.

"You've lost the Major," Casey whispered over his shoulder.

I thought of Sandhurst, Dienbienphu, and those years in the Orient, and wasn't so sure.

We were just then passing the Morley intersection; Joanne pointed to a ruins on the left. "Can we take a look there?"

The Major pulled up short, and we all threaded our way through scattered debris to a spot that looked like it had been leveled by bulldozers. Joanne shaded her eyes against the sun. "There was a house here where I'm standing," she said, "and over there"—she pointed to the left beyond a ravine—"was a barn."

She closed her eyes. "There should be a well right about there."

The Major stooped over and examined the surface of the soil. He came up with a rusty nail, square-shafted, about five inches long, and we found crumbled bricks, shards of pottery, and bits of steel—and, rather amazingly, a well where Joanne had signified.

"When did this Susan live before?" the Major asked.

"Oh, about a hundred years ago."

He handed me one of the square nails. "Well, you might inquire about the age of this one."

I had scooped up a couple of nails of varying size myself. "There was a house here," I agreed, "but whose house?"

Joanne was still poking around, edging closer to the ravine, when I caught a blur of fur on a crest beyond, Two deer stood paralyzed for a moment, a sculptor's dream, then bounded off into the woods.

Joanne gazed fondly after them, as though they were old friends.

The sun had receded by now and the Major consulted his watch. "Getting on to dinner," he said cheerfully.

Joanne looked wistfully up the road.

"I think Tommy's house was a half-mile up or so."

"We must have gone by it," I said.

She nodded. "I got that feeling."

"How about the Twin Churches?"

"We didn't go quite far enough up for that."

The Major had had enough for one day. "You can always come back," he said. "Just give me a jingle."

It had been a long arduous day, though it didn't seem so in the summing up. Joanne had manifested some recollection near the so-called Ganier property, visualizing a home and picking out a nearby church, in the area of a virtual colony of Browns. Somewhere between the Ganier and the Marrow we located a spot, the Mountain, where Eagles had placed a Yancey. In a clutter of debris, on the township line, Joanne had picked out a well, on roughly a line from where Eagles had stood and pointed diagonally southeast. However, we had found no graveyard with the names we were seeking, nor the remains of the Twin Churches and an adjacent cemetery, nor the Marrow house, which should have been close by.

As the Major said, though, we could always have another try at it. Meanwhile, taking advantage of his kindness, we stopped by at the Officers' Club, and the promise of the pause that refreshes.

The Major's versatility intrigued me. "You've had an unusual career?" I said.

"We've moved around a bit, the wife and I," he acknowledged.

"Did you like the Far East?"

"It was an education," he smiled.

"So we can't win in Vietnam?"

"Not and leave anything there to build on."

He shook his head. "It's an entirely different way of life, and we don't understand it any more than we understand"—he hesitated—"your project. The point of view depends on where you're at. And they think differently than the West. Everything in Vietnam is for sale, and they keep selling the same thing over and over again to different people." He thought a moment. "I can remember the Chinese—the merchant class—bringing their goods through Vietnamese checkpoints. The guards would stand there as big as life, and shake their heads—against regulations. The Chinese would slip something in their hands, and the goods would go through. Regulations had just changed."

With a laugh, he turned briskly back to the present. "As regards this project of yours," he said, "you might check the Meaford *Express*. Their old files could very well list the old-timers living on the property before the Army took over. Then there's the Meaford Museum, they have old voters' lists, back before the turn of the century, I believe."

He stood up suddenly, took Casey's hand, then Joanne's, and eyes twinkling, said, "You might even check the Irish block—she's a right pretty lassie."

During the next few days, my mind turned gratefully to the Major, for an interest that made my own interest seem less ephemeral.

Actually, though, the more remote the area—the less intellectually oriented—the more open-minded its people appeared. With even the most routine Orillians, the psychic seemed taken for granted, local journalist Jim Pauk pointing out that this was not at all unusual on the Canadian frontier, where the harshness of the land seemed to demand intuitive rapport of the settler. Nothing of a clairvoyant nature apparently surprised anybody, though a healthy skepticism was everywhere apparent. Many were fascinated when Dr. Rolph Alexander, a notable metaphysician, stood confidently in Couchi-ching park, presumably dissolving overhead clouds with the magnetic action of his mind. In the nearby Indian reserve of Rama, they spoke of the Indian artist who dreamed of a destructive fire, shortly before an Orillia building housing his art was destroyed by flames. What if skeptics did suggest a careless cigarette had more to do with it than any vision of the future.

Even the local airwaves reflected the fascination with the occult. I was intrigued one day by a horoscope report from Orillia station CFOR, a gently persuasive voice announcing, "There are those who say destiny is written by the stars and that every day there is a message. Come with us as we scan the twelve houses of the Zodiac. Listen carefully for your sign as designated by the days and month of the year of your birth."

I listened for my own Taurus, and wondered how many Orillians with birthdays were tuned in for the star-watcher's birthday bonus: "If you were born today, a special message awaits you."

And then, after all the fanfare, the lame apologia: "Your daily horoscope is presented solely for your entertainment. It does not propose to suggest a belief or judgment on any science or pseudo science. It acknowledges that it is man's will and not fate that determines the future."

Cowards!

Just as the airwaves recognized destiny, they also acknowledged destiny's end—death.

Staring out moodily on Couchiching one day, I was startled to suddenly hear the radio roll of those "gone to their just reward." The background music was eminently suitable:

> *O light that followest all my way*
> *I yield my flickering torch to thee.*

It was a sad day that the Voice of In Memoriam proclaimed: "There are no deaths to report today."

In this rarefied climate, I had the feeling after a while that anything was possible, as long as it was bizarre. I still made occasional forays into Grey County for old-timers, hunched over stacks of records, and kept checking back with the MacIvers. I had no luck locating the nonagenarian Mrs. McDonald, who had lived on the township line as a girl, but after a most unrewarding experience with Henry McCutcheon, a contemporary of Arthur Eagles, I questioned how much I could count on direct testimony.

Young Bob Fournier, who had done much prying on his own, had told me of McCutcheon, saying the old man had vaguely remembered a Ganier and a Marrow, but McCutcheon, when I finally found him near Balaclava, had trouble remembering even Fournier.

I did turn to the Irish block, as the Major had suggested, but since it had been solidly Catholic, and Joanne had stressed Mason Ganier's Protestantism, it appeared idle to linger here.

My meetings with Joanne were invariably pleasant but brief, except for one notable evening at the local inn, the only Orillia dining place stressing jacket and tie. She was demurely dressed, but still self-conscious in the unaccustomed formality. I was amused, privately, of course, at her uncertainty as to what fork to use with the salad, a sharp contrast with her extreme sophistication in the more unschooled aspects of life.

As a matter of course, we discussed our proposed return to the range. "If we go north a bit from Morley, I'm sure I can pick out the Twin Churches and the cemetery," she said.

"And whose body shall we find?" I asked.

She chose to take me seriously. "If bodies are all you're

looking for, you should have no great problem."

I was reminded of the distinction between body and spirit made by the most pragmatic of reincarnationists, that exemplar of thrift and prudence, Benjamin Franklin. He had put it very well in his epitaph: "The body of Benjamin Franklin, the printer (like the cover of an old book, its contents worn out, and stript of its lettering and gilding) lies here, food for the worms. Yet the work itself shall not be lost, for it shall, as he believes, appear once more in a new and beautiful edition, corrected and amended by the Author."

Joanne listened politely. "This," she said, "is no revelation to me."

"If you were buried in that Twin Church cemetery," I said, "then you obviously lived close by."

She mused a moment. "I felt a terrible feeling of familiarity at the place where we saw the deer."

"One deer looks like another," I said.

"Please," she groaned.

The food was good, and she was silent for the rest of the meal, enjoying her dinner. But after dessert, she regarded me with a contemplative eye.

"Have you ever watched a colony of ants?" she asked abruptly.

"Human ants or ant ants?"

"No matter how close scurrying ants get to a person they don't seem to notice him until it's too late. Their world is so small that they aren't aware of anything as big as a human, until his action affects them in some way."

I was still waiting.

"That's how people are; in their smallness, they can't see God or His plan, until His actions are somehow dramatically reflected in their lives."

It was rather interesting analogy from a girl who wasn't quite sure of the right fork.

"And how," I said, "do you find God?"

Her eyes met mine gently. "In everything around me, in what I do and see, in glimpses of my own past and my destiny."

And was it part of her destiny that she not only marry young and have children, but somehow be the vehicle by which a doubting world would be given a glimpse into its own destiny through a manifestation of reincarnation? As Crowley had suggested, we were here to remember, and Joanne MacIver, aged seventeen, unknown, could remember with Wordsworth.

> *Our birth is but a sleep and a forgetting:*
> *The soul that rises with us, our life's star,*
> *Hath had elsewhere its setting,*
> *And cometh from afar:*
> *Not in entire forgetfulness,*
> *And not in utter nakedness,*
> *But trailing clouds of glory do we come*
> *From God, who is our home:*
> *Heaven lies about us in our infancy!*

A marveling Ralph Waldo Emerson had called this the "high water mark which the intellect has reached in this age," and yet, with no stress on intellect, Joanne might very well have a greater impact on human thought.

"All people work in some measure towards the ends of Providence," said Marcus Aurelius, "some with knowledge and design, though others are not sensible of it."

Although I was to think long of what Joanne had said, I did not see her again until we were finally ready for the trip back to the Tank Range.

She was in a jolly mood, again singing to herself, "We're off to Dublin in the green . . . " and then, "You can't be loved unless you want to be, peaches won't grow on a cherry tree."

"You're in fine spirits," I said.

"Why not, it's a wonderful day, and I have my whole life before me."

"And a few behind you."

She wrinkled her nose. "Can't we forget all that until we get there?"

"Sure, we'll stop off in Meaford for breakfast, then look at the cemetery . . . "

She moaned. "I've been through more cemeteries than a grave robber."

"Who knows, you might find Tommy Marrow there?"

She gave me a scathing look. "You don't listen . . . Tommy is buried on the farm where he lived with Susan."

Her face was flushed, her eyes sparkled, even her teeth gleamed. She was radiance personified.

"You and Tag must have ironed out your differences," I said.

"We have no real differences."

"The perfect romance?"

Her lips puckered thoughtfully. "We're friends."

"Did you know him before?"

"I'm not sure I know him now."

"In rating a potential husband," I asked, "what is the chief requirement?"

"Somebody I respect."

"How would you know somebody was right?"

"I'd know."

"But how?"

"I would love him."

"And how strong would this love be."

She frowned slightly. "Sex is a part of love, but love is not a part of sex. Love can wait, or not wait, as the situation demands; it means putting the other person ahead of one's self. So sex would never be a problem, really, when two people love one another."

We rode silently for many miles, drinking in the scenery. "Wait till the leaves change," she said finally. "People drive all the way from Toronto to see our trees change color."

Soon we were in Meaford. The town, with its population of 3800, had become a radiating point for the search. Owen Sound (formerly Sydenham), the Grey County seat, was a few miles west; Massie was not far south; Morley, Annan, Balaclava (near Eagles' farm) were close by, and the Tank Range was a short ways up Route 26. The Meaford cemetery, within walking distance, was spread over several acres. As far as the eye could see, there was a sea of graves, some simple markers, others grandiose vaults, all jammed together without regard for station or temperament.

Joanne considered the graves thoughtfully. "There's nothing really under those stones," she said, "that's why they're called the remains."

"There may be a name we're looking for."

She shook her head. "I would feel it if there were."

I laughed. "There are so many graves that even the wrong Marrow or Ganier may be here."

The cemetery superintendent, Wilfred Barr, a veteran of World War II, had been tending graves for thirty years. A friendly man, he was very much the philosopher. "We keep growing," he said proudly. "We're seeding another four and a half acres, and we'll need more." He looked around with a practiced eye. "We already have a bigger population than the town, some five to six thousand."

"May I browse around?" I asked.

"You can't bother anybody here," he said dryly.

"Are you sure of that?"

"Never surer." He chuckled reminiscently. "Every once

in a while, after a service, a minister asks me what I think
about it all?"

I was truly surprised. "You mean a minister wanted
your opinion?"

He nodded affably. "Oh, yes, some ask where it all ends
up?"

"And what do you tell them?"

He pointed to the stone at our feet. "Right there."

"If that's the end of it," I said, "what's the purpose of it?"

"Enjoy yourself while you can," he said. He looked
over at me quizzically. "Anybody in particular you looking for?"

I spelled out the names—Marrow and Ganier, or Gainer.

He wagged his head. "Relatives?"

"Not mine."

Curiously, the curator for the departed was as sure
about the finality of death as Joanne was about the survival of the spirit. And, ironically, on less evidence. How
could any custodian of bodies determine whether there
was a human soul or not? What special proof did he have
that death was the be-all and end-all. How did he know
that the invisible spirit had not moved off on its ap-
pointed course, as unlikely as it might seem? Obviously,
all he knew was that a stockbroker or a farmer or a carpenter was laid to rest, and their peculiar function ter-
minated with nobody, or almost nobody, hearing from
them again. Still, this was only evidence by inference,
and the soul could live on for all anybody knew to the
contrary.

"What is death?" Marcus Aurelius had asked. "It is a
resting from the vibrations of sensation, and the swayings
of desire, the rambling of thought, and a release from the
drudgery of your body."

The curator was no philosopher himself. "What do
you think about reincarnation?" I asked.

His face turned blank. "What's that?"

"The soul returning in another body."

He laughed. "I never saw one get up yet, but I suppose there's always a first time."

With a wave of his arm, he put the cemetery at our disposal.

I had never perused so many gravestones in my life, getting a feeling after a while that I was walking among old friends.

"You develop a compassion for the whole human race in a cemetery," Joanne observed.

"Don't you have the feeling their problems are over?"

"Not me," she smiled, "I have an idea their headaches are just continuing."

After two hours plodding in the hot sun, we were ready to leave philosophy to others and take nourishment. The tour through the vale of death had not affected Joanne's appetite in the least.

"You eat," I said, "as though you didn't get enough in the last life."

She smiled self-consciously. "I guess nobody can say that about me this time around."

Had she felt my sense of recognition here in Meaford?

She shook her head. "Not in the least. Of course, things have changed over the years."

After lunch, we dropped by the Meaford *Express* to check old files. Publisher Walter B. Brebner, a former advertising executive, greeted us warmly.

"The Major mentioned your project," he said.

His eyes fell on Joanne. "I guess she's the one."

Joanne smiled uncertainly.

"Any luck so far?" he asked.

I shook my head. "We can't even find graves with the right names."

He smiled sympathetically. "We're having trouble lo-

cating the graves of many of the fathers of the Confed-
eration, and they were not obscure citizens in some obscure hamlet, but the most prominent leaders of their
time."

He showed us a recent editorial:

"The grave of the first Speaker in Canada's first House
of Commons, James Cockburn, is difficult to identify in
a Toronto cemetery. The ravages of time and weather
have obliterated his name from the simple stone that
marks his grave . . . perhaps it is even now too late to find
and identify the graves of some of the Fathers of Confed-
eration."

It was worse, he conceded, in rural areas. "The farther
you go from the big cities, the more difficult it gets. Fortunately, Canada's Boy Scouts are looking for the graves."

I sighed. "If you see any Boy Scouts, send them to me."

There was a new disappointment. Brebner's paper
only went back sixty years. However, the files of a prede-
cessor, the Meaford *Mirror,* were in the Meaford Museum. He had still another suggestion: "Look up Vina
Ufland, our librarian. She's from a pioneer family herself, and a bit of a local historian."

The town hall housed the police department as well
as the public library. It was a sedate red brick structure
of Victorian vintage, decorated by an imposing figure of
an infantryman and a bronze plaque with forty-four
names: "In honoured memory of the men of the town of
Meaford and St. Vincent Township, who died for king and
country in the Great World War."

There were no Marrows, no Ganiers among these
dead, or on a smaller bronze panel for the thirty-five in
World War II "who gave their lives in defense of Canada
and the Empire."

The library was small but compact, like its supervisor,
the spinsterish Miss Ufland.

Her owl-like eyes regarded Joanne with unblinking interest. "So you're the girl with the dream?"

Joanne blushed prettily.

"Do you know anything about reincarnation?" I asked, diverting her attention.

"It'll take some proving," she said, with an emphatic cluck of her tongue.

"I'm trying to track back on some early settlers," I said.

She nodded toward the crowded book shelves. "I have a couple of journals and diaries you might find something in."

"Even so, I'm still not sure how significant it would be."

Her eyes shone benevolently behind their glasses. "Why not use your imagination?" she said. "I was a newspaper reporter once, and I must say it's a help."

She turned back to Joanne, regarding her doubtfully.

"You really have a recollection of things?"

"Some things," Joanne said shortly.

Miss Ufland beamed approvingly. "This young generation has so many talents."

"You don't remember any Ganiers or Marrows yourself?" I asked.

She smiled. "I'm not quite that ancient."

She shuffled over to a shelf, and pulled down a small journal. It was the diary of Peter Fuller, a Meaford bank manager, who had emigrated from England in 1852, at the age of twenty-six, settled in St. Vincent, where he built a sawmill, got into banking, and died in 1890.

"He mentioned a lot of people," she said, "and he may have mentioned the people you want to know about." She contemplated me with a maternal air. "Anyway, it should give you the flavor of the times. He was quite a gentleman, was Peter Fuller. Grandfather Bumstead knew him well."

Joanne and I plumped down at a corner table, and

were soon in another century. Banker Fuller had the facility of vividly re-creating a land where money and sentiment were equally sparse.

Not one to waste words, in June 1859, he noted:

"Hired a girl today at a dollar and a half for a month." Again, "Sold potatoes at 37 1/2 cents a bushel."

We were leafing idly through Fuller's pages when Joanne's eyes suddenly stopped:

"Mr. Stephenson buried in his garden in the back of the house."

It seemed to take her back to another time and place. "I guess," she said slowly, "Tommy wasn't the only one who was buried where he belonged."

Swiftly, I skimmed the pages, looking for clues, and found instead: "Attacked by Jarman's bull on my way from the barn. Mr. Bull altered into a stag in the evening."

Many names were sprinkled through the journal: Carney, Ayling, Purdy, Watkins, Chandler, names I had encountered nowhere else, each adding its touch to the picture of the times. "Traded my rifle to Jess Wright for a cow, assisted Mrs. Aberg with a concert in the evening."

"Too bad," I observed, as Joanne flipped a page, "that you didn't pick out a common name for yourself."

Joanne bridled. "I didn't pick out any name."

I returned to the last entry.

"What concert would that be?"

"Hardly the Philharmonic," she snapped. "Somebody brought a fiddle and a guitar, and they may have had a piano."

"How would you know?"

"Nostalgia."

Peter Fuller showed himself something of a philosopher. As the New Year rang out uneventfully in 1868, he noted solemnly, "Another year has hasted its course along, and whether used or wasted, is now forever gone."

Joanne was reading ahead of me, with an expression of dismay. I soon found out why. Peter Fuller's wife, Frances, had died in the spring of 1870, and in October, that same year, "Mrs. Mary Foster became my partner in life."

"He didn't waste any time," I commented.

She grimaced. "I suppose he had to have somebody to take care of the house and farm—the beast."

I recalled that Susan Marrow hadn't remarried.

"She didn't want to settle for anything less than she had," Joanne decided.

"I don't see where she had so much."

Joanne regarded me pityingly. "That's because you're a man."

The watchful Miss Ufland trundled over with another book. "Keep at it," she said cheerfully, "you never know when you may find a friend."

Three or four books later, there was still not a clue. The authors had known a lot of people, but, unfortunately, the wrong ones. I had not come across a reference to the Eagles family, and I found that encouraging.

"If they didn't know Eagles, why Marrow or Ganier?" I whispered to Joanne.

"Please don't belittle my people." She smiled broadly.

We had run through the available books, and there was nothing to stay for. Miss Ufland trailed us to the door. "Come again," she said warmly, "and use your imagination."

She gave Joanne's hand a gentle squeeze.

I really had not expected much. Even if we did find a familiar name, the difficulty of tying it meaningfully to the present was an obvious problem. Still, one never knew when a moment of illumination might strike. And so we moved on hopefully to the Meaford Museum, a structure quaintly resembling a summer playhouse. In

the guest book we spotted a familiar name: Julius Cae-
sar, Rome, Italy.

I nudged Joanne. "Would you consider that evidence
of reincarnation?"

She gave me a sour look, and moved away.

Many visitors were browsing through books and
newspapers, examining photographs, fingering ancient
articles of dress and appraising furnishings which
seemed to have popped out of the Victorian era.

One wall featured tintypes of early St. Vincent settlers.
There were Breadners, Wrights, Richmonds, Wards, but
no Ganiers or Marrows; nor were there Eagles or Browns,
Watsons or Urquharts, families that had left a definite
mark on the land.

They were a rugged-looking group, these pioneers, all
out of the same tough mold.

"See anybody you know?" I asked.

Joanne shook her head.

We were approached at this point by a gray-haired,
pleasant-faced woman, filling in for the curator. She was
familiar with the old voters' lists but couldn't find any
before 1909. "They're not very accurate anyway," she
observed. "My husband's name was left off once, though
he voted in the previous election, and tenants weren't
listed, only landlords."

I browsed through some old directories, including the
Ontario *Gazetteer* for 1903, and stopped at "McMillan,
sawmill."

Joanne's brows arched. "There's a familiar name."

"In what sense?"

"As if I knew it from somewhere."

"But how and where?"

She shrugged. "I don't know, except I have that feeling
you get when a name eludes you."

"You remember just short of enough," I said.

"Would you like me to make it up?" Her voice had an edge to it.

"I would just like a nice connected series of facts."

"All wrapped up in a nice convenient little package."

She was still in a bit of a stew when the curator brought over some old copies of the defunct Meaford *Mirror.* Leafing through the issue of May 27, 1892, her eye was struck by a corset advertisement: "Reasons Why Our New Ladies' Waist Corset Should Be Worn."

"Just think," I said, "Susan Ganier may have bought a corset from that."

Joanne sniffed. "It came along too late for her to care."

She read on with mock seriousness:

" 'Ladies ever so frail can wear them with ease and comfort.

" 'They can be worn with or without steels in front as desired.

" 'They never break down like ordinary corsets.

" 'They have given universal satisfaction to every lady that has worn them.' "

Joanne, laughing, was obviously no corset girl.

The next stop-off was the Major's. It being an off day, we found him at home, only a few minutes from the Museum. He was casually clad, relaxed, as hospitable as ever.

"I've made arrangements for you," he said, cocking one eye. "Any luck so far?"

"I'm getting to know the country."

He grinned. "Stay on the roads and don't hit any deer. By the way, did you check the Irish block?"

I nodded toward Joanne, in rapt conversation with the Major's wife. "Her Twin Churches were Methodist or Quaker."

"Good luck," he smiled.

Once on the Tank Range, Joanne drove with uncanny direction, passing the Administration Building, rows of tanks, and heading for Vail's Point, at the top of the town line dividing St. Vincent and Sydenham.

From Vail's Point on the bay, south, we would retrace the route Arthur Eagles' father would have taken to the Widow Marrow's, some three miles from the water.

Joanne took the dirt roads with remarkable sureness, and it wasn't long before we were looking out on the blue haze of Georgian Bay. As we proceeded slowly south on the line, instead of coming up as before, Joanne recalled our last visit. "Another half-mile or so north," she said, "and we might have hit the Marrow house."

"Which Marrow house?"

"Tommy's house, our house."

"And the churches?"

"That would be another mile or so up the road."

"North of the Marrow house?"

She nodded. "Yup."

We had now come to an intersection, a mile or so south of Vail's Point, stretching off to our right, to nearby Balaclava.

She stopped the car. "I have a feeling the Tommy Marrow house was not on the Tank Range, as my father thought, but just opposite it in Sydenham."

Arthur Eagles had stood near Silcote, just south and west of us, and pointed south and east for the Widow Marrow's house, where she had presumably moved after Tommy's death.

Joanne frowned. "That could very easily have been where we saw the deer."

"All right," I said, "let's head west toward Balaclava then south on the Sydenham side."

We drove a quarter of a mile over bumpy road, to a Tank Range barrier. Immediately beyond, narrow tracks stretched south, into spotty cow pasture.

"We'll have to walk it," I said.

"You're kidding?" Joanne said. "It's one hundred in the shade."

I grinned. "We can rest under an apple tree in the family orchard."

I hurtled over a wire barricade, and Joanne reluctantly followed, sliding down the side of a gully on the seat of her slacks.

We trudged south in the sun for about two hundred yards or so, until we came to a wooden gate, separating us from a small herd of peacefully grazing cattle. As we passed through the gate, the cows perked up their heads and began to warily sidle off. Two bulls, however, stood their ground, tails twirling, front legs tentatively poised.

"You don't have to worry," I said, "until they paw the dirt."

"They're Herefords," Joanne cried, slurring her words in her excitement.

I misunderstood. "They're the strangest heifers I ever saw."

"Herefords," she repeated, in some exasperation.

Meanwhile, the lead bull was edging toward us, a red-flecked eye rolling angrily, as we cautiously angled for the Tank Range fence.

"If he starts to run," I said, "we'll go over the fence."

Suddenly the bull, now about fifty feet off, began to paw the dirt. I shouted, "Hit the fence."

Joanne got one leg over the barrier, and then with a desperate glance over her shoulder, gasped, "They ought to call this place Bullaclava."

"Very funny," I said, following her over the fence. We sprawled in the tall grass for a few moments, trading stares with our four-legged adversary, who gave us one last baleful look before stiffly backing off.

Retreating discreetly, we were soon back at the car, continuing south on the town line. We had proceeded but a short distance, when, consulting a Tank Range map, I said, "Your Twin Churches should be right about here from what you said."

On the left, even as I spoke, was an old ruin, little more than a shell, with a remnant of stone wall, and four unusually wide window embrasures. There was no flooring, no ceiling, nothing but the foundation and fragment of wall. I measured the foundation carefully with my eye. There were no subdivisions for rooms, it was obviously all one space. "This could very easily have been a small church," I said.

Joanne looked around at the rubble underfoot. "There's no sign of a barn," she said, "so it couldn't have been a farmstead." She gestured through the ruins toward the rear. "That is where the churchyard must have been."

"What churchyard?"

We were shuffling through the debris now toward the spot she indicated. Suddenly, even as I looked at her, her eyes took on a glazed, faraway look. "The cemetery," she said. "They buried their dead behind the church."

I looked about helplessly. "Then there should be some markers around."

We were now in the middle of a pile of rubble, turning the dirt with our shoes.

"I don't know whether we'll find anything," she said, "the ground's been pulverized by tanks." Her eyes, I noticed, had resumed their normal expression.

Suddenly, my toe encountered something hard and resisting. I managed to loosen it, and then tugged. It was a slab of stone, four inches square, two inches thick, and crystal white where it had jaggedly broken off. It was clearly a piece of a gravestone. On one side were the numerals 66, and the lower portion of two letters not readily discernible. On the reverse, the letters G and O.

I examined the foundation with renewed interest. The

church could have seated perhaps fifty to sixty worshipers in comfort. There would hardly have been a need for more in 1866.

Joanne was still viewing the site reflectively.

"Was this Methodist or Quaker?" I asked.

"Methodist," she replied.

"And was Susan married here?"

"No, in a hall."

"Then what happened here?"

Her face grew suddenly wistful.

"Susan was buried here."

"Shall we look for her gravestone?"

She shrugged. "It was only a wooden cross and you saw what was left of stone."

I found myself suddenly irked.

"How would you remember all this now, even if it were so?"

"Ever since I was first hypnotized, certain landmarks, names, words even, seem to touch off other impressions." Her blue eyes regarded me evenly. "That's one of the reasons I don't like going over everything again—it keeps bringing up what I would sooner forget."

We turned back to the car. The stone, weighing three or four pounds, I put in the glove compartment, with three rusty nails from the earlier expedition. I was building up quite a collection.

As we continued south, stopping now and then to examine a ruin, Joanne kept shaking her head. "There should be apple trees, and a little gulch, and a barn bigger than the house."

"How do you figure that?"

"The house was small; we never had to add on to it."

Knowing the answer, I still asked why.

"No children," she replied.

We were now three miles from Vail's Point, and perhaps a half-mile above the Morley intersection. Having left the car at this point, we were sauntering down the town line road, when Joanne started walking briskly across the dirt road, to a ruin beyond a wire barrier, "Do you see that old orchard?" she said tensely.

I saw a few gnarled old fruit trees on the Sydenham side, and a cluster of ruins little different from any other local ruin. Joanne's stride quickened to a jog as we passed a wooden gate to a pathway hidden in the brush. She walked slowly through a crumbled ruin, peeked over the low walls, and pointed to a larger ruin across a narrow gully.

"That was the barn," she said slowly.

She rummaged around the foundations, studying the layout, and occasionally frowning. It looked a shambles to me, and could only have been a modest house at best.

But Joanne seemed thoroughly at home. "This was the pantry," she said, touching a patch of a wall. "And this," frowning over a solid slice of stone, "was the porch."

Her eyes glowed. "This is the kind of a place I'd like to live in."

Our eyes met over the scattered rubble and we burst out laughing.

She pointed airily toward the gate. "There was a well there, and another by the barn."

She stepped out into what must have been backyard, and jogged a few paces to where a walkway bridged a small creek. "How many farms have a walkway like that?" she said proudly.

She circled leisurely, standing in the middle of an apple orchard and then pointing to a terrace back of the house, plumped herself on the broken edge of a wall and rocked her legs. "This is the only place I feel comfortable."

Restlessly, however, she jumped up and started poking through the ruins again, scooping up rocks, bits of steel, slats of wood, casting them away with a grimace. "There's nothing there of mine."

Frowning now, she again studied the outlines of the rooms. Seeming to have lost some of her sureness, she pointed to what I would have assumed to be the living room, since it was the largest area, and called it the bedroom. The smaller room incongruously became the living room.

It just didn't seem logical.

She wandered around the interior, shaking her head as she passed from one room to another. "Strange," she said, "but this isn't quite the way I remember it." She stopped at the stone remnant of a staircase. "I don't recall anything like that. But the site, the walkway, the terrace, the room spaces give me a definite feeling."

"What kind of feeling?"

"As if I could reach out and touch another part of me."

I looked around at the ugly ruins, marveling what she could see.

"You felt something in Orillia that Dave Manuel had no conception of," she countered mildly.

She kept moving about, occasionally checking the angle of the landscape from a window position. "That ridge," she said, "is just where it should be, and so are the apple trees."

She stepped out on the make-believe porch again. "The trees are very old now," she said, looking at the gnarled apple tree growing out of the ruins. "The house was neat and compact and it was white."

"How do you know it was white?"

Her eyes kept roving about. "Because it was her house. Not having children, she put in the walkway and terrace to beautify things and keep busy in the summertime. She would sit out in the afternoon sun, enjoying the view, waiting for Tommy to come to dinner."

As she reacted again with that faraway look I had come to know so well, it was obvious that Joanne had projected herself into Susan's subconscious personality—or was Susan. Watching her, I could understand now for the first time how she had been so impressive under hypnosis.

Suddenly now, she sat down on a slab of stone, and I could sense the sadness in the droop of her head. Tears had welled in her eyes, and she quickly averted her head. She sat motionless, head bowed, for five minutes as the birds chirped overhead and the chipmunks played in the rocks.

Slowly, she raised her head. "Why do I all at once feel so horrible when I felt so good at first?"

"Perhaps, because of what the scene represents."

"I haven't tried to do anything, it just came over me."

I helped her to her feet.

"What came over you?"

"The terrible feeling that Tommy had died here, and was buried here." She gestured vaguely toward the barn. "Over there where the pathway crosses the creek."

I took her by the arm. "Shall we leave by the gate?"

She kept her voice firm. "By all means, let us depart in style."

We made it slowly back to the road. As she got into the car, she said in a voice huskier than usual, yet oddly highpitched, "I don't think we have to look any farther."

I marked the site, and noted the surrounding landmarks. There was an apiary a hundred yards away; and near the barn, closer to the road, the remains of a timbered house which I had not noticed before.

We drove silently, each preoccupied with his thoughts. I thought more deliberately now of the possible explanations of the recent scene: Joanne had dramatized her subconscious to where she actually believed she was

Susan Ganier, and was playing out the fantasy of a previous life. Or it was all an act, expertly contrived to gain attention, and profit through this attention. Or, having incredibly been Susan Ganier, she did have God-given glimpses of another time and place, with a dramatic impact she could neither anticipate nor control.

On Route 26, we soon came to a highway arrow to Bognor. On an impulse, thinking of the nonagenarian we had missed before, I took the turnoff, saying, "Let's call on Mrs. McDonald, it's on the way." We soon found the house, and a woman of perhaps sixty, with a friendly face, came to the door of the modest dwelling. She was Mrs. Duncan Lourie, and it was her mother I wanted to see.

In a few moments, a very old woman, with straight gray hair, and an austere countenance, walked into the living room and coolly acknowledged our presence.

She was joined by her son-in-law, Duncan Lourie, an amiable heavyset farmer.

Mrs. McDonald seemed unusually alert. But when I asked about the Ganiers and Marrows, she only shook her head. The names were totally unfamiliar. Tommy Marrow would have been long dead when she was born, but Susan's widowhood would have overlapped her girlhood.

"Did you know Arthur Eagles?" I asked.

"Not well, he lived up toward Vail's Point then."

She spoke clearly, precisely, distinctly, asking no questions. A shawl was loosely pulled around her shoulders and her hands were calmly folded in her lap.

Her father, Thomas Hughes, a Welsh immigrant, had settled on the township line in 1880, first renting one hundred acres, then acquiring a farm just north of it on his own, and building his own house. Even as recent as the 1880s, however, many settlers didn't know who had the land before them, nor did they much care. "Nearly every old house had people living there," Mrs. McDonald recalled. "They'd move in and work nearby, and stay as long as nobody bothered them." She had never known any of these squatters. The landed "gentry" were something else. She remembered a MacGregor, at Vail's Point just south of Eagles; William and John McMillan, who had a sawmill; a Jack Watson, who kept a grocery at Balaclava, and had the post office there, and a Margaret Speedie, on the way to Owen Sound.

"Exactly where did you live as a girl?" I asked.

"At a spot called Morley, where my father had his farm." She would have been almost on top of the Marrows there, though twenty years after them, and should subsequently have known an old woman living only a half-mile or so down the line in her own time.

"I would have thought so," she agreed, "but there was quite a flow of traffic."

"Didn't people get together to amuse themselves?"

"Oh, the young people had their dancing and sleigh rides in the winter, and in the summer we worked. There wasn't much summer in those days."

"Do you remember the Twin Churches?"

"Yes, they were up the road a bit."

"Methodist and Quaker?"

"Methodist and Baptist."

She seemed so calm and self-assured, I wondered whether she had resolved whatever doubts and misgivings she had about the timeless unknown. Did she feel her own little drama was over with her final breath, or had she accepted the revelation of everlasting life, believing that to enter the gates of heaven one must be reborn again?

And so I asked, "Do you believe in reincarnation?"

Her lips tightened. "I don't believe in spirits."

"Then all of life begins and ends here?"

She regarded me evenly. "I have my own ideas about that." The words precipitately ended the conversation.

My eyes met Joanne's, and we got up to leave.

Mrs. Lourie gave me a friendly smile. "You're not a Canadian?"

"No, but the young lady is."

"You mentioned New York, but I thought you might be from here originally."

"I have never been in this part of Canada before, not knowingly anyway."

She smiled. "We've been to New York."

"How did you like the skyscrapers?" I asked rather fatuously.

"That wasn't what impressed me most." She touched her spectacles lightly. "A lens fell out of my frames, and I took it to an optical shop. The man was busy, but he put the lens back in and then wouldn't take anything for it."

She smiled. "He had never seen us before, and yet in that busy city he could stop to do something for strangers."

I smiled back. "I guess we're not as heartless in New York as we think."

We shook hands. "If you need anything more," Mrs. Lourie said, "I'm sure Mother won't mind."

Mrs. McDonald's stern features relaxed, and she gave Joanne a piercing glance. "I hope you find whatever you're looking for," she said.

Back in the car, Joanne looked rather pensive.

"What?" I asked.

"You know," she said, "I wouldn't mind getting old if I could stay like Mrs. McDonald."

"Did you have any feeling about her?"

She shook her head. "Susan Marrow wouldn't have known her."

"But why wouldn't Mrs. McDonald, even as a child, have heard of an eccentric so close by?"

Joanne laughed. "These people were like your Vermonters, they had no interest in anything but their own circle, and Susan would have been just another squatter."

She thought a moment. "There's something else, the distinction between landowning farmers and those who only worked the land—there was no communication."

"But Arthur Eagles' father was friendly with the widow."

She shrugged. "He wasn't that friendly. Besides, his status was that of an itinerant thresher."

We were now retracing the route, along Nottawasaga or Georgian Bay, approaching Wasaga Beach, the Coney Island of the North Country, where Joanne's interest in the psychic had been earlier piqued by a fortuneteller's sign.

"I've never had my fortune told," she said, blue eyes gleaming. "Have they ever told you anything?"

"Thousands of things."

"Do you believe in them?"

I shrugged noncommittally. "The particular reader may be a fraud, or have an off day like anybody else."

She pursed her lips. "Once we were passing this woman's house, and suddenly, without knowing why, I saw that she was going to die soon."

"How long did it take?"

"A few days."

"Maybe you hexed her."

"No," she replied seriously, "I saw it."

She gave me a sidelong glance. "Did you ever have an experience like that?"

I shook my head. "I generally see brighter things."

The day couldn't have been nicer if we had ordered it,

and the rolling hills wore their foliage proudly.

I looked at the pretty girl next to me. "Is all this scenery familiar to you?"

She wrinkled her nose. "I have no feeling about it—that seems to make the difference."

"You had no feeling about meeting Arthur Eagles, and yet you supposedly knew him before?"

"It was obviously only a fleeting acquaintance with a small boy, so why would I react any more sharply than Susan would have?"

In a few minutes we were on the outskirts of Wasaga Beach. As we drew up to the seeress's house, we saw several people on the porch, waiting for "readings."

"How is she?" Joanne asked a dark-faced man, whose wife was inside.

He regarded her solemnly. "I was here once before, and she told me there would be three deaths close to me in the next few months."

"And what happened?" Joanne asked.

"I lost my wife, father, and brother."

Joanne shivered with anticipatory delight. "I can hardly wait to get in there," she said.

In forty-five minutes she walked in, and a half-hour later she came out.

Her face was radiant.

Waiting now were several newcomers, chiefly unmarried women. "Well?" they asked, almost in a chorus.

"She's interesting," Joanne replied nonchalantly, but she could hardly contain herself until we got back to the car.

"I'm going to live till ninety-five," she enthused, "and I'll know my husband the moment I meet him."

"I suppose you're getting married young?"

She looked at me sharply. "How did you know that?"

I smiled. "I know you."

"What else?"

"You will marry nobody you now know."

"Why do you say that?" She had quite forgotten the fortuneteller.

"It's your pattern."

"What do you base it on?" Her preoccupation with marriage was refreshingly female.

"Your own karma, as you visualize it. You are looking for somebody stable, somebody older, somebody who will like having children; that's what the reborn Susan would want."

She looked at me questioningly. "But you really don't believe I was Susan Ganier."

"No," I smiled, "but you do."

She was not to be put off. "What else do you see?"

"By this same pattern, you should marry before you're out of your teens."

"And how old will he be?"

"Considerably older—about thirty or so." It was my turn to look at her quizzically. "And he will remind you of Tommy in looks and temperament."

"How many children?"

"Three or four," I laughed.

She seemed pleased. "I'd like four, anyway, a good-sized family."

We drove silently for a while. "By the way," I asked, "what else did the fortuneteller say?"

"Just about what you said." She smiled wryly. "Can you see anything else?"

"I'm really not very psychic."

She hesitated. "Will I live in Orillia after I'm married?"

"You really don't want to, do you?"

"I like my family, but I want my own life."

"That's quite natural. Susan Ganier, your alter ego lived in the wilderness. Joanne MacIver came into a similar world, streamlined but still provincial, still confining."

"It's not that bad," she remonstrated. "Not bad—only monotonous."

"You want to make up for the widow's terrible years of loneliness, marry a man like Tommy and have children quickly, far from the bleakness of the North Country."

She nodded thoughtfully. "I do want to get out of this part of the country when I marry, so I suppose I would have to marry somebody I don't know yet."

"Stability, somebody you can lean on, like Susan did Tommy, that's what you want." I laughed. "Your new husband may even look like Tommy, that's how strongly the picture is shaping up from the past—wherever that past comes from."

"How soon will I marry?" she asked.

"Before twenty, and most likely eighteen."

"Why do you say that?"

"Because that's what Susan wants, and you're an extension of the Susan personality."

She looked at me curiously. "You have no idea who you were before?"

"I have no idea of before."

"You're sure?"

"Positive."

Had she somehow mesmerized herself into thinking I was Tommy Marrow?

She suddenly burst into a gale of irrepressible laughter, "Why of course not," she said, "you're a perfect Yancey."

As a cynical hypnotist, Joe questioned everything—life, death, taxes, love. People were motivated purely by self-interest, and truth was an anachronism. "Anybody can say she's lived before," he grunted.

"Do you think she made it all up?" wife Ruth asked.

"Why not? It must get dull in Orillia."

I felt a flutter of anticipation. "It won't be dull long."

Joe growled, "She'll have to prove it."

"I do feel she's sincere," I said, "but I'll leave the rest to you."

Joe's lip curled. "You're a brave man."

I recalled my own reaction as I first gazed into those bottomless blue eyes.

"Wait until you meet her."

He looked out calmly at the flowing rows of maples. "I can hardly wait."

The motor trip from the Toronto airport took under two hours, but it was already dark when we reached Orillia. The only restaurant open was the Chinese.

We quickly got rid of dinner, and headed for my cottage on Big Chief Road, grating to a stop, finally, on the front lawn. Clambering out stiffly, Joe stood off and took a long look at the house and the shadowy moonstruck lake beyond. "What a place for spirits," he grinned.

I pointed out to the lake. "They even have some kind of monster out there."

"Have you seen it?"

"It looked like an empty canoe to me."

"Maybe the spirit was paddling its own canoe."

"Oh, Joe," Ruth groaned.

Tired after the trip from New York, they were ready to call it a night. Upstairs, Joe tested the bed, bouncing up and down on the mattress.

"How about tomorrow?" he asked.

"I'll show you the town, then you can meet the MacIvers, father and daughter, and arrange the sessions. That should kill the first day."

All the way down the stairs, I heard him laughing to himself.

I fell off to sleep quickly. In the morning, I was awakened by a rustling noise outside my room, and there was Joe, building a fire against the early September frost.

When Ruth collected herself, we headed downtown, rolling past quaint old Victorian houses and storefronts. As I turned into Mississaga Street, Joe's head was hanging out of the car. "It must have looked this way a hundred years ago," he said, wide-eyed.

"The storefronts might vary a bit, the streets may have lost their telegraph poles, but essentially attitudes and outlooks are what they were a century ago." I waved toward the dock, directly behind us, "That's very familiar."

"And getting more familiar all the time," Joe grinned.

"I can close my eyes anytime and see the waterline more clearly than my own backyard."

"How long has the marina been there?" Ruth asked.

"Since 1872, and the railroad before that."

I was not at all sensitive about my *déjà vu* experience. It did not necessarily imply a belief in reincarnation. In a clairvoyant moment, the subconscious may have tuned into what Jung called the collective unconscious, and Cayce the Universal Consciousness. The explanation was no more fantastic than the event.

Joe's bantering voice cut short my reflections. "You may have known this girl right here."

"I may have known everybody I've ever felt strangely at ease with the first time I met them."

Ruth nodded thoughtfully. "Whenever this instant feeling occurs, it invariably happens to both people."

"Love at first sight," Joe snarled.

"And even the poets can't explain it," Ruth smiled.

After breakfast, we took a roundabout route to the Mac-Ivers', passing a vast sprawling complex, conspicuously incongruous in the surrounding small-town atmosphere. "The Ontario Hospital School," I advised, "provincial headquarters for nearly three thousand retarded persons—all born that way, for no conceivable reason."

Joe snorted sarcastically. "I suppose it's karma; they did something in a past life, and now have a lesson to learn in this one." His eyes darkened. "What can you learn being an idiot?"

"Maybe others had to learn," Ruth said softly, "the parents or others in the family."

We had now approached the MacIvers'. The children came curiously to the door. Ken and Joanne were inside waiting. Joe's eyes quickly brushed past MacIver and rested on Joanne. She smiled and took his hand, and they chatted for a while.

I sensed a subtle change in Joe's manner. "So you've lived before?" he said with a smile.

"I guess so," Joanne countered good-naturedly.

"What makes you think so?" Joe asked affably.

"Oh, I remember some things. As a small girl, I kept telling my father about a farm I'd lived on, and described the apple orchards, the rows of corn, and things like that."

"And had you lived on a farm?"

Her blue eyes held his without flinching. "Not in this lifetime."

Joe seemed taken aback by her directness. "All right," he said, "now how do you feel about being hypnotized?"

I was again impressed by Joanne's easiness with grown-ups. "If it will settle it, once and for all," she said.

Joe was incredulous. "You have no curiosity about Marrow?"

"My curiosity has been satisfied."

"You wouldn't like to know a Tommy Marrow in this life, or who Yancey was, or what happened to your father?"

She gave me a sly look. "We know about Yancey."

Joe shook his head, and then turned to MacIver. "Would the cottage on the lake be all right for the hypnosis?"

MacIver nodded. "If it's all right with Joanne."

"It'll be painless," Joe promised.

Joanne regarded him placidly. "I'm not worried."

Joe was strangely quiet as we drove off.

"Well?" I said.

"Those eyes," he said. "You look into them and see centuries!"

Winding back to the cottage, we dropped off at Casey Jones's. The psychiatrist and the hypnotist measured each other briefly, and then Casey guided us into the kitchen for an intimate chat.

He seemed to have taken to Joe. "Perhaps you can get something out of her that smacks of evidence," he said.

"Like what?" Joe said.

"Some tangible information, the prices of everyday staples that she could not possibly have had any knowledge of."

"That seems reasonable," Joe said. "However, while people never really forget anything, even under hypnosis they can't suddenly remember something they never thought worth remembering."

The impending sessions had revived Casey's interest in Joanne's experience, and the possibility of regressing the retarded for indication of a past life. "It might be very revealing," he said, "if their present condition could be linked to a previous existence."

Joe was dubious. "The feebleminded are virtually impossible to hypnotize, as they have little attentive ability."

As it had before, the thought struck me. "Does the truth invariably come out during hypnosis?"

Joe pursed his lips. "Because of the censor ban, a question may shake up a subject, and so violate his sense of propriety that he will either not answer or answer obliquely."

How did hypnosis open up the subconscious?

Joe thought a moment. "Hypnosis allows the subconscious to function without conscious interference. So many memories are piled on top of one another that confusion is the conscious result."

How did some little fellow, with puny muscles, become a karate champion after a few sessions of hypnosis?

"He's just using more of his potential, perhaps four or five times more, because conscious interference has been removed."

The next question was a specific. "Will hypnosis make Joanne brighter, sharpen her memory?"

"Only in bringing out that dormant in Susan's or Joanne's personality."

I looked up bemused. "Susan's personality?"

"After four years of thinking she's Susan, regardless of how she got that way, Joanne has a definite Susan personality."

"Maybe this is the way reincarnation works, if it works at all."

Our little prelude ended, Casey cheerfully invited us to review the facilities at his institution. "They really are very happy people—perhaps the only happy people I know."

And so we made a date.

That night, as he was charcoaling a steak in the fireplace, Joe wheezed unhappily.

"What's the trouble?" I asked.

He sighed. "I'd like to get that girl away from her family, particularly the father."

"Why?"

"I don't want her thinking she has to please him or anybody else. Actually, I don't want her thinking about anything, just relaxing and letting the subconscious take over."

"Will she know what's going on?"

"Oh, she'll be hazily aware, but the subconscious will dominate."

That night I tossed restlessly, and in the morning was a little weary. But it being H-day—for Hypnosis—I did my yoga, and was ready when the participants began trickling in.

As Joe rolled up his shirtsleeves, and set the tape recorder, the living room was taut and alive with bright-eyed observers: Ken MacIver and his wife Edna, Casey Jones, Professor Julio Molinaro and his wife Matie, and, of course, Ruth Lampl and Dave Manuel.

It was hardly an occult setting. The spectators sat around in casual attire, Joe darkly boyish in a sleeveless gray sweater, shirt open at the neck. Joanne was the radiant bobby-soxer, snug in her shorts and blouse, precociously attractive but still a child in many ways, announcing sheepishly that she had to go to the bathroom.

Joe smiled approvingly. "Shows you're sensitive."

She laughed uncertainly. "As long as we're hypnotizing you," Joe said, "shall I suggest that you concentrate better in school, and get better marks?"

"You can do that?"

"You," stressed Joe, "can do that."

Joe took a chair near Joanne's head. His voice was clear-cut and conversational. "I want you to relax, cooperate, and listen, and you will feel at ease, comfortable, and secure. I want you to close your eyes. At all times, your eyes will remain closed."

Joanne's eyes fluttered. "I can't," she began. "It's hard . . . I try to keep them closed. But they pop open."

"That's good. Now just listen, let yourself go, enjoy it, and have fun."

Joe was oblivious to everything but the girl. "Your legs are heavy, your arms are heavy, your entire body is heavy, and you are going deep, deep asleep. Your legs are relaxed, your arms are relaxed, your entire body is relaxing, you are relaxing deeper and deeper with every breath you take." His face hovered over the girl's. "As I touch you on the forehead, you will relax and go deeper and deeper asleep. Any sounds will tend to make you relax even more and send you deeper and deeper asleep."

Unruffled, solicitous, vitally alert, it soon became apparent why Joe was a hypnotist's hypnotist. "Whenever I talk to you, you will respond easily to the suggestions. You will be able to answer, speaking clearly and distinctly, and as you give answers, you will go deeper asleep. Your subconscious mind will aid to bring about feelings of well-being, so that all functions of the body will continue to be normal. As you answer questions, you will feel more sure of yourself, you will go more deeply asleep, you will be able to understand the questions."

Joe's powers were immediately evident. As Joanne subsided into a light trance, I felt my own head nodding, as Joanne's had when she was inadvertently hypnotized by her father.

Joe quickly established the girl's conscious identity. She was Joanne MacIver, she was seventeen, a high school senior, living in Orillia. She spoke in a low measured voice, clearly recognizable as Joanne MacIver's. He got into her contemporary life slowly.

For a healthy teenager, she had an unusual sense of isolation or apartness. Among hundreds of schoolmates, she had no intimates.

"Any close friends in the school?" Joe had asked routinely.

She shook her head.

"No close friends in school?" he repeated.

"No," she replied evenly. She preferred to keep her own counsel, travel her own way, with many acquaintances but no confidantes, feeling older than her classmates. Certain teachers resentfully attributed her remoteness to a feeling of superiority, but all she felt was different.

I half-expected because of Susan's French origin that French would be Joanne's school language. Instead, curiously, it was Spanish.

"Why Spanish?" Joe asked.

"I didn't do too well in French and I had to have a language."

"Does Spanish come easier for you?"

"Than French? Yes."

As a reincarnation holdover, it would have seemed that French would have been easier. However, as Susan Ganier, her father had discouraged her speaking French.

Joanne considered her schooling a takeoff point. She had many secret hopes and aspirations, all taking her out of Orillia. She wanted to go to college, to get away and expand her horizons.

"But Orillia is so beautiful," Joe pointed out.

"I just want to develop," she said slowly, "can't be in a small town all the time."

Nobody could have been more definite about a husband. "Somebody like your father?" Joe asked.

"A male male," she replied firmly.

"Have you met anybody like that?"

She grimaced. "They all seem sort of feminine to me."

"What is a feminine characteristic?"

She groped for a moment. "They're soft."

"You're going to find a rugged man, right?"

"I don't know if I'll look too hard. We'll bump into each other."

"You're not aggressive, right?"

"Oh, yes, I am."

"When did you discover this?"

"I always have been."

Joe proceeded lightly. "Now I know why you need a strong man."

Just as she had definite ideas about a mate, Joanne knew what she wanted in a marriage. It was as though she had hashed the whole thing over, and had come up with her own recipe for a rewarding union.

"I don't want to be told everything," she said. "I want a bit of consideration."

I whispered in Joe's ear, "Was this the relationship before, with Tommy?"

Joe whispered back, "She's Joanne MacIver, she's seventeen, and she's still very much in this life."

I had forgotten. Joanne, subconsciously, could not range beyond her subconscious point. She was a creature of the hypnotist. Now, Joe gently began the regression. "Joanne, you're going back—you're sixteen years old, fifteen years old. Very quickly. It happens so quickly. You are now fifteen years old. Now you're fourteen years old. How old are you, Joanne?"

Time flew under hypnosis. "Fourteen," Joanne replied equably.

"What day is it today?"

"Sunday," a little pensively.

"What did you do today?"

"Played football in the front yard."

"Who did you play with?"

She recalled the names easily. Paul Torrance, her brother Ian, Wayne, down the street; Tommy (not Marrow) and Fergie, other neighborhood friends.

The regression moved on. At eleven years, on June 10, she recalled a swimming lesson.

At six, she was playing in the sand, in the Canadian Niagara Falls.

I glanced across the room. MacIver was beaming proudly, as though Joanne had discovered America. The others were listening intently, even as Joe kept testing her at six. "Do you have brothers and sisters?"

"A brother, Ian."

Ronald and Warren were not yet born.

"All right," Joe said, "I'm going to take you farther back now. You're five years old, you're four, you're three, two, one ... "

I felt an anticipatory tingle.

"Now I'm going to take you farther back, farther back in time. You'll drift farther back, back ... " He paused dramatically. "Now you're farther back. Where are you?"

Joanne stirred under her blanket. When she spoke, finally, her voice was lighter, airier, entirely different, the voice of a child on a lark, and that child was not Joanne.

"Where are you?" Joe repeated.

"On a road."

"What do you see?"

Her eyes were closed but she had no trouble visualizing. "The road is sort of like tracks. There are bushes on both sides and grass in the center."

"Any houses?"

"No."

"Country?"

"Umhm."

"How old are you?"

"About eight."

"Eight years old."

"Umhm."

Her name came as no surprise. "Susie, Susie Ganier." She pronounced it Gay-nyay.

"Susie, you're walking down this road, right? And you're eight years old?"

"Umhm."

Despite her age, she was not in school, though she had attended some classes. "It's a ways," she explained, "and I have to help at home."

Previously, she had mentioned two playmates; brother Reuben and Tommy Marrow. She now added another, Jed—a dog—also the name of her collie in this life.

Joe proceeded to explore Susan Ganier's childhood, beginning with a significant relationship.

"Did you play hide-and-seek with Tommy?"

"Not very often. He couldn't come all the time."

"He lived far away?"

"Pretty far."

Her intimate circle remained the same. Mason and

Catherine Ganier were still her parents; brother Reuben was enamored of Rachel Brown, and Old Man Mac-Gregor was her friend.

When she mentioned Rachel, there was a current of dislike in her voice, and Joe quickly seized on this.

"Yes, Mother and Father like her, but I don't. She's a sort of smart aleck."

So deeply did her dislike for Rachel cut that she eventually shunned their wedding.

"How did your mother and father take this?" Joe asked.

"They thought I was sick."

Like other St. Vincent farmers, the Ganiers had their crop problems, as even the children's play indicated. "Once we were playing hide-and-seek in the field—in the cornfield—because you can really hide in the corn," Susan confided, "but we got into trouble."

Her father had scolded them because they were knocking the corn down.

"What did he tell you?"

"Not to do it again, because it was food."

"Food was important?"

"Sometimes it got so hot and there was no rain and it wouldn't grow. So we had to store it."

"Do you have any animals?"

"Some cows, and some pigs, and some chickens."

So far the session had gone easily, revealing a girl with few amusements and no friends, except for the visiting Tommy.

Susan was eight, then fourteen, then sixteen. She recalled how the Ganier farmhouse had been built with timber from the surrounding forests, how she helped with the chores. There were only eight cows, and the barn was small.

Joe picked this up. "What does the barn look like?"

"You go in the back door, and the cows are right up at

the back, against the wall. And you walk up between the cows, and there are pigs in the corner."

"What does the house look like?"

"It's wood, and sort of square . . . "

"If I wanted to visit you, how would I get there? What roads would I take? What's the road outside of your house?"

Everybody in the room leaned forward, but her answer was an inarticulate murmur.

This was our first inkling that not everything was to be neatly packaged together. Still, there seemed a pattern in what she remembered most vividly, what was most important to her as Susan. Church and school held little significance. Formal religion was makeshift, services improvised by lay preachers or itinerant parsons, and it was as difficult to get to services as to school. So few had shoes, and the distances were great.

Education was no aid to survival. Tommy could not read or write, and Susan only scantily.

She had only gone to grade school "a couple of times."

"Why didn't you go to school?"

"Because I had to help at home."

"But in the winter there wasn't much to do?"

"Well, there was the barn. And it was too hard to go to school in the winter. And my clothes weren't warm enough."

"Didn't your father want you to learn the [English] language?"

"Well, he knew the language."

"Did he teach you at home?"

"I just learned from them."

"Did they have any books?"

"The Bible."

"Any other books or almanacs?"

"There were some calendars."

"Were there any schools nearby?"

"One."

"Who went to that school?"

"People who were closer. People who had money . . . "

"How far was the church?" Joe asked. "Did you have to go by wagon?"

"Umhm."

"How far? An hour, half-hour?"

"About a half-hour."

"Was there a name for the church?"

"The Methodist church."

"You make friends with people at church?"

"Umhm."

"Tell me some of their names."

"Umhm . . . there's the Watsons . . . Umhm . . . the MacPhersons."

"You put on your nice clothes to go to church, right?" Joe asked.

Joanne's voice dropped a couple of registers. "They weren't very nice," she said dolefully.

English was the prevailing tongue, and the Ganiers spoke it faithfully. "Sometimes people were French like I was, but they spoke English."

"Why didn't your father want you to speak French?"

"Everybody else was English, and he didn't want us to be known as French people."

"Well, was there any coolness or separation between people because one was French and one was . . . "

"Yes."

"Did your father feel different from the others?"

"He made us speak English."

"Did he like the English?"

She hesitated. "He felt inferior because he wasn't."

"Tell me how your father spelled his last name."

"Ga . . . n . . . " Joanne faltered.

"Difficult for you to spell?"

"I can't remember some . . . " She brushed a hand across her brow.

"Your father had a French name?"

"Yes."

"Did he ever change it, use another name?"

She moistened her lips and tried again.

"G . . . a . . . i . . . n . . . er."

In the search for Ganiers, I had not seen any Gainers, so this was no help.

At seventeen, marrying Tommy, Susan had taken the Marrow name. Did it jog memories of the only Marrow we had documentary evidence of—Archibald Marrow? She would have been eight or nine, when Archibald made his claim in 1840, only months older when he defaulted.

Joe progressed her well into her marriage. "Did you know somebody named Archibald Marrow?"

"I think I heard . . . "

In the half-gloom, I could see the heads crane forward.

"Was he a relative of Tommy's?"

"I think he was a cousin, a second cousin."

"Was he a farmer?"

"Sometimes Dad would talk about them . . . about people. And I think he said something about Archibald. Something to do with his crops."

"Was he having trouble with his farm?"

"There was a fire in his field and some oats burned."

"Did you see that from your farm?"

"I just heard Dad talk about it."

"What happened to Archibald Marrow?"

"I don't know. I just heard about him a couple of times."

Susan showed no greater familiarity with Tommy's parents. She recalled the names, Jacob and Margaret, but had them vaguely living at a distance.

Only where she was emotionally involved did Susan become vividly alive to the girl on the couch. She went over ground well traveled before, without enthusiasm or precision. Tommy took grain to the mill at Massie, and brought back flour and sugar. The store was still "Mac-Gregor and . . . uh . . . Milligan, or something." What difference did it make? She came away periodically with dresses, boots, socks, blankets. Once, they picked up a saddle for ten dollars and bags of sugar at ten cents.

In marriage, she was subconsciously vulnerable. Mindful of Joanne's belief that she had come back primarily to marry early and have children, Joe took her to age twenty-two when she would have been married five years.

"Why don't you have any children, Susan?"

"We couldn't make them yet," she replied.

Across the room, I noticed Professor Molinaro nudging his wife, without knowing why.

Joe moved on. "We'll take you to twenty-three, Susan; you're twenty-four . . . you're thirty-two years old."

He checked back. "Susan, how old are you?"

"Thirty-two."

"You have any children?"

She shook her head slowly. "No."

"Were you lonely living on the farm?"

She sighed. "Just miss children."

"Is there any reason you don't have children?"

"We try." Her voice dragged.

"Did you talk to anybody about this?"

She was horrified. "No, no, no."

Was anything wrong with the marriage?

"You married Tommy," Joe said. "Do you like him?"

"No," unhesitatingly.

For a disconcerting moment, the love story of Tommy

and Susan threatened to erupt. Even Joe seemed taken aback. Insensibly, the personality of Susan had so taken shape that we all gradually identified with her.

Joe paused uncertainly. "Then why did you marry him?"

Was it because Tommy had a farm . . . because there was nobody else . . . because she wanted to get away from home . . . ?

Her voice rang out musically. "Because I love him."

I looked up and saw the smiles of relief.

Joanne's voice was now blurred with fatigue, and Joe set about bringing her back. "Now all those thoughts are fading from your mind, leaving your mind completely, completely faded. You are coming up through time to the present, to your present age level." Having felt from earlier regressions that Joanne had not been effectively returned to this life, Joe reinforced the suggestion. "You're going to be seventeen years old very shortly now. All your memories, all your thoughts and ideas that have real meaning for you as Joanne are now returning, returning completely. Now you're seventeen years old. Seventeen, you're Joanne and you're seventeen."

His voice turned brisk. "All right, how old are you?"

"Seventeen."

"What is your name?"

"Joanne."

"Where do you live?"

"Orillia."

She slowly sat up, rubbing her eyes. "Gee," she said, "I'm hungry."

Suddenly, everybody was out of their chairs, chatting gaily and laughing. Matie bore down on me in suppressed excitement. Husband Julio, a true skeptic, had been startled when Joanne observed, "We couldn't make children yet," an idiomatic French expression.

Still, it was all rather disappointing. The session had turned up nothing revealing in the way of names, dates and places. Surprisingly, Joe was more optimistic than I. "Granted reincarnation, which I don't," he smiled, "there would be no reason for Susan to be any brighter under hypnosis than she was a hundred years ago."

After the last guest had left, Joe fixed the fireplace. "At least," he said, turning a log, "she never lived in Atlantis. Usually, they're exotic kings or queens, or nobility. I don't know what they did for peasants in those days."

He took a last lingering look through a picture window at the pale yellow moon shimmering on the clear surface of Couchiching. "Mighty spooky out there," he said, shivering. "Must be ghosts."

"I haven't seen any."

"Okay," he grinned, "close yourself off." I looked out on the lake for a while before drowsiness came. The power of suggestion was strong. Suddenly, in the uncertain light of the yellow-cheese moon, I made out the filmy outline of a strangely bobbing object. And then, just as suddenly as it had appeared, the image vanished. It was time for bed.

In the morning, refreshed, I considered questioning Joanne myself, when the sessions resumed.

"Why not," Joe said, "you're a reporter."

That morning we toured the countryside, admiring the reddening leaves, and headed for a house west of Orillia which, in local tradition, we understood to be haunted.

"Legend has it," I explained, "that an Indian boy was tossed out a window into deep snow and allowed to freeze to death. For this breach of hospitality, he returns each fall to haunt whoever's living there."

Joe assumed a professional air. "How does he haunt?"

"Sometimes he shows himself on the steps, or he just rattles around in the attic."

Joe nodded approvingly. "Sounds like a nice ghost."

We headed for the Owl Pen, the celebrated honey trove, which was the nearest landmark to the haunted house. Joe and Ruth bought some honey, fresh from the bees, from a tall, rangy extrovert named Bob Miller, and then Joe inquired with customary tact, "Where's the haunted house from here?"

The honey curdled on Miller's lips. "How'd you know about that?"

"We have ways of finding out," Joe said mysteriously.

"You passed it down the road. Nobody stays there long." Miller grinned. "During the winter, they say, the lids on the stove clatter."

"That's all?" Joe said.

Miller shrugged. "That's enough."

"How about the attic?"

Miller shook his head. "You got me there."

"Who's there now?" Joe asked.

"A young fellow, new to the neighborhood, named Barnes, Mel Barnes." Miller's eyes twinkled. "He doesn't know about the ghost."

Miller directed us to a red brick house on the crest of a hill, a mile down the road. "He's got some cows grazing out front." He pursed his lips reflectively. "He's young, and he's got a lot of work in the house; he won't scare easy."

As we drove up to the side of the house, a young man bounced out of a back door.

"Just like to see your house," Joe announced.

"Fine," Mel Barnes said, "have some coffee."

Inside, we were greeted by Mrs. Barnes, a teacher in the Orillia school system.

Barnes showed us the cellar, then the kitchen, with the latest appliances. The house was more than a hundred years old. With luck, it would last another hundred years.

"Who lived here before?" Joe asked.

Barnes shook his head. They were comparatively recent arrivals, and were happy with their 150-acre spread, purchased at bargain rates. They mentioned the price, a remarkably good buy.

"No wonder," Joe commented darkly, sniffing around the house like a dog in a meat market. "Anything strange happen here?"

Barnes looked puzzled. "Not that I know of."

His wife edged closer.

"Sure?" Joe said.

"What do you mean?"

"Have you heard any peculiar noises?"

Mrs. Barnes moved a few steps nearer.

"What are you driving at?" Barnes asked.

Joe measured Barnes nonchalantly. "I guess you don't know this house is haunted."

Barnes chuckled. "By what?"

"A ghost, what else?" Joe was indignant. "Haven't you heard him rattling around the house?"

Barnes guffawed. "Maybe that's why we got a good price."

Mrs. Barnes caught her husband's eye. "Remember those noises we heard in the attic?"

Barnes laughed. "It's an old house, and it creaks."

Joe wagged his head. "You can't be sure," he said wisely.

Ruth was tugging peremptorily at Joe's sleeve, and the Barneses, coffee forgotten, waved an uncertain goodbye.

Ruth gave Joe a withering look. "You beast."

"She may as well know," Joe said serenely.

There was still time to drop in on Casey at the Ontario Hospital School, and get back for the afternoon session. In a few minutes, passing into the institutional grounds, we encountered small groups of older patients standing around idly. Some stared vacantly, with slack jaws; others giggled uncertainly. When we asked directions, they waved their arms frantically toward a large building, repeating, "Dr. Jones, Dr. Jones."

Casey was ready and waiting. "I hope you're not feeling squeamish," he said genially, starting the tour.

The immense complex was outwardly immaculate. The halls, dormitories, classrooms were bright and clean; the work force attentive, even solicitous with their charges, though obviously not expecting visitors. Here were the hopeless derelicts of a subterranean world. Even in the halls we saw nearly every variation of genetically defective individuals, some with mental ages scaled down to infancy. The interest in our arrival was communicable. Many pressed forward and took our hands, or stroked our clothing, giving us shy, wistful smiles.

A tall, gangling boy of fifteen, with a vacant smile, loose-jointedly bent down to kiss Ruth's hand, fondling it tenderly, unwilling to let it go. "Mother, Mother," he kept repeating, his eyes glowing. Ruth's own eyes were moist.

Another youngster, with black pits for eyes and a twisted back, kept hobbling after Ruth, pulling on her sleeve and demanding chewing gum, pointing to the wad in his mouth, so she would surely understand him. Casey finally shooed him off.

Still another, grotesquely stunted, except for an abnormally large and misshapen head, pleaded tearfully to leave with us. "I'll be good," he promised. Others could not articulate at all. In a roomful of women, the oldest no more than thirty, one poor creature stood up, pressed both hands to her groin, and jumped up and down gleefully. The babble issuing from her mouth was hardly human.

I could not shut off her guttural, animal-like cries. Shuddering, I wondered at the purpose of this manifest injustice. Born without sin, these wretched unfortunates were little more than vegetables. Medically, of course, there were explanations. Many were afflicted with anoxia, an oxygen deficiency arresting mental development. The pragmatists could explain everything and nothing. Some didn't exceed the mental age of three, and had to be supervised through life. Others, mental age three to seven, could be taught simple tasks; reading or writing was beyond them. Still others, eight to twelve years, could use uncomplicated lathes and sewing machines, and some, few advanced, trained in the institution, took jobs outside.

The feebleminded, generally, were no threat to others, only themselves. Some, fleeing the wall-less grounds, were found helplessly sprawled in nearby streams, on the verge of death. They couldn't get out of their own way.

Anything after our last stop in the grotesque tour would have been anticlimactic. Many of the patients there were in cribs with high railings. They were skimpily clad to avoid entanglement in their own clothing. Some were preoccupied like monkeys with their own bodies, too engrossed to look up. Others hauled themselves to standing position, regarding us blankly. However, one boy, no more than three feet high, clutching the rail of his crib, began jabbering in an effort to engage our attention. Bare to the waist, with a diaper-like cloth about his midriff, he looked like a chimpanzee. His face sweeping out from a tiny neck narrowed into a peak at the crown. His eyes danced excitedly, and he kept gesturing to his own squeals of delight. He may have been fifteen or sixteen years old.

On his crib, as the others, there was a family name. He couldn't read it himself, and didn't know what it was there for, but even perversely, it gave him a tenuous identification with the human race.

Joe watched him with morbid fascination. "He's a Monkey Boy. Would you say he was in God's image?"

Casey must have seen my dismay. "The boy's really very happy," he said, "probably happier than you are."

"How do you know?" I asked.

"He sleeps and eats well, never cries, and is in high spirits. It's the parents who suffer. Some have guilt pangs, and compensate by visiting regularly, suffering through it. For others, it's too much."

In the hall outside, we passed a television set, screening a game of charades, and the participants were making the same motions as the patients on the other side of the door. The gestures, the blank looks, the movements were similar, and the studio audience responded with applause.

Joe blinked. "No wonder," he said, "they call it the Idiot Box."

Silently, we returned to the car, Casey leading the way. Never was the fresh air so clean and clear, and freedom so inviting, but I felt only a sense of depression.

"How old is this place?" I asked Casey.

"More than a hundred years," he replied. "Why?"

"Oh, nothing."

I could not get the child Joe called "Monkey Boy" out of my mind. I saw him gesticulating, jabbering, squealing, coaxing. Could this aberration be truly part of a Divine pattern, a phase of a complex plan in which death was but a beginning?—"Master, so did sin this man or his parent, that he was born blind?"

There was no conversation all the way to the cottage, and we had hardly got there before Joanne arrived with her parents. She was bubbling with good humor—ready, eager, almost anxious to lie down and become Susan

Ganier again. Slipping off her sandals, she stretched out on the couch, and purred as Joe threw a light blanket over her.

As Joe pulled the drapes and doused the lamps, we took the same stations. Putting her under quickly, he took her to the year 1854. The questions came like a barrage.

"How long have you been married?"

"About . . . four years."

"You love your husband?"

"Yes."

"Do you have any children?"

"No."

"Any special events coming up?" Joe inquired.

"Going to bake . . . lots of things."

"What are you going to do with all these things?"

"Take them to Mrs. O'Leary's house."

Joe recognized a new name.

"Where does Mrs. O'Leary live?"

"Not on the same road."

"Why are you taking these goods to Mrs. O'Leary's house?"

"Going to sell them."

"What are you going to do with the money?"

"Buy material for quilts."

"Is Mrs. O'Leary a friend of yours?"

"I know her."

"How long have you known her?"

"Um . . . five years."

I jogged Joe's elbow.

"All right, Susan," Joe said, "I'm going to let a friend talk to you; he will ask you some questions, and you will enjoy talking to him and giving him answers."

I slid into Joe's chair.

Remembering Major Malone's reference to the Irish

community near the Tank Range I asked, "Susan, have you heard of the Irish block?"

"Um . . . a block . . . with farms . . . on the corner . . . about a half-mile . . . maybe a mile away."

"Did Mrs. O'Leary have any children?"

"She was . . . older." The children had grown and gone off.

She was no more interested in the O'Learys than in the Watsons, Urquharts (presumably her Urketts) or the Eagles.

As a sidelight of the times, Tommy farmed when weather permitted, and with the approach of the winter foraged the white wilderness for fur-bearing animals to augment the family income. Beaver was the main quarry. "And once . . . " Joanne hesitated " . . . once he got a bear."

"How did he catch this bear?"

"He had a snare."

"What did it look like?"

"It was steel." Susan—or Joanne—had apparently confused a nooselike snare with the traditional claw-trap.

"How did he prepare the snare—did you see him do it?"

"With a spike in the ground, by chain to the snare. Then he covered it up with leaves, then the snow."

"What time of the year would that be?"

"In the fall."

In Upper Canada late August nights were frosty and snow came long before winter.

Susan's childlessness had intrigued me. "How did Tommy feel about not having children?"

Joanne twitched slightly under her blanket. "He pretended that he didn't care."

"He tried to make you have children?"

"We didn't talk about it very much. And if I did, he would laugh and say it didn't matter."

Had she ever consulted a doctor? No, but she remembered a doctor, a tall, gaunt individual with a big stomach and a black hat. He had called on a neighboring tenant, Hilda Black. Susan hardly knew her, for she lived two miles away. There was obviously little importance to any of these relationships, and only to important associations did she seem to significantly respond.

"Who," I asked, "was your closest friend?"

"Mrs. Speedie."

"What was her first name?"

"Margaret."

The Speedies lived in Annan, perhaps two miles from the Marrows.

"Did you go any place with her?"

"To . . . uh . . . to a bake . . . and quilting sometimes."

"Where does this quilting take place?"

"At somebody's house."

"Was it ever held at your house?"

"I wanted it there."

"Then why didn't they come?"

Her voice was sad. "I don't know."

"Did you ever invite them?"

"But they all said they'd go somewhere else."

She had visited the Speedies, the O'Learys, the Browns, but never the Blacks, the Hilda Blacks, not socially.

"They were poor," she explained.

Apparently, even in the wilderness, social lines, based on worldly success, were tightly drawn, and snubs were not uncommon.

Tommy was, of course, her most meaningful relationship. At eight, when she first met him, she felt she would one day marry him. He was already farming when they set a date. He had paid one hundred dollars down for his land, leasing from a man whose name "started with A."

"Would you have married him if he hadn't owned a farm?" I asked

"No," she said flatly.

I peered down into her face. Her features were as placid as ever, a trace of a smile on her lips.

"I thought you were in love?"

"Not till he got the farm."

I felt a gasp in the room, approximating my own reaction.

"But you always knew you were going to marry him?"

"Yes, when he got the farm."

"Was it important to you to have a farm of your own?"

Her voice registered surprise. "Why, where would we live, what would we do, if we didn't have a farm?"

"But you didn't marry him just because he owned a farm?"

"No, I didn't marry him because he had a farm. I was going to marry him when he got his farm."

I could almost feel the sighs of relief.

"Was anybody else interested in you?"

She grimaced, "Yes."

"What were they like?"

"Awful, like dogs."

"In what way? Running around after women?"

She shook her head. "Me."

Two or three would drop in, as though visiting the family.

"How did you know they were there to see you?"

She sniffed. "Because they always wanted me to be there."

The most memorable event in her life was her marriage. Even so, she was vague. The ceremony took place in July 1849. She was seventeen, and Tommy four years older. They were married in a hall by a lay preacher. His name was McEachern, and he had no church. "He was staying on somebody's farm."

At this point, Joanne appeared to be responding reluctantly, and I returned the questioning to Joe, who had been watching with an enigmatic smile. "You pressed too hard," he whispered, as he resumed command.

His voice was brisk and authoritative. "Now we're going to take you forward in time. Now you're thirty-three, you're thirty-four, you're thirty-five years old. Thirty-five, thirty-six, thirty-seven. You're thirty-seven years old. Thirty-eight, thirty-nine, forty. You're forty years old. You're forty-one. You're forty-two years old."

As I watched, she seemed incredibly to age. The muscles in her face sagged, and her voice became thin and reedy. She seemed terribly tired.

"Do you feel old?"

"Yes," she sighed.

"Feel all of forty-two?"

"Feel fat."

"How do you feel?"

"Lost."

"Why lost?"

I could anticipate the answer, but not the note of utter desolation.

"Because Tommy died." He was dead seven years.

"How did he die so young?"

She faltered. "Accident . . . in the barn . . . I couldn't believe." Her voice broke off.

Joanne seemed loath to relive the agonizing moment. With a nod from Joe, I took over the questioning.

"Did you call the doctor when they found Tommy?"

"No, I didn't."

"Somebody called the doctor, do you recall his name?"

"Dr. Black."

"And what was the cause of death?"

I leaned forward to catch her answer.

"He bled."

"There was a man named Brown with him at the time?"

"Yes."

Tommy had been cut by a sharp blade, which had fallen from a hook. He was dead when the doctor got there. They brought his body into the house, and buried him the next day. Only a handful of people were at the funeral. Reuben and Rachel, Old Man MacGregor, the Ganiers, and Rachel's parents. The services were by the ubiquitous McEachern.

They had buried him back of the house.

"Who helped to dig, the neighbors?"

"Yes."

"How deep did they have to dig?"

"About five feet."

"Did you put a marker on the grave?"

"Wood."

"Now what was the distance from the road to the grave?"

Susan hesitated. "About a hundred and twenty feet."

"Were there any indications from the road that you would know exactly where to go to that grave?"

"About . . . straight back from the gate."

"Why did you bury Tommy so quickly?"

"I . . . didn't want him in a box."

I tried to visualize her picking up the threads of her life after the initial shock had worn off.

"Did you think of marrying again?"

"No, I wouldn't have been happy."

"Didn't you feel that you could love somebody else?"

"No."

"What year would you say that Tommy met his death?"

"Um . . . Eighteen sixty . . . three."

She was still young enough for children. "Had you

given up the idea of having children at the time Tommy
was killed?"

She shook her head, "No."

"You still thought you might have a child?"

"I hoped."

"Did you feel that if you had a child now, life would
have been easier?"

"Yes." It was almost a sigh.

Yet she wouldn't remarry just to have children. Obviously, there would never be another Tommy. She got rid
of the farm, sold the stock off, collecting three hundred
and forty dollars, and kept a few pigs. Of the hundred
Tommy had originally put up, she got seventy back.

"Why did you sell so cheaply?" I asked.

"Because it wasn't mine."

Anxious to get away from her memories, she moved
into an abandoned shack about a mile down the road.
She didn't know whose it was. "Nobody owns it." This
house had a terrace, a well, and a garden for vegetables.
She lived simply, helped occasionally by neighbors. A
pig, killed by a Mr. Thompson, lasted a year, smoked. "I
buy it when it's small. He feeds it and it grows up big,
and then he kills it and brings it over."

Thompson was youngish, married, black-haired, tall.
He dropped by occasionally on the way to the store. But
he never seemed very much more than a name. She was
terribly alone now, and obviously dwelling in the past.
Her mother had died before Tommy, and her father
shortly after Tommy. Curiously, though, she had mentioned her father visiting her.

"Didn't you go to his funeral?" I asked, struck by this
contradiction.

She shook her head. "No, I didn't want to see him buried like Tommy."

"Then how do you see your father?"

"After he died . . . he talks to me."

It seemed a rather obvious compensation. "And you talk to him?"

"Yes," she replied faintly.

As I looked at her now, the color had drained from her face. She was wan and woebegone. Joe hovered over her solicitously. "She's had enough for the day," Joe announced, as he brought her back to the reality of being Joanne. "Now, Susan, all the thoughts you've had are going to fade completely from your mind. You're relaxing, you're feeling wonderful, coming up through time to the present . . . back to the seventeenth year as Joanne. Coming up now all the way, back to seventeen years old . . . Joanne."

His voice turned crisp. "How old are you, Joanne?"

She rubbed her eyes. "Seventeen."

"Do you feel fine?"

"No," she said accusingly. "I have cramps, my side hurts." She got up and stretched, easing the pain.

"What time tomorrow?" she asked.

"Right after school, before you're fagged from homework."

Joe had decided to work hereafter without the distraction of an audience. "Under hypnosis," he observed, "Joanne appears to be sensitive to the thoughts and vibrations of others in the room. I would like a minimum of outside influence."

MacIver was visibly disappointed.

"I don't want anybody influencing her mind," Joe stressed, "and that goes for me, too."

That night, Joe, Ruth, and myself sat around the fireplace, Joe discussing the burgeoning personality of Susan, as I expressed disappointment at her maddening vagueness about names and places.

"You want it all neatly tied together," Ruth laughed,

"like a reporter checking a courthouse record. If there is such a thing as reincarnation, it certainly wasn't designed expressly for the edification of the investigator."

"I have no idea of what the yardstick is," I said.

My mind turned back to the recent session.

"How did she happen to come up with a cramp?"

Joe smiled slyly. "She'd been through quite an emotional experience. Her mother died, Tommy died, her father died, then came back and talked to her. Wouldn't that twist your insides?"

I found the transference difficult. "If she thinks she's Susan Ganier, that doesn't make her Susan Ganier. She's probably Joanne MacIver having an hallucination."

"No hallucination to her. She's living it."

"But is this evidence of reincarnation?"

Joe cocked his head. "The girl's experience is coming out of somewhere, and it could be past experience of some sort for all we know."

We had a few new names to consider—Old Man MacGregor, Mr. Thompson, Urquhart, Watson, Mrs. O'Leary, Jacob Marrow.

"Why," I sighed, "didn't she have first names for Mac-Gregor, Thompson, Mrs. O'Leary, Brown, Urquhart?"

Joe chuckled. "She's a poor, ignorant girl, doing well to remember anything. She may have been pretty, but she never had much mind. Her whole life was two men: her father and Tommy. When they went, that was it."

In view of her great love, why hadn't her dramatic subconscious materialized Tommy in spirit, instead of her father?

Joe shook his head. "It may have been a reversion to childhood. Anyway, if Tommy had come back, one way or the other, she wouldn't be searching for him now."

Interwoven as they might be, they were two distinct personalities, Joanne and Susan.

As a personality extension of Susan, for instance, Joanne was intent on spreading out, and broadening herself.

"With two successive lives in this wilderness," Joe said, "this girl—Joanne—can hardly wait to be carried off by some Lochinvar. She won't marry anybody from around here, you can bet on that."

Ruth nodded thoughtfully. "That's one of the principles of reincarnation, the crystallization of new attitudes and goals from subconsciously remembered lessons from previous lifetimes."

Why did she talk freely about some things and not others?

"Would you like to talk of a previous life," Joe said, "if you came from the slums?"

I looked at Joe curiously. "I thought you didn't believe in reincarnation."

"I don't like labeling things. Scientifically, nothing is destroyed; only changed, and just as human matter continues altered into perpetuity, the energy force that makes up the human spirit may live on in fragmentarily remembered experience."

With hypnosis, I had expected a clearly connected panorama of remembered experience.

Joe laughed. "It doesn't work that way. She is obviously trying to block out her other life. The little remembrance she had was enough to put her guard up."

"We should get more into Tommy's death," I said. "It might bring out more about the marriage."

I was still troubled by inconsistencies of dates and places.

"I'd worry more," Joe said, "if it was all pat."

Ruth, silent a while, now chimed in. "Dates aren't particularly important when she can re-create a scene so completely delineating her relationships. How woebegone she was when the neighbors didn't come to her house for the quiltings. The Marrows were tenant farmers, obviously struggling, and the homeowners probably never considered her place."

Another thing had bothered me: her moving into an abandoned house, and remaining there, undisturbed.

Joe shrugged. "Why not? She wasn't bothering anybody. They could have farmed all around her." He looked up with a frown. "Didn't Mrs. McDonald report people moving in and out of abandoned shacks all the time?"

There was something rather cozy about the next session. With only Joe and Ruth and myself in attendance, Joanne would be in a trusting mood. She turned up at 4 p.m., immediately after school; alive, vital, sure of herself, and quite grown-up in a form-fitting sweater. She eyed Joe reproachfully. "I didn't do well at math today. But at least I wasn't sleepy."

Joe was unabashed. "Rome wasn't built in a day."

She took off her shoes, threw a blanket over herself, and stretched out, yawning even before we started.

As before, Joe dimmed the lights and pulled the drapes, a sliver of sun slanting through the folds to cast an eerie glow over Joanne's head. Joe varied his routine slightly, in response to Joanne's complaint of a raspy throat. "As I touch you on the forehead, you will relax completely and go deeper and deeper asleep. As we go back in time, you will become more deeply hypnotized. You will have pleasant, comfortable feelings in your throat area, circulation will be improved, bringing about healing forces, so that you will have new cells and tissues forming and these cells and tissues will be strong and healthy. The throat area will be normal and will function normally at all times."

He swiftly drifted back to a period following Tommy's death. "Now you will feel and be and act the year 1864.

All the information, all the material is there. All things will come about for you, in the year 1864. The way you feel, think, act will be 1864."

His voice was casual. "How old are you, Susan?"

"Thirty."

"Thirty years old?"

She hesitated, "No . . . four, thirty-four."

"How did you get this house you live in?" he asked.

"A man owned it . . . and I asked if I could live in it."

He said you could?"

"It was rundown, and he thought that if I went and lived in it that I could fix it up."

"Did you make it livable?"

"Yes."

"What do you do all day?"

"Look after the garden in the spring and summer and fall. And read the Bible sometimes."

She usually got up at nine, late for that country, fed her three cats, and brought in the firewood and water. Sometimes she cut her own wood, but Mr. Thompson often helped. He also supplied her with flour, sugar, and tea. She had very little money.

"How do you prepare for the winter?" Joe asked.

"I bring all the vegetables in, and cover the vegetable garden up with manure, and put the vegetables in the shed behind the kitchen. And get more wood. Mr. Thompson brings the pig."

"How would you describe yourself?"

"Sort of heavy. My hair is brown, faded now, in a bun at the back."

Her voice had turned tired and listless.

"What clothes do you wear?"

"They don't have much shape."

"Where does your dress come to?"

"A skirt . . . down to my ankles."

She received a few letters, and wrote fewer, occasionally hearing from Reuben, who had moved off to a gentler clime with Rachel.

"Why don't you live with Reuben and his wife?"

Her lips tightened. "Because I don't like his wife."

Mr. Thompson brought her the mail, picking it up at the Annan post office presided over by Mrs. Speedie.

Having put her at ease, Joe was now ready to fire away. "Do you recall the day," he began, "when Tommy got hurt? Were you in the house?"

"Yes, in the kitchen."

"And your husband was with someone in the barn?"

"Yes."

"Who was he with?"

"Mr. Brown."

"Why was Mr. Brown with your husband?"

"It was summertime . . . and . . . Mr. Brown came over."

"What time of the day was it?"

"In the afternoon."

"Late afternoon?"

"Yes . . . I . . . think he just came over to visit, and talk about farms."

"Did you ever hear your husband talk to Mr. Brown?"

"No, not often."

"Did they ever talk in front of you?"

"Just hello . . . and he'd ask me how I was, and I'd ask how his family was."

"So he was just passing the time of day. What was your husband doing? Why was he out in that barn?"

"They were upstairs."

"Upstairs in the barn?"

"The loft."

"What's up in the loft?"

"Grain and some tools."

"And how did you know about the accident?"

"Because Mr. Brown yelled and came running out of the barn."

"What did he yell?"

"That Tom was hurt."

Here was the scene we had all wondered about.

"And what did you think happened?"

"He said that he was cut and dying."

"And what did you do?"

"I screamed that it wasn't true."

"Did you go to the barn?"

"Yes." Her voice faltered.

"And what did you see there?"

"He was on the floor, bleeding."

"Which floor?"

"Upstairs, in the loft."

"Where was he bleeding?"

"From behind the neck and shoulder."

Joanne's face suddenly twisted in horror.

"And what caused this accident?"

"It was heavy, it fell. And sharp." "It" was apparently the blade of a scythe.

"Was it a . . . ?"

"A cut . . . to cut things."

"What did you do to help?"

"Mr. Brown went to get the doctor."

"And how did he go?"

"By horse."

"And what did you do while he was gone?"

"I'm not sure if I used my skirt."

"You wanted to bandage him up?"

"Yes."

"When the doctor got there, was your husband still on the floor?"

She now had difficulty articulating. "Mmm."

"What did the doctor do?"

"He . . . said he was dead."

"And then what did you do with Tommy?"

"I didn't think he was . . . "

"So what did you want the doctor to do?"

"Make him better." She was like a child speaking of a precious possession.

"And what did the doctor say?"

"He said he couldn't."

"Who helped take Tommy into the house?"

Joanne's lips trembled. "I don't know."

Joe, looking uncomfortable for the first time, gave her time to collect herself. He then pushed on to the funeral.

"Why did you bury him the next day?"

"Because I didn't want him to be put out like Mother was . . . funerals didn't mean much to people."

"Why not?"

"People didn't like to make fools of themselves when somebody died." Where nature was harsh, there was little sentiment.

Brown had made the coffin, contacted the minister, and comforted the widow.

"Mr. Brown seems to have done quite a bit?"

"He was almost my only friend." Her voice cracked. "A good friend of Tommy's, too."

Joe adroitly shifted tack, returning providentially to the irrepressibly jolly MacGregor.

"He told you stories, is that why you liked him?"

She now giggled happily.

"Could you tell us one of his funny stories?"

Her gaiety was infectious. "Once he was drunk . . ."

"What did he get drunk on?"

"Cider. He got drunk at the wedding."

"And what happened when he got drunk?"

"He was walking home one night and saw a bear. And he climbed up a tree and he screamed and yelled . . . because he was afraid . . . and he stayed up there all night."

"Was it a big bear?"

She broke into a laugh. "When morning came it was a cow."

She described MacGregor at length: Gray hair and beard, short, wiry, considerate even when obstreperous.

"Did he ever tell you stories about when he was young?"

"Just about getting drunk."

"Why did you think he was so funny?"

"Because he was a friend."

"He was much older than you, though?"

"But he lived not far away. I always knew him."

After Tommy's death, MacGregor helped the widow with chickens, eggs, and other food.

"Did he ever bring cider?"

"I wouldn't drink it, not after Tommy died."

"And what did you talk about mostly?"

"About what he did at his farm, who he saw, and what was new."

"You liked gossiping?"

"He did."

"Tell me the things he'd tell you, about the neighbors."

"Sometimes one man would tell stories . . . they weren't true, made them all up. And how one man would try to sell something for too much money. And sometimes he'd talk about men fighting . . . and drunk."

"Where was all this taking place?"

"On the farms."

"You enjoyed hearing about these things?"

"Yes, because I wasn't out."

"You didn't go out much?"

"Not from my place."

"Did you know who usually got into the fights? What men drank the most? Did everybody drink?"

"Most of them drank."

Joe was searching about for names—names that obviously had no meaning for her.

"What would they say?"

"Sometimes one man would say something about another man's wife. And they'd get mad." She elaborated. "One man would say . . . um . . . 'Your wife's sure got a good figure for her age.' Something like that."

"And that would start a fight?"

She laughed uproariously. "Yes, he would fight."

"Anybody ever get hurt in these fights?"

"Not really. They were usually too drunk to hurt anybody."

"Did MacGregor tell you the names of the people who got into these fights?"

"Yes. Mr. O'Leary got into a fight once. Not over his wife, though. About somebody else's. Don't know who, because she was really young."

"MacGregor knows the O'Learys?"

Her voice rang with pride. "MacGregor knew everybody."

"Did you know these people when he told you their names?"

"Just knew the Browns. But he'd tell me what they were like."

"Did any of the well-known people get into fights?"

"Mr. Brown never did."

"Did Mr. Eagles ever get into fights?"

"Too far up. I didn't hear very much about him."

"Who else would MacGregor tell you about?"

"The Watsons had lots of children."

Sometimes MacGregor would stay for supper.

"Did he eat much?" Joe asked.

"No. Just as much as I did. He was small."

"Did MacGregor do anything besides drink?"

"Just looked after his chickens and pigs, and sometimes he helped people on their farms."

"They knew he drank though?"

"They drank too, but not as much."

"MacGregor was well off?"

"His house was dirty . . . a dump."

"How do you know that?"

"I've seen it, when I was small."

"Oh, you visited him?"

"He was different, that's why."

"Than what?"

"Other people, they were all married."

Joe decided to progress a responsive Susan in time. "The year is 1872. Just drift around. Your memories will help you . . . 1872 . . . 1872 . . . 1872. The year is 1872."

His face hovered over hers. "How do you feel now, Susan?"

"A little better. Because I know how to look after myself a little better now. Feel more sure."

"Do you ever see Mr. Thompson?"

"Yes. He made the garden bigger."

"Do you still see Mrs. Speedie?"

"Speedie . . . no, I don't go out any more."

"Is she still alive?"

"As far as I know, she's still at the post office."

"Do you have any other people visiting you?"

"Once in a while Mr. MacGregor still comes."

"Do you think about Tommy much?"

"No, talk to Dad, though."

Joe brought her along to 1879.

"How are you doing?" he asked.

"Getting old."

"You're getting older?"

"Tired." Her voice reflected her weariness.

"How old are you now?"

"Forty-nine."

"You're forty-nine? Is that old?"

She corrected herself. "Forty-eight. Yes."

"How do you feel?"

"Getting stiff. Got arthritis. My legs hurt."

"Do any of the neighbors stop by?"

"Some people stop, but MacGregor is dead." He had died two years before. She still had her house and garden, Mr. Thompson still brought supplies, but with age she didn't eat as much, and was subject to colds. She sensed changes about her, without sharing their impact. New people were moving in, children growing up, farms abandoned, people dying, without her feeling any of it. Sometimes she recalled dates with apparent accuracy, her sureness increasing with the date's significance.

The year 1885 seemed to have special meaning.

"Any local activity going on?" Joe asked. "Anything new happening that you've heard about?"

"People moved from across the road."

"They moved out, or they moved in?"

She thought a while. "In."

"Could you tell how many?"

"Four children."

"Four children? Mother, father?"

She nodded.

I could see Joe's interest rising.

"Why did they move in?"

"They bought the farm."

He leaned forward. "Who did they buy it from?"

She replied impassively, "Nobody."

"Nobody?" Joe's face fell.

"They built a new farm." She spoke with assurance, placing the property near Morley. "It's fairly big. It has some rocks though. And they built a new house."

"A new house?" Joe exclaimed.

"Yes, and a new barn."

"All by themselves?"

"No, people came over and helped them."

"Was this exciting for you?" Joe couldn't quite fathom her sudden interest.

"I went over."

"You went over and watched them build the house?" She nodded emphatically. "Yes."

"And how big a house did they build?"

"Medium size."

"Did they build it out of wood?"

"Yes. Stone around the bottom."

"Did they have any farm animals?"

"They bought them after."

"Did you meet them?"

" . . . No, I saw them. Everybody was there."

"Did you become friendly with them?"

"No, they were across the road and down a bit."

Joe asked bluntly, "What was the family name of this new farm?"

I could see her straining under her blanket. Did she know, had she ever known? Only a glimpse was given, if at all, before the door closed on the misty past. Had she remembered this name, every other name, I am sure, would have tumbled out long before.

As Joanne squirmed restlessly, mumbling to herself, Joe sank back in his chair. "All right, just relax," he said with a note of resignation. "Now you're Joanne, and feel wonderful, and you're going to wake up very shortly. You're going to feel better than you've felt in a long time. Now, slowly . . . open your eyes and be wide awake."

Joanne stood up uncertainly. Her eyes had a dull, glazed look. "I feel as if I've been through something, without knowing what."

"You'll be as good as new tomorrow," Joe assured her.

She was rather subdued during the ride home. At the door, she turned to me. "How much more will there be?"

"Just enough for Joe to explore all corners of Susan's life."

That night, as the fireplace snapped against the early frost, the discussions at Big Chief cottage resumed before a visitor, Sally Steacy, a pretty secretary from the northern mining country. She listened puzzled for a while. "You mean this girl, this Joanne or Susan, lived before?"

"Something like that."

I was prepared for an outburst of incredulity. But Sally only said matter-of-factly, "Well, what's so unusual about that? Every time I walk down the main street, I find myself saying hello to all kinds of people I've known from some other time."

Joe grinned diabolically. "Orillia must be a stop-off place for spirits."

Sally saw nothing funny about it. "I don't know why there should be so much excitement about some girl having lived before. Everybody has."

Ruth laughed. "Proving it is something else."

Sally sniffed. "You'll never prove it." She put a hand on her heart. "Here you know it's true."

The conversation shifted to Tommy's dramatic death scene. Ruth was sympathetic as usual.

"Can't you see this poor thing, stricken as the lifeblood drained out of the only man she ever loved?"

Joe looked up slyly. "I don't know about that. Mr. Brown was around an awful lot for a stranger."

Ruth was disgusted. "Oh, Joe, you always see the worst."

Thompson puzzled me. "Why should he be so helpful? He obviously didn't charge her for the pigs and other supplies. After all, she had no money."

Ruth's eyes flashed. "Men," she exclaimed.

"Now, love," Joe countered silkily, "we all know that people are self-seeking. When the phone rings, it's invariably somebody wanting something."

Ruth was fully embattled. "I remember a poor old recluse like Susan Marrow back in Indiana. Nobody even knew her name, but people cheerfully brought her food and did her chores. This was their good deed for the day and they felt better for it. She was never put off the land, it would have been inhuman."

Sally Steacy got up to leave, with a final word. "Living again is fundamentally an emotional experience and that's as real as real can be."

Even in the framework of her own subconscious, I often found Susan's behavior puzzling: her pointless preoccupation with Old Man MacGregor, for instance.

"He was rather childish," I pointed out.

"Exactly," Ruth said. "They were on a level."

"How could a brawl result from remarks about a woman having a good figure for her age?"

Ruth laughed. "A woman would understand that. In those days, you couldn't possibly discern a woman's figure without the outer clothes off." She smiled. "Didn't you notice how Susan's voice changed at that point? She was being devilish."

Joe pursed his lips dubiously. "I just can't see a woman surviving alone in that country."

Ruth snorted. "The men helped her because she was a weak female. MacGregor had chickens, so she had chickens. Thompson had pigs . . . "

Joe got up and stirred the fire.

"Joanne," he said with a frown, "hasn't made much progress. Her mind gravitates to what she knows. She remembers Watson and dates a young man named Watson. Jed was her dog's name before, and still is." He regarded me with a mocking smile. "And Jess was Yancey before, and he's still Yancey."

I laughed. "How do you know I'm not Tommy?"

Joe looked more malevolent than ever. "She doesn't like you that much."

They trudged upstairs, and I sat around a while, watching the yellow moon play its flickering shadows on old Couchiching. The giant willow, framed in the picture window, bent gently before the north wind, its branches weaving in the moonlight. Suddenly, a tiny shiver raced up my spine. Out there on a wave something was tossing about. I was sure of it. But as I pressed against the window, the obscure outline seemed to fade. I passed a hand over my eyes, and decided to call it a night. But it was dawn before I finally fell off to sleep.

By midmorning, when I peeked into the living room, Joe was already at his fire, stacking the wood on the hearth. The lake was a bluish green, and smooth as glass. There were no strange objects, only a couple of motorboats swiftly receding from shore.

I dismissed an impulse to discuss my apparition with Joe, but did open up a discussion of the supernatural.

Joe was in his element. "There are all kinds of spirits," he said equably, "just as there are all kinds of people."

"They're certainly not real?"

"Real?" His voice cracked with incredulity. "They can drive you mad. They may not haunt anybody, but they make their presence felt."

"In what way?" I asked, more curious about him than the spirits.

He lit the fire, then stood back admiringly as the flames went roaring up the flue. "Sometimes," he frowned "they're like Susan's father, seen only by those they have a message for."

"You really don't believe he came back?"

"Spirits aren't in flesh—that's why they're spirits."

"But this was all in her mind."

"And who put it there?" He cocked an eye at me. "Demons, evil spirits, often get into people and make them mad."

"Now, Joe . . . "

"Christ drove out the devil."

"But wasn't that figurative?"

He shook his head. "That's the trouble, people take from Scripture only what they want to believe."

"Do you think Joanne has a demon in her?"

He snorted. "She has Susan, and that's more than enough."

I mentioned a minister in town who reportedly exorcised demons.

Joe's eyebrows raised. "They have everything in Orillia."

"Let's drop over and see him," I suggested.

Ruth strolled in, dressed for the street. "We're shopping for Chihuahuas. Joe has enough demons at home."

And so we went our separate ways. The Reverend Crighton's (pronounced Creighton) pastorate, the Anglican Church of St. James, was in the Orillia business district, opposite the main post office. Gravestones more than a century old studded its well-tended lawn, and I couldn't resist wandering among them, automatically checking names. There was no Marrow or Ganier. The church was of dull-toned reddish brick, and the irregular architecture gave it an English county look. I found the rector, a youngish man with a thin face and ascetic features, in his study, hard at work.

After briefly introducing myself, I made a direct approach. "I understand that you have met the devil and mastered him."

His austere face relaxed into a smile.

I disclosed my preoccupation with Susan Ganier and reincarnation. He nodded noncommittally. "Have you read the Reverend Leslie Weatherhead?"

The stories about the priest and the devil were slightly exaggerated. On only one occasion had he driven out a demon. "Our Lord said that what He did, others could do with the Father's help." And the Reverend Crighton had taken it from there.

"You actually believe in a devil?"

He smiled. "He must exist to be driven out."

To confound the devil, Reverend Crighton had responded to an appeal from a parishioner whose fourteen-year-old daughter had apparently suffered epileptic seizures. The confrontation occurred at her hospital bedside, before witnesses in accordance with Christ's injunction.

The man of God had spoken out bold and clear. "I commanded the devil to leave the body."

"It was that simple?"

"Faith, faith in the Father is what did it, without that we could do nothing. 'Whatsoever ye shall ask the Father in My name, He will give it unto you.' Or as Jesus had further elaborated, 'He that believeth in me, the works that I do, shall he do also and greater works than these shall he do, because I go unto my Father.' "

There was no mistaking the priest's ardor. "We either believe what Jesus did, or we don't." The Reverend Crighton recalled how the disciples, unable to eject the demon from a lunatic child, had asked Christ, "Why could we not cast him out?" Christ had responded, "Because of your unbelief; for verily, I say unto you, if ye have faith . . . ye shall say unto this mountain, Remove hence to yonder place, and it shall remove, and nothing shall be impossible unto you."

And what had happened to the fourteen-year-old girl?

Unaware of the fight for her soul, she nevertheless began to improve immediately, and was soon completely cured. A miracle!

Crighton's story recalled a modern parable. A ten-year-old girl had been told that faith could move mountains. She prayed faithfully one night before retiring that God would move a large boulder from the front of her house to the backyard by morning. Waking early, she popped her head out of a window. The boulder still stood on the front lawn. The little girl shook her head and cried, "I knew nothing would happen."

The rector was in a philosophical mood. Lack of faith, he felt, was man's primary problem, leading to more specific problems—war, crime, divorce, sickness, delinquency. "Without the conviction that man is part of God's world, living becomes meaningless," he observed.

My thoughts turned to the Ontario Hospital School. "What part of God's world are these children?" I asked.

He regarded me evenly. "God is perfect, but we have distorted His image. Instead of wasting ourselves in destructive wars, excessive drinking and drugs, we could be using our resources to help these children. God gave us the capacity, but we are out of tune with God."

Was reincarnation, with its principle of karma, a part of God's plan?

The rector smiled. "Living is for now, regardless of what went before or later. We can only learn about our purpose as we try to find God."

While pointing out that his church did not accept reincarnation, he was still familiar with the Reverend Weatherhead's remarks: "I think it possible not that all have to come back, but that some have to, and that many may be allowed to return when it dawns on them that such is for them the path of progress. Perhaps they are even allowed to choose . . . they will doubtless choose in a way which gives them maximum opportunity, so they will choose the parents with the right makeup. What looks like heredity, then may be partly wise choosing on the part of a spirit eager in new circumstances to realize his possibilities."

He stood up and bowed. The interview was over.

I found Joe and Ruth waiting at the cottage. "How are the demons?" Joe asked.

"Is it possible," I asked, "to explore the area of Susan's communication with her father?"

Joe grinned. "No dates, no places? You're taking those demons seriously."

Before anything more could transpire, there was a rattle at the door, and Joanne came sauntering in. She struck me as being a little moody. Her eyes had lost their striking vitality, and were subtly opaque. She moved about restlessly, nervously chain-smoking as Joe adjusted the tape recorder and darkened the room. Finally, she stretched out on the couch, mentioning her sore throat was gone.

As before, Joe regressed Joanne gradually back to the year 1872. She was about forty then, already "visiting" periodically with her father.

Joe was sympathetic. "Is life hard for you?"

"It's boring."

"What do you think about mostly?"

"When I was small, and when I was married."

"Do you talk to your father still?"

"Yes."

"When do you do that?"

"In the evening."

"He keeps you company?"

"He sits in the rocking chair."

"Did you ask why he came to talk to you?"

"He said that he just came to visit."

"Did he stay long?"

"About an hour."

"Did he come back every day?"

"Not always."

"How long has it been since he's back?"

"About a week," she murmured. "I know when he's going to come now." She expected him that night.

"Did you ever have a visit from Tommy?"

"No."

"If your father comes back, why couldn't Tommy?"

"I don't know."

"When your father visits you tonight, what are you going to talk about?"

"Talk about what I did and how we used to live."

"I'm going to take you forward now in time; it's evening, and your father's going to come." He paused. "Now your father is there. You talk to your father."

I was on the edge of my chair.

She stirred without replying, and Joe tried again. "Are you in the kitchen or the living room?"

"In the kitchen."

"Where is your father?"

"In the rocking chair."

"Are you talking to him? . . . Talk out loud so that I can hear."

She spoke in a faint whisper. "The kitten died today. I found the kitten dead in the shed, so I buried the kitten outside . . . in a box . . . a little box that I put in the ground."

She kept her head cocked, as though listening. "I'll make some tea, but you don't want any because you can't drink it, can you?" Joanne's eyes suddenly had a faraway look. "He rocks in his rocking chair. He smokes his pipe. And I make my tea. Then I come back . . . "

Whatever Susan—or Joanne—saw was all in her mind,

I told myself. And yet there was no questioning the sub-conscious reality of the scene, bizarre as it was.

"He says that he sees lots of people, people that have died . . . and he talks to them, too . . . but he hasn't seen Tommy anywhere."

"Ask him why."

"He thinks Tommy's in a different place, a different part. Dad doesn't think he can get there."

"Ask why he went where he is, and Tommy went else-where."

"Tommy developed differently."

"And so he would go to another place?"

"Yes."

"Is the place Tommy's at as nice as where your father is?"

"Also heaven, but a different level."

Joe now turned to Susan's mother. "How is Catherine doing?"

"She's very happy. Nothing to worry about."

"But she doesn't visit you?"

"I can't see her."

"Oh, she comes, but you can't see her."

"I think so."

"Ask your father if you could do anything so that you could see Catherine."

Apparently the spirits were on different frequencies. "If I don't think very much maybe I can see her. But she's not strong enough."

"He's stronger?"

"Yes."

"And he's able to let you see him?"

"Yes."

"Where does your father stay now, and what is he do-ing?"

"He just talks to people, and if he wants to visit somebody, he just thinks about it, and he's there."

"What world is he in, do you know?"

"Heaven, he's in heaven."

"Is that what he calls it?"

She shook her head. "Doesn't call it anything."

"Could you ask him to describe it to you?" Joe and Joanne seemed in great rapport.

"There are trees and fields and everything the earth has. It's always sunny, and they don't eat or drink anything. They never want anything."

No wonder they called it heaven.

"What direction would you go to get there?"

"You have to go up, but not far. There are different layers on top of each other."

"Is Tommy above him, or below?"

"Think he's below."

"Where they are, are they solid or spirit?"

"Spirit."

"When you see him, of course, he's dressed?"

"Yes, they wear clothes. But not for warmth."

"Could you ask your father why they wear clothes?"

"They just wear clothes, something like what they wore when they were alive."

From his face, I thought Joe unduly impressed. "It's all a dramatization of her own subconscious," I whispered.

Joe waved me off.

"Does everything stay the same there?" he continued.

"Except sometimes more people come when they die."

"And do they have some kind of religion?"

"No, because everybody knows what they did that was wrong."

"There are things you do that are wrong?"

"When you are alive."

"Does your father believe in God?"

"He knows that something made him get there. And

so he thinks it's God. But he never sees God."

"How long is he going to stay there?"

"He's not sure."

"Your father hasn't gotten any older . . . looks the same?"

"Yes."

"Is he ever going to come back to life again?"

"He thinks that he waits for a while and then they"— she broke off—"he wants to come back."

"Ask how he could bring that about?"

"He doesn't do very much. God does it."

"He said that?"

"Yes. He said some day he won't be there any more. He doesn't know when."

"Does your father talk about people leaving there? Does he know of anybody who left where he's now staying?"

"He knows some people have gone." She hesitated. "But he . . . he knows they're missing."

"Why do some return and others don't?"

Her head bobbed. "They do."

"They all do?"

"They will."

"They'll all return, everyone?"

"Where he is."

"The level he's on, right?"

"Yes."

"All of a sudden it happens?"

"Uhmm."

"And the others know that it will happen because they've seen other people missing all of a sudden?"

"Yes, they'd know when they die. They just know that they'll go back."

"Do they have a choice?"

"No, God knows where they should go."

Irony crept into Joe's voice. "So they still believe in God? . . . And though they like the place where they are, they may return to earth again?"

"Uhmm."

"And they all will come back, everyone that's where he is?"

"Yes." Flatly, freely, unfalteringly.

Joe took a deep breath. "All right, your father had a nice visit with you. He's left now, and it's getting dark. It has become night." He peered down at her. "Were you pleased that your father visited you?"

"I'm always happy when he visits me."

"Did he say when he might return?"

"No."

"Do you think you'll see him tomorrow night?"

"Possibly. I don't know till . . . " Her voice trailed off.

One subconscious gap required a little clarification. Told she would not join Tommy in "heaven," she still wanted to die. How then would they be rejoined?

"Did you have a feeling that you could see him in another earth life?"

"Yes."

"That you would marry him again?"

"I don't know about that."

"What would he be like?"

"Same as he was."

"How would you know him?"

"I'll just know."

"Because he would look the same?"

"His eyes."

"Would you search for him in your next life?"

"I'd just wait."

Joe's eyebrows arched. "You'd wait, and it would happen?"

"Yes."

"It's going to happen for you in the next life?"

"Uhm."

"Does that happen for everybody?"

"I don't think so."

"Even though they dearly loved each other?"

"Maybe if they did love each other."

"If they really loved . . . ?"

"Most people don't."

The soft hum of her voice wove a spell in the gathering gloom.

But Joe was not easily spellbound. "Why," he asked, "would you be able to come back and find your loved one again?"

"Because our love is eternal."

"When you went to heaven, they told you it was eternal?"

"You don't have to ask it. You just know everything."

"You know everything?"

"But then, you come back and you forget."

"Did you see your next life when you were in heaven?"

"Not the whole life. You just see where you go."

"Could you tell me what you saw?"

"Just Mother and Father."

"Did you have to go back?"

"I wanted to go."

"But even if you didn't want to, you would have to go back."

"You want to go back, if you have to go back."

"Did you remember your whole life when you were in heaven? Your past life, did you remember it all . . . all your memories?"

"The important ones, just like I remember now."

"Did your father stay with you all the time?"

"He left."

"Before you did?"

"Yes."

"Do you know where he went?"

"You just knew yourself where you were going."

"And when did you know in heaven that you were coming back?"

"Just before I was born. I knew I would come back but I didn't know where I was going back."

"You just knew it?"

"I saw."

"What did you see?"

"My new mother and father, the MacIvers."

"Anything else?"

"Mother was pregnant."

Joe's jaw dropped. "Your mother was pregnant, and you knew that was you?"

"Going to be me," she corrected.

"And when did you enter the body?"

"Just before I was born."

"Where was the baby when you entered into it?"

"Inside Mother."

"Still in the womb?"

"Uhmm."

"And what happened when you went into this body?"

"Just waited to be born."

"And when you came out, what happened?"

"Then I forgot everything."

"Is that the way it was supposed to be?"

"When I was small I knew, but then I forgot."

"Everybody forgets slowly?"

She shook her head. "Fast."

"Before they can talk?"

"Sometimes they still remember when they can talk, when they're just learning."

"But couldn't they remember after they've forgotten, like you can remember . . . ?"

"Some people do, but not very many."

For vivid detail, Joanne's—Susan's—portrait of heaven surpassed the clairvoyant revelation of the mystic Swedenborg, who claimed an astral projection two centuries before.

But what did it all mean? Were we to believe that her spirit had actually survived to experience the heavenly adventures she had dredged out of her subconscious? I had never heard heaven described before, nor had Joe, and there wasn't the smallest grain of evidence in her narration. Yet, in speculation of life on other planets, it seemed possible the form would differ greatly, and might even be an energy force—pure mind. Could not this be true of any extraterrestrial heaven?

Joe seemed reluctant to wind up the session on so fanciful a note. He got Joanne back to earth, and the winter of 1883, when she was in the winter of her own life.

For the first time, he went deeply into the Eagles connection.

At this time, Susan had known Mr. Eagles slightly for ten years, knew vaguely that he was married, and knew of only one son, who would have been Arthur Eagles.

She had met the older Eagles when he offered her a lift to town.

"How did you get to town?" Joe asked.

"In . . . uhmm . . . a democrat."

Joe looked bewildered.

"He was a democrat?"

"No, the wagon was."

I explained, "It was a style of carriage."

"Oh." Joe seemed relieved.

The son, then three or four, had accompanied the father. "Was he a nice boy?"

"Quiet."

"Do you know Mr. Eagles' first name?"

Although consciously, Joanne was very much aware

that it was Charles, she replied subconsciously now as
Susan, "No."
"Did you meet his wife?"
"No, I just asked how she was."
"Where was his farm in relation to you?"
"It was north."
"And what did he do for a living?"
"He had money."
"How did he make his money?"
"I think he had a mill."
"What kind of mill?"
"To cut up trees."
"Did he ever tell you about the mill?"
"Had a big saw."
"When you went to town with him, did you have to
pass his sawmill?"
"No."
"What road did you take into town?" he asked.
"You go east on the one I live on, and then south . . .then
you go east."
This was the way to Meaford, on Georgian Bay, not
Owen Sound, which was south and west.
"How long did it take?"
"Half an hour."
Eagles had made several stops, the hardware store, the
blacksmith, the grocery. Susan bought groceries and
cloth.
"It was a small town . . . right?"
" . . . on water."
"Were there many buildings there?"
"A street."
"Did it have a name?"
Her voice wavered. "I think we went to Owen Sound."
"Was that the town called Owen Sound?"
"I know there were two towns, but I don't know

which . . . " She sighed. "Maybe it was Sydenham."

I peered into her face curiously. A hundred years or so ago, the county seat, Owen Sound, was actually named Sydenham.

"You're not sure?" Joe pushed on.

"We just call it the town."

Even when the information was readily available in libraries, Joanne was often contradictory and vague. Most disconcertingly, too, she died twice, once in 1884, again in 1903.

Joe had progressed her swiftly to 1903, when she would have been seventy-one or seventy-two.

"Where are you, Susan?" he asked.

Her voice was sepulchral. "Dead."

"Now, did anybody come to get you?"

"Dad."

"How old were you when you died?"

"Older than sixty, seventy . . . "

"Do you remember being very sick?"

"No . . . I was just tired and cold."

"What happened to you when you died? What happened to your body?"

I edged forward.

"It stayed in bed."

"Did you stay around after you died?"

"No."

"You went right away?"

"Yes."

"Do you like it there?"

"I liked it better when I was married . . . I want to go back."

Subconsciously in suspension now, Joanne was made capable of roaming wherever her boundless mind would take her.

"Tell me," Joe asked, "when did you leave there to come back?"

"I just left," she barely whispered.

"Who did you come back as?"

"Joanne."

"When you became Joanne, what year was that?"

"Nineteen forty . . . eight." Joanne was born October 22, . . . 1948."

"What did you want to do on earth?"

"I wanted to live."

"Why did you want to live again?"

"I like to live."

"You did like that period when you were married to Tommy?"

"If he didn't die."

Joe was now able to move Joanne around from one life to another with a simple suggestion. He took her easily back to 1846, when she was presumably fifteen or so.

"You'll soon be sixteen?"

"Yes."

We had now explored Susan's attitude in virtually all subconsciously meaningful relations but one. And from the faintly mocking smile on Joe's lips, he was now considering that. Nodding across Joanne's prone form, he said ironically, "With your permission, naturally."

And so we came to the interlude in Susan's life, which, apart from Tommy's death, had stirred the sharpest reaction in the sleeping Joanne.

"All right," Joe said, frowning now, "do you remember Yancey?"

She shook her head.

"Now you're seventeen. Do you know a Yancey?"

No response.

"All right, you're living with Tommy now, you're twenty-three years old, you're on the farm with Tommy . . . Do you know a man by the name of Yancey?"

She hesitated and for a fleeting moment I thought she was about to say no. But she finally gulped out a yes. As ephemeral as it was, the whole experience was still no more evanescent than life itself. For as the dying Thoreau once told a patronizing condoler, "Death is as near to you as it is to me."

Like a bloodhound on scent, Joe burrowed ahead. "How long have you known Yancey?"

"About three years."

"What is this Yancey like?"

"Tall and slight."

She didn't like him. "He's sly."

"Has he ever harmed you?"

"No . . . he's sneaky."

"Why do you have him around?"

She grimaced. "He helps Tommy."

Obviously, the crisis hadn't occurred yet, so Joe progressed her another three years; Susan was now twenty-six.

"Has he harmed you ever?"

Her face was now distorted with emotion. "He grabbed me once."

"What did you do?"

"Pushed him away."

"Did you tell Tom?"

"No."

"Why didn't you?"

"I was afraid."

"What were you afraid of?"

"That he might hurt me."

"Yancey might hurt you?"

"Yes."

"What was Yancey's last name?"

" . . . I just know Yancey."

"Was he born there, near you?"

"No."

She knew little about him, except that he lived alone, and hired out to farmers. He spoke English with an unfamiliar accent.

Joe advanced Susan another four years. "Now you're thirty years old . . . you're thirty years old. Do you still know Yancey?"

"No." She sighed her relief.

"When he would grab you," Joe said, "where would you be, what part of the house."

"In the kitchen."

"Did he leave because he used to grab you?"

"No . . . " uncertainly.

"He just left?"

"Maybe he did." Her voice suddenly rose in anger. "Hit him."

"Did you hit him hard?"

"Uhmm."

"Weren't you afraid he might harm you?"

"That's why I hit him."

"Oh, he was trying to harm you."

Somehow, obliquely, he had removed the blocks Susan had built up around the traumatic adventure.

"I'll take you back to that day now. You're going to go back to that day and relive that episode with Yancey. You will be on that day . . ."

"In the summertime . . ." she filled in slowly.

"And . . ." Joe prodded.

"And Yancey came up to get something. I was in the kitchen, and he came in."

"Did you know what he came into the kitchen for?"

"Didn't come into the kitchen for anything . . . he was supposed to go to the barn."

"And what did he do to you?"

"He grabbed me."

"Where did he grab you?"

"Around the waist."

"Then what happened?"

"I started talking to him."

"What did he say?"

"He got excited."

"What did he do?"

"Just pulled me toward him."

"What else did he do?"

"Then I hit him."

"How did you hit him?"

"With my arms and I kicked him. Then I ran . . . " Her tongue ran nervously over her lips.

"You ran," Joe prompted.

" . . . over by the stove."

"Then what, did you scream?"

"Then he came over, and I grabbed the shovel."

"And hit him?"

"Uhmm."

"Did he leave the kitchen then?"

"Yes, he . . . left."

"And what did you do?"

"I was scared."

"So what did you do?"

"I ran . . . ran down and told Tommy." He was in the field cutting trees.

"Did Tommy believe you?"

"Yes."

"And what did he say?"

"He was really mad. And he said that he [Yancey] was not going to work any more. And he came back with me. But he [Yancey] was gone."

"He ran away?"

"Yes."

"You never saw him again?"

"No."

"What," asked Joe, "would Tommy have done if he had found him?"

"He would have beaten him up."

She had no more to say about Yancey, or anything else. She was used up. As she opened her eyes, she stretched languidly from head to toe, and yawned. "I feel tired."

"You should," Joe laughed, "you were fighting for your honor."

She stifled another yawn. "Oh, Yancey still giving trouble?"

Her face was pleasantly flushed.

"Who," Joe asked, "do you think Yancey is?"

She laughed mirthlessly. "He could be anybody. They're all like him today."

"I thought the men were effeminate, and that was the trouble."

"They're trying to prove they're not."

Joe gave her a paternal pat. "All right, Joanne, go home and rest. Big day tomorrow."

Watching Joanne relive the horror of Yancey's attack, I realized she had only been teasing me before. I felt no involvement myself, aside from being a fascinated spectator of a fantastic drama from which the pallid curtain of time had been miraculously lifted.

How had the Susan experience, subconsciously so deeply felt, cut into Joanne's own life. She seemed to have a normal healthy attitude toward sex, and then with a start I suddenly recalled a remark she had made one day on the road as we discussed her reactions toward young men. "If any date of mine touches me, I feel like climbing a wall."

Had the conscious impression of the assault remained, while the attack itself was providentially forgotten—until hypnosis.

That evening, as Joe and I traded notes, we tacitly glossed over the totally unpleasant incident and moved on to the girl's more pleasantly intriguing portrait of a heaven that sounded like heaven. Her description was clearly the product of her subconscious, for consciously she spent little time pondering the hereafter. How much validity was there to her spiritual impressions? I had recently been struck by the experience of a friend, at death's door for days after an accident. In coma, she saw her dead mother standing by her bed, grave and unwelcoming. Then, with an expression of love, the mother suddenly vanished, just as the patient opened her eyes, and heard a doctor saying, "She will live."

The experience had jarred my practical-minded friend, a veteran of the Israeli struggle against the Arabs, who felt with so many others that God helped those who shot first and fastest, and His influence ended there.

Convalescing, she was visited by a brother, who eyed her curiously. "You know," he said, "I suddenly see in you a resemblance to Mother."

Tingling with emotion, she described her vision.

He snorted. "You were delirious."

She could not be budged. "I knew I saw my mother, and that she was letting me know they weren't ready for me."

Joe had heard me out. "These impressions are more subjectively real than anything in the conscious," he commented, "but whether they have objective reality is something else." He frowned. "But what is real? If it is what influences the conscious life, then your friend's vision was terribly real. And with Joanne, the same should be true. Nearly everything she is getting points to early marriage and motherhood."

We swung easily from marriage to death; namely, Susan's (or Joanne's) confusion about her demise. Joanne must certainly have known that 1903 was the death date established by Arthur Eagles. Yet, she had twice mentioned 1884.

Joe didn't share my misgivings. "Dates are meaningless to old people whose lives stretch out meaninglessly."

I wasn't quite satisfied.

"She seemed to remember Yancey, and heaven she discussed like an angel."

"Yancey was a tangible personality, but even with Yancey she was hazy on dates. But there was no question about her feeling the reality of Yancey." He laughed. "She even avoided using his name. He was invariably *he.*"

I turned to her celestial junket. "There is certainly nothing evidential about her trip to heaven."

He grinned impishly. "They're always talking about nobody coming back to say what it's like. Well, they can't say that any more."

"If she knew so much about heaven," I persisted, "why not a little more about next door?"

"She obviously became a little pixilated," Joe observed. "Mental changes, accompanying a change of life, may have occurred by 1884. She would have been the right age, about fifty. And for practical purposes, she was dead; she could no longer bear children."

The loneliness of the Canadian bush was capable of unsettling even resolute minds. In a contemporary chronicle, *A Gentlewoman in Upper Canada,* early settler John Langton met a disconsolate stranger who had just finished clearing off his land two miles away. He "had come down to the Lake," Langton reported, "for the chance of seeing a fellow creature."

With all Joe's probing, we hardly knew enough of Susan's marriage at this point to know what karma was building up. For in the context of their relationship, we hardly knew the kind of husband Tommy was, or Susan, a wife.

Joe nodded appreciatively. "We've had to move gradually, but we'll take it from the wedding tomorrow."

To know how Joanne was eventually to fulfill herself, shouldn't we know why there had been no children as Susan? Was it through some psychological—or physiological—malfunction, hers or Tommy's? Would there be opportunity in this lifetime to profit from the last?

Thus, Joe thought it imperative that the marital relationship be thoroughly explored. "Women fearful of sex frequently have difficulties having that first child." He anticipated difficulties, hypnotically, with the Victorian Susan. "Victorian women didn't discuss sex problems, even with their physician; the censor ban will be getting a workout.

"Remember, too, whoever she is—Joanne or Susan— she's only seventeen."

As the new session began Joe rapidly regressed the seventeen-year-old Joanne back to Susan at seventeen, just before she married.

No prospective bride could have been happier. Tommy was kind and gentle, irrepressibly gay and happy, and she loved him.

Only once did she seem sad, in discussing Tommy's love for animals. Subconsciously, Susan may have already sensed she wouldn't have children, just as Joanne was sure she would.

Joe's questions were rather basic.

"Are you strong and healthy?"

"Yes."

"Do you expect children?"

"Yes."

"Do you know the way children come about?"

"Of course."

"Would you tell us about that?"

"No."

"Does Tommy know how children are made?"

Disdainfully, "If you're on a farm, you know that pretty young."

Joe hesitated, "Do you have any personal knowledge of this, any personal acquaintance with making children?"

Joanne stammered, and gave a subdued, "No."

"Looking forward to that?"

"Not thinking about it much."

Joe was incredulous. "Do animals think about it?"

"I don't think animals think about it. They . . . the farmers make them."

"Why did you want to marry Tommy?"

"Be happy with him."

"And how do you expect to be happy with him?"

"Because I love him."

"How do you love him?"

"Very much." It wasn't quite the expected answer. Joe swung back to the courtship.

"Do you kiss?"

"Uhmm."

"Do you hug?"

"Uhmm."

"Before you got married?"

"Uhmm." Dreamily.

"It was pleasant?"

"Yes."

"Do anything he wants with you?"

"No."

"Didn't let him?"

"He hasn't tried."

"He never tried? He wanted to wait till you got married?"

"Uhmm." Her head bobbed for emphasis.

"All right, we're going to take you to your wedding day.

Now it's your wedding day . . . where are you?"

"At home."

"Who's home with you?"

"Tom."

"This is your wedding day?"

"Yes."

"Who else is at home?"

"Nobody."

"When were you married?"

"This afternoon."

"What time is it now?"

"Four o'clock."

"And you're already married?"

Dreamily, "Uhmm."

Susan was a lovely bride.

"What color is your hair?"

"Brown."

"How tall are you?"

"Above five . . . four, or five."

"Are you fat or thin?"

"No, just right."

"And what color are your eyes?"

"Blue."

"How do you know that?"

"I know they're blue."

"Very blue?"

"Light blue."

"Do you have rosy cheeks and a nice skin?"

"Darker than Reuben's skin . . . hair's down."

Tommy was medium height, but strongly built, fair with dark blue eyes, thick-cropped hair, "a short nose" and "sort of heavy" cheeks.

"All right," Joe said easily. "Now tell me a little bit more about how you look . . . what your clothes were like?"

" . . . Dress pink."

"You have a pink dress on?"

"Umhm."

"That's pretty."

"It's full."

"You have some beads on?"

"Yes . . . from Mother. And I have a veil, a white veil, and flowers."

After the wedding came a reception in a hall. A few farmers and their wives had paid their respects. There were the Browns, Watsons, Thompson, the Urquharts. Old Man MacGregor, tipsy as usual, put his foot in the cider bowl.

Later, the newlyweds shyly retired to their farmhouse. Tommy carried his bride over the traditional threshold, and swung her merrily around the kitchen. As she made tea, Tommy made the fire. And they sat and chatted—to Joe's obvious consternation.

"Then what did you do?" Joe inquired, with a shake of the head.

"Went out for a walk."

Joe was speechless.

" . . . because it was still early. We'd been for lots of walks before, but we weren't married then. So I wanted to go for a walk when we were married. Around five . . . then we came back . . . had some biscuits, some more tea . . . and looked around the house. Small."

"Then what did you do?"

"Then after a while it got late."

"Then what?"

Her voice dropped. "Went to bed."

"And what happened then?"

"You'd be surprised." Her voice snapped.

"He did what?"

"You'd be surprised."

"I want you to tell me about it."

"No."

"No?"

"No."

Teasingly, Joe tried another tack. "Wasn't any good?"

"I won't tell you."

"Did you talk?"

"Yep."

"Did you like it?"

"What?" she parried.

"Whatever you were doing that was so surprising," Joe fenced back.

"I didn't say it was surprising."

"Oh, you mean I'd be surprised?"

"Yes."

"Was it something different?"

"What do you want to know for?"

"I want to know how much you loved him."

"Very much."

"That doesn't mean anything. What did you call what he did with you on your wedding night?" Crude as it seemed, Joe was after a clear, objective understanding of the relationship. "Is there a name for it?"

" . . . Nope." None that she could use.

"Everybody knows about it, though, right?"

"Umhm."

"Everybody does it?"

"Lots of people."

"What comes about because you do this?"

"Mmmmm . . . sometimes children." She was relaxed now. "I know, because we have cows."

"Cows do it this way, too?"

"Umhm. And pigs."

"And so you had a good evening, right?"

"Umhm."

"And you discovered you loved him even more, right?"

"Umhm." An almost ecstatic murmur.

"It was just the way you thought it would be?"

"Better."

At this point I got up to answer the phone; Joanne's eyes were staring glassily into space. She could have been a million miles away.

But Joe was still on scent. "Did you have a good night's sleep?"

"Yep."

"And he didn't wake you up during the night?"

"Nope."

"Are you hoping to repeat this every night?"

"I don't think it's very nice, what you're talking about," she said warmly.

"Didn't you enjoy it?"

"Yes, but it's not for everybody to know about."

"All right, just relax," Joe said placatingly. "You'll feel wonderful."

Somehow all this probing seemed outrageously personal, and I finally waved Joe down.

"All right," he said reluctantly, "back to the ranch."

We still didn't know where Tommy had acquired his farm. The Alexander Fraser properties stood about where the Marrows presumably lived and Fraser was an absentee owner. Significantly perhaps, Joanne had begun the owner's name with an A. Now Joe was hoping to pry out the rest. "Tommy must have said the owner's name many times . . . you must know his name."

She began uncertainly. "A . . . l . . . "

"Al, did you say Al?"

"No . . . " faltering. "Aln . . . son?"

"Would that be Allenson?"

"Maybe."

"Could it have been Alexander?"

"Maybe that was it . . . Al . . . something."

Joe threw up his arms and turned to the farm itself for clues which might jog some hidden chord of memory.

It seemed like a good hunch, for she was now quite graphic. The farm came caressingly to life under her loving words. Oats and hay were planted in fields back of the house; their own trees provided firewood against the cold; fresh water flowed bountifully from a well near the house; the barn was small but sufficient for their livestock. The house itself was a white frame dwelling, with kitchen, fireplace, bedroom, living room, and a table and a couple of chairs. Light came from candles, the fireplace—even the stove—and served the dual purpose of providing warmth.

Susan did her best to produce a wilderness version of the house beautiful. She had a garden with flowers, a fringe of lawn, and a fence to keep the cows from the living room. There were some unusual features for the period: a porch, pathway, and terrace.

Joe was impressed in spite of himself. "Whose idea was the terrace?"

"Mine," she said. "I went and found some stones."

"Did most people have terraces?"

"No."

"It would be nice then to have a terrace?"

Proudly, "New idea."

Not in the commonplace, but under stress of great events, did the subconscious personality of Susan Marrow fully express itself.

And so Joe proceeded in this realization. "You're in your seventies, in your house. You're all alone."

Susan spoke of a racking cough, and a leaden cold chilled her bones. She was consumed by one thought— death.

"Do you still think of Tommy?" Joe asked.

"No, not now. I want to die." Her voice was a dull gray.

"Why do you want to die?"

"Sad."

"Does your father come to visit you still?"

"Umhm."

"Is he going to take you over?"

"As soon as I die . . . been waiting to die."

"Did you feel badly about not having children?"

"At one time. Not now."

"After Tommy died, did you still want children?"

"Didn't think about them . . . wanted them when Tommy was here."

"You wanted to be alone?"

"I just didn't want children without Tommy. I wanted Tom's children."

"Are you going to see Tom when you die?"

"I don't think so."

"But you want to come back again, so you can marry Tom again?"

"Maybe."

"Who," Joe asked, "was the last person you saw before you died?"

"Two men."

"Did they come into the house?"

"Yes. They wanted to see if I was all right."

They were strangers. "They came to see how I was. Somebody told them."

"Who would tell them that?"

"Mr. Thompson would."

They were to bring food, but she never saw them again, apparently dying before they could get back.

After death, Susan seemed to gain an awareness she never had in life, and she realized an ambition nearly everyone secretly dreams about. She turned up at her own funeral.

She had died that winter, but remained unburied until spring.

Joe was aghast. "They didn't bury you that winter?"

"No, the ground was frozen."

"Where did they keep you?"

"I don't know. I didn't come back until my funeral."

"And when you came back, where was your body?"

"In a churchyard . . . at the back . . . near the pines . . . the church."

"How did you know it was a church?"

"It was a graveyard."

"How far was this graveyard from your house?"

"I don't know. I don't even know where the church was. But I was there."

"Did your father come back with you?"

"No, I watched it myself."

"Alone?"

"Mr. Thompson was there . . . some minister."

"Did they say any words over you?"

"Sprinkled sand on the casket."

"Were you sad when you saw your funeral?"

"No, except nobody was there." Nobody who mattered.

"And did they lower the box into the grave?"

"Not until people left."

"Oh, there were some people."

"Mr. Thompson."

"Mr. Thompson wasn't old?"

"Middle-aged." She paused. "I don't know if Mr. [Charles] Eagles was there."

"Would you know him if you saw him?"

"Yes, I think so . . . but I wasn't interested in the people, really."

Joe was obviously fatigued. "All right, Joanne," he said, "you have left heaven and gone into a new life. And you're seventeen years old. You're Joanne with memories of Joanne. When I awaken you, you'll feel better than you have in a long time. And as you remain awake, you will feel more relaxed, more sure of yourself, more stable, more adjusted."

Joanne bounded off the couch, alive and vibrant.

"Whew," she said, "I feel good."

Joe regarded her equably. "Only one more session."

That would be the last, except for a scene at the presumed site of the old Marrow homestead.

He viewed Joanne's receding figure rather grimly. "Tomorrow," he said, "we'll tie up a few loose ends."

"Like what?"

"Sufficient unto the day . . . " His voice trailed off.

That night, we again sat around discussing the gaps Susan had left unresolved.

"Strange," I said, "that she doesn't remember the number of the lot she lived on with Tommy, or later alone."

Ruth demurred. "I can't recall all of my previous street numbers."

I had felt like a Peeping Tom at Susan's wedding night. Still, why hadn't Joanne, as a modern teenager, been able to discuss sex easily?

Joe smiled. "It's Susan we're dealing with here, not Joanne. Susan didn't even know *what* she was doing. She didn't know the word *intercourse*. The dog was in heat, horses mated, but humans were above that, and the censor ban went up."

In *The Phenomenon of Man,* De Chardin had postulated that in the half-light of his consciousness—the subconscious—man "has a cosmic extension, and as such is surrounded by an aura of indefinite spatial and temporal extensions."

Did Joanne's subconscious, in hypnosis, reflect this infinity? Was her spirit personality a deathless part of some timeless, spaceless infinity? Or, death being the end, did we vanish after one brief excursion seemingly meaningless in itself? What then was the meaning of the infinity that we saw everywhere around us in the skies, earth, seasons, even in a humanity constantly regenerating?

Joe threw up his arms. "All I know is that Susan's experience comes out of somewhere. You could read a dozen books, and not get the picture she's giving us of a wilderness that couldn't even communicate with itself."

He stepped to the big window, and stared out moodily on the lake.

Ruth's eyes followed him with concern. But suddenly his mood changed. "Tomorrow morning," he said heartily, "we visit the haunted church."

As they climbed the stairs together, Ruth squeezed his hand and his arm circled her waist. They knew what Tommy and Susan were all about.

I peered out at the lake for perhaps fifteen minutes, then floated off to sleep, dreaming of a Loch Ness monster. It had two heads, and somehow resembled Ken MacIver.

Joe was his usual irrepressible self in the morning, bombarding me with questions about the legendary ghost of St. Columbkille's Roman Catholic Church. I told him as much as I knew. The legend had begun sixty years before with the untimely death of a youthful pastor said to return periodically to brood over the fortunes of his flock. The last known visitation had come just before Easter two years previously, and was carefully reported by the Orillia *Packet and Times,* a daily affectionately known as the *Racket and Crimes:*

"A shadowy figure floated across the gallery and, sitting down at the keyboard, started playing the organ. He played beautifully. Some of the watching girls screamed and fled but others stayed to see the figure vanish mysteriously into the belfry. The legendary 'ghost' of St.

Columbkille's Roman Catholic Church had returned."

Joe grinned. "Any witnesses?"

"Two girls, I understand."

One girl had told a *Packet* reporter: "We were all cleaning the church when suddenly this figure floated across the gallery and started playing the organ. It was dressed in a black choir gown and black hat with a white face. Only the eyes were visible."

A carpenter, racing up a stairway to the gallery, lunged for the gauzy figure, but it miraculously eluded him. Later, Orillian Wayne Birch and six companions noticed the apparition in the balcony. At their shouts, it quickly disappeared. "It looked," Birch said, "like it went through the wall."

The Reverend Frank Voorwerk laid the ghost to rest from his pulpit, but not before sightseers from all over Canada had visited the church and tramped its aisles.

There were no ghosts, the priest said, with all the conviction of his background. But Joe thought he would see for himself. The church was just outside Orillia. We could spot it from the road, a stately structure set well back, with a cemetery next to it. With a glance at the headstones, Joe observed wryly, "At least, the ghost doesn't have far to travel."

An elderly man toiled in a field behind the church. He looked up dourly as we cut across the grass toward him.

"Hello," Joe called, "any ghosts?"

The dour look became a scowl.

Joe went on amiably. "Heard about your ghosts, and came over to see for ourselves."

"People need something to gossip about," the man growled.

"You mean there are no ghosts?"

"None that I ever saw."

"A priest came back, wasn't that it?" Joe said.

The man motioned to the graveyard. "The priest, Henry McPhillips, is buried out there in the yard." He singled out the headstone. "There was some silly story that, because he died young, he'd keep coming back to watch over the church."

"Could we look inside?" Joe asked.

He shrugged. "I guess so."

It was a simple but gracious interior, and rows of hardwood pews negated any impression of any unusual supernatural presence. In the balcony, behind a rail, sat the organ, silently brooding.

Joe's eyes roamed through the church. "No ghosts here now," he said authoritatively.

The man was still in the fields when we came out. His name was Bill Henshaw, and he was the caretaker. "I've been here a few years," he said, "and I never saw anything."

"Maybe, you didn't look hard enough," Joe suggested.

The caretaker's eyes hardened. "We have an idea who it was."

"Who?"

He hesitated a moment. "Some nine-year-old boy playing a prank, and if we ever catch him at it . . . "

"How can you be sure?" Joe asked.

"He must have sneaked behind the rail, and kneeled unseen by the organ, fooling with the keys."

"But if there were a lot of ladies present," Joe remonstrated mildly, "why didn't they notice him?"

The caretaker squinted into the sun. "Only two impressionable girls heard the organ."

Joe regarded the caretaker curiously. "If a boy was actually playing the organ, then why didn't all the women hear it?"

The man's jaw dropped. It was a new and obviously baffling thought. "Anyway," he said stubbornly, "we know it was no ghost."

The ride back to Big Chief Road was uneventful, Joe seriously contemplating the approaching session with Joanne. "Do you wonder," he asked abruptly, "what this girl thinks about you—or of your own feelings for her?"

"I'm quite detached."

He snickered. "You weren't detached at first."

"Perhaps not," I conceded.

"But you are detached now, right?"

"As much as anybody can be."

"How about those blue eyes?"

"How about them?"

"Do they look back into the centuries?"

"You said it."

His eyes had a speculative look. "Do you think the father's brainwashing her?"

"Why not ask her subconscious?"

He chuckled. "Today is the day."

"What do you mean, love?" Ruth inquired.

"You'll find out," he said ominously.

The session started later than usual that afternoon. Joanne had come bouncing in, depressing us with her adolescent vitality. We spoke of ghosts for a while and while curious, she was understandably more preoccupied with her own activities. As she slipped off her jacket, revealing an attractive sweater, one thing was sure: Joanne was certainly no ghost.

She smacked herself down on the couch, pulled the blanket to her neck, and was ready. And so was Joe. Almost immediately, I noticed a variation in his routine. "All right, Susan, I'm going to give you the ability to see your life very clearly. All through your childhood, all your adulthood, being married, your friends, everything is going to be very clear. The information you give will be *truthful* and *accurate*. You'll be able to see your whole life from the time you were born to the time you died."

He surrounded her, suggestively, with a blue light of truth. "As this light engulfs you, you're going to have great ability to recall about your life from the time you were born to the time you died. Now this light is growing brighter and brighter, and the more brightly this light glows, the more you will be able to see clearly."

He turned first to the conflicting death dates. "You felt you had died in 1884. You felt you had died around fifty years of age. Is there any reason why you said that?"

The voice was Susan's, tired, old, defeated. "I wasn't living."

"What do you mean you weren't living?"

"I had no reasons . . . "

"To live?"

"No, I'm alive."

"You felt dead inside?"

"Yes."

"What gave you that feeling?"

"I was sick of life."

"Any other thing?"

"I wasn't well."

"Anybody think you strange, different, or mentally disturbed?"

"I don't know what they thought."

"Do you know what it means to have a change of life?"

"No."

"Do you know what it means to have menstruation?"

"Yes."

"Did you menstruate?"

"Of course, I did." The blue light apparently outshone the censor ban.

Joe hesitated briefly. "Did you stop menstruation when you were about fifty-one or two?"

"Yes."

"When you stop menstruating, what does that mean?"

"Can't have children any more."

Joe now took her beyond death. "Was there anybody in heaven by the name of Jess Stearn?" I had had no warning of the line of questioning, nor had Joanne.

"No, I don't know anybody."

"Was there anybody in your past life that was like Jess Stearn, or later became Jess Stearn?"

"I don't know who became who. I don't even know where my father is. Just know where I am."

Joe soon realized the name was in the wrong life. "I'm going to take you forward to the present time. You're now seventeen years old. You're going to remember all your time in heaven, and you're going to remember all your time as Joanne . . . All right, seventeen years old. Do you know Jess Stearn?"

"Yes."

"Do you know anybody in your past life that was like Jess Stearn?"

She stammered, "Uh . . . yes."

"Who?"

"Something like my father."

"Like your father, as Susan?"

"Yes."

"Tell me, what made Jess Stearn and your father alike?"

"Looked like him. Tall, light, same temperament." She certainly wasn't talking about MacIver, who was short, paunchy, and rather extroverted.

"Although he looked like your father, he could have been somebody else?"

"Could have been anybody else."

"Do you remember a man by the name of Yancey?"

"Yes."

"What was he like?"

"Not very clever."

"Is there anyone in this life like Yancey?"

"In certain ways, a lot of people are."

"Do you know anybody in particular like Yancey?"

She hesitated. "Won't say."

"You can say."

"No, you don't know who he'd be."

"That's more reason why you should say."

"He lived at our other house."

"What was his name?"

She recalled an unfamiliar name. At any rate, I was no longer Yancey. But at last I knew why she had wanted me to go to Massie—thinking it might strike some familiar chord. Hadn't her Ganier father traveled and perhaps lived there?

Had Joanne MacIver's life any specific purpose, aside from blindly continuing the evolutionary process that seemed the destiny of most of us?

"Is there a Tommy Marrow in this life?" Joe asked appropriately enough.

She shook her head. "Don't know."

"Would it be Jess Stearn?"

"No."

"Could it be Tag Watson?"

"Maybe."

"Why do you say maybe?"

"He's like him a lot."

Tag was hardly our idea of a romantic figure, but then we had only seen Tommy through Susan's love-struck eyes.

"Why did you say that you knew Jess Stearn before?"

"I recognized his eyes."

"How did you feel about recognizing him?"

"It was sort of fun knowing somebody without ever having seen them."

"You were happy about it?"

"Umhm."

"What were your other feelings about it?"

"That we must have had something in common . . . personalities, way of thought."

But almost as quickly as it had come, recognition had faded.

"What happened that caused you to lose the recognition?"

"When I first saw him, I recognized his soul in his eyes. I can't see his soul now, the way I could the first time."

"Why not?"

"Because he's different, it's a different life."

"What did you recognize in his eyes?"

"It was his soul."

"What does that mean?"

"A soul that keeps reincarnating all the time."

"You liked what you saw?"

"Yes."

"And then you didn't recognize that any more?"

"No."

"Whose else's eyes did you look in and recognize their soul?"

"Nobody's."

"Why have you lost that ability?"

"I haven't lost the ability. It's just not the same."

"What changed?"

"His soul was hidden, and I saw it." In that one fleeting moment, had she been given a glimpse of something I was not even aware of?

"And now it's hidden again."

"What makes it hidden?"

"I recognized his eyes . . . recognized his bare self. But now he's built a barrier around himself. Can't recognize him any more."

"Would you like to tell us anything about his soul when you saw it?"

"Was very happy."

"How many lives had it lived?"

"Seven . . . maybe."

"Is that the truth?"

"I don't know the number for sure, but it's more than five."

"How do you know it was more than five?"

"His soul is old."

"How do you know it's old?"

"I could recognize it in his eyes."

Listening now, I was certainly detached. Whatever the reaction of our first meeting, it was long since extinguished, perhaps deliberately on my part, and I had only the friendly, impersonal attitude of a dispassionate chronicler for an attractive subject. I no longer attached importance to her feelings about me, nor was I especially concerned at this point.

If anything, Joe had prior claims on my sympathies. For days we had been listening to the subconscious proliferations of a seventeen-year-old, and now Joe was about to examine the authenticity of this subconscious.

I sat back to watch the duel.

"Do you know what truth is?" he asked peremptorily.

"You can't make one definition for truth," Joanne replied rather shrewdly. "It applies in different circumstances."

"Truth changes?"

"In a scientific discovery, sometimes they base their theories on fact, what they call fact. And at the time it's truth and everybody believes it. But after a while, it changes and that's another form of truth."

"So a truth could be a lie today, because tomorrow they found out what it actually was?"

"Some things . . . If I told you something that was true about myself, what I did, that is already done, and can't be changed."

"How is it," Joe came back, "that you told us you died at one date when you really died at another?"

"When I'm trying to remember, sometimes the dates aren't clear."

"Then you could possibly have lied about knowing it?"

"If I'm purposely wrong . . . if there's intent."

"If you don't remember correctly, it's not a lie?"

"But that's only on dates that I'm . . . "

"On things that you've said to us, are you interested in finding out if they're true or not?"

She was remarkably assured. "I know they are."

"Was it truthful when you told me that you were back in a past life?"

"Yes."

"How do you know?"

"Because I can remember."

He plunged ahead. "Who told you what you were in a past life?"

"Nobody."

"How old were you when you remembered a past life?"

"When I was in grade nine . . . fourteen."

"How old were you when your father hypnotized you?"

"Fourteen."

"Have you been hypnotized recently?"

"Yes."

"When?" Joe's voice quickened.

"Yesterday."

He shifted tack slightly. "What did your father say when he hypnotized you?"

"He said I was getting very tired . . . relaxed . . . I feel that way now."

"And then what did he say?"

"That I was going to be able to remember whatever he asked me."

"Yes?"

"And he took me back to my birthday. But I didn't have one. And he kept saying, 'You're going back in time.' Then he asked me for another birthday, and I told him, but it wasn't the same birthday that I'd had."

"Do you know why that came into your mind?"

"Because he went too far."

"What else did he tell you?"

"That's all for that time, except when he woke me up."

"What did he tell you then?"

"Just told me that I'd feel fine, but he didn't say that I'd be Joanne."

Just as he had bungled in taking her back, MacIver had erred in not removing the spell of the previous life.

"Who were you?" Joe asked.

"I was Susan for a while."

"Where did that name come from?"

"I just knew my name was Susan, the same as you know what your name is."

"Do you think your father might have planted some suggestions?"

"How could he plant suggestions?"

"The way I plant suggestions with hypnosis."

"No, because I'm aware of what's being said."

"Did your father ever tell you about Susan?"

"Never."

"Did he ever tell you about the lot . . . the place she was born . . . the things that she did?"

"No."

Only after the search got under way had he mentioned Susan to her, and then merely seeking clues.

"Did he ever take you up where Susan came from?"

"Yes."

"Did he ever give you names of places up there?"

"After I gave them."

"Why would he do that?"

"Because we were looking for the farm."

"How many times did your father hypnotize you?"

"About seven times. Sometimes two hours, sometimes one hour. All he did was question."

Her voice was barely audible now. "I'm tired," she said faintly.

"Tired of what?" Joe asked.

"I want to forget it."

"Forget what?"

"The other life . . . "

"Do you think you should know about it?"

"I don't think it's right to be thinking about it all the time."

"Would you like all the memories of the other life removed for you?"

"I don't think about it, if it's not forced upon me."

"And this will all slip away once they stop talking about it?"

"Yes."

"All right, Joanne. All thoughts and ideas about your previous life and lives will fade from your mind, and will become part of your memory and act on your life as they are meant to act. Now when I awaken you, you will feel rested, refreshed, relaxed."

Joanne sat up, rubbed her eyes, and yawned. Suddenly, she looked around and got her bearings.

"You sure pushed me." She turned resentfully to Joe.

"We have to ask the questions anybody else will," Joe replied evenly.

"I wish that were the end of it," she said.

"Just on the range now," he said, "and that's it." He looked at her quizzically. "Would you call it home on the range?"

She snorted. "What's the difference what you call anything?"

The last session at Big Chief cottage was over. In two days, she would be briefly resurrected near the old Marrow homestead, and that, hopefully, would be the end of Susan Ganier.

Joanne approached the last test casually. She had no objection to being hypnotized on the scene. Indeed, she seemed to prefer following the trail of her own subconscious to its dramatic finale, but for a reason of her own.

"I'd just like to end it."

As before, I was struck by her disinterest.

Her blue eyes were faintly amused. "You really don't believe it, do you?"

"I don't understand your lack of interest."

"I accept it, there is no doubt in my mind. So why put on?"

"You have no desire to convince others?"

"They will believe what they want, anyway."

Nevertheless, she gave no sign of elation that, at last, four years of seeking would be over. But MacIver, not as phlegmatic, obviously viewed the trip to the old homesite as a family lark. He announced on the telephone that, besides Joanne, he was taking his son Ronald, and Tag Watson, Joanne's boyfriend, and the dog.

"Should we bring a shovel and dig for Susan's or Tommy's grave?" he asked. "It would be terrific if we found a skull, or something like that."

It seemed a little premature for cadavers. "The property owners might raise some objection," I temporized.

As I put down the phone, Joe was eying me with an enigmatic expression. "Shall we bring a picnic lunch?" he said sourly.

"Just hypnotize her, and let her roam," I said.

He picked up a map, studying it with a magnifying lens screwed into one eye like a monocle.

"Now, as I understand it, we're going to the lot where

Joanne lived as Susan Marrow with Tommy until his death."

"She'll either have some sort of recall there, or not," I observed.

Joe was trying to refresh his own memory.

"She got married at about seventeen, so that would mean they moved in about 1849. They were married about a dozen years, so that would take them to the early 1860s."

Ruth broke her silence. "You might ask her about the Civil War."

Joe grimaced. "This woman didn't care who was living next to her, so why should she know what was going on in another country?"

"But somebody may have told her about the war."

As I recalled, MacIver was the first to suggest Joanne be hypnotized near the range, pointing out that if she could lead a search party to Tommy Marrow's grave, a pick and shovel brigade might well do the rest.

It was legally out of the question to engage in such a ghoulish pursuit, and, furthermore, improbable that anything would remain of a crude pine box and a set of bones moldering in damp ground for a hundred years. Actually, there was only one point to hypnotizing Joanne on the spot, as Joe saw it: the actual terrain, the ruins, the whole atmosphere might be conducive to jogging her subconscious into some specific recall.

From her conscious recall, we had established the Marrow site tentatively as the north half of Lot 33, on the First Concession Line of Sydenham Township, directly opposite the range. This site, near Morley, was practically on a line from where Old Man Eagles had once so dramatically pointed. It was approximately three miles from water, Vail's Point, as Susan had said it should be. The apple orchards were there, so were the ruins, and the land was rolling. Susan had recalled a road from the

Ganier farm to the Marrow, and such a road cut across the Tank Range at Morley. "Go up from the Ganier farm," she had said, "turn left then at the crossroads [Morley] turn right, and the farm is on the left."

The present owner of North 33, Milford Johnson, had never heard of Marrows or Ganiers, but didn't find that odd. "There were quite a few tenant farmers on the land, but there just weren't any records, and people were moving on and off all the time."

MacIver was sure that the ruins remembered so dramatically by Joanne were on land that had come down from the Frasers, through Walmsleys, and eventually to the Johnsons. He pointed out that North 33 had changed hands four times in two years in the 1860s, just before 1867, roughly when Susan Marrow got off.

On a crisp sunny morning in late September, traveling in two cars, we were ready for the final jaunt to the Sydenham-St. Vincent town line. It was quite an expedition. Besides Joanne, there was Tag Watson, one of the Nut Brothers, Joe and Ruth, Dave Manuel, up from Toronto, myself, and the collie, Jed. Casey Jones was not feeling up to going. We lunched as usual in Meaford, chatted with Joe Walker, briefly saw the Major, and headed for Silcote and the turn into the Johnson place, Dave deciding to stop off for permission to traverse the ruins.

Dave and Joe were at loggerheads all the way. In Meaford, Joe had quietly visited a drugstore, inquired about various points of local interest: the cemetery, an abandoned sawmill, the old town hall, and then entranced everybody with his "recollections."

"Migawd," Dave said, "it must be contagious."

I regarded Joe with a jaundiced eye, but old Joe Walker, who couldn't remember Marrow or Ganier, did recall an old mill, just where Joe put it, down by the Meaford waterfront. "Burned down when I was a boy," old Joe said, scratching his gray thatch.

Later, with a Machiavellian grin, the hypnotist cheerfully confessed his hoax. "How easy to fool some people," he chortled.

Dave had thought it dirty pool.

They had also disagreed mildly about Joanne's future. "There's no point going into her background on the site," Joe had said. "She's already established as a poor ignorant girl."

Dave observed thoughtfully, "That must be why she wants to go off to college so badly."

Joe had smugly shaken his head. "Marriage is the first thing on the docket for our little country girl, and it won't be anybody in these parts."

Dave had nodded at Joanne and Tag in the car ahead. "They seem pretty thick to me."

"Not in a million years," Joe snorted. "She's looking for a father for her children, not a roommate."

As we turned into the Johnson driveway, Joe sang under his breath, " 'Home, home on the range . . . ' "

Milford Johnson, the farmer son of farmers, was working in a neighboring field, but his wife received us warmly. Her face was seamed, and she was near seventy, but a light still twinkled in her faded eyes.

She was from old pioneer stock. Grandfather Michael Fettes, migrating from Scotland, had settled in Sydenham in 1847. He had intended to lay claim to land in St. Vincent, where the Tank Range was today, but was dissuaded. They told him, she recalled, that there hadn't been any bread in Vincent for ten days. He had settled instead near the water, not far from Balaclava.

The name still intrigued me. "Were the original settlers veterans of the charge of the Light Brigade at Balaclava?"

Mrs. Johnson looked puzzled.

"Balaclava—the Crimean War," I elaborated.

"Oh, no," she laughed. "A couple of Scotchmen got in a battle up that way, and they spilled so much blood that the folks called the place Balaclava."

Grandfather Fettes had received a fifty-acre Crown grant, with options for fifty more at fifty cents an acre.

It seemed odd that settlers should rent when they could obtain free Crown lands.

"Renters," she pointed out, "didn't have the cash to clear and seed the land, and get the farm working."

She was not at all curious about our mission. "There isn't much to look at, but look all you want, and keep anything you find."

"You have a right to know what we're after."

"Suit yourself."

"We're looking for a grave."

She chewed her lower lip thoughtfully. "No graves there."

"How about spirits?"

She only shrugged.

I found her lack of interest challenging. "Do you believe in reincarnation?" I asked.

She regarded me doubtfully. "You mean all of us coming back one day?"

"Something like that."

Her tired face suddenly brightened. "Well, Christ said He was coming back, so how can we greet Him unless we're here?"

She moved an arm down the road. "The house you want is the King house, they got it from the Hughes family, and Mrs. King moved it to Owen Sound a few years back."

I stopped in my tracks.

"Then it isn't the same house?"

"Oh, the foundation's the same."

"What lot number would that be?"

She smiled. "Oh, I wouldn't know about that."

"But you own the property now."

"Oh, Milford might know. I never think about things like that."

She pointed down the road. "Just turn left at the Tank Range, and up a ways, you can't miss it. There's apple trees out back, and a bee-yard right by."

At the site, we all piled out of the cars. Jed, the collie, seemed the most excited, scurrying about frantically, nose to the ground. "I guess," drawled Joe, "he sees a squirrel he knew before."

I laughed. "At least, he remembers it's something to run after."

With the dog barking excitedly, we headed for the ruins Joanne had earlier called home, passing through a wooden gate. As we poked around the debris for a while, Joanne scooped up an old doorknob, and Joe caustically announced, "It looks like it came from an outhouse."

He turned to Joanne curiously. "What kind of stone was on Tommy's grave?"

"A wooden cross," she said, her eyes still combing the ruins.

Joe's eyes swung north, across the ravine. "There's another house up there, beyond the barn—the place is crawling with ruins."

Joanne nodded. "Yes, a smaller house, it was there first." She turned back to the ruins, as the company restlessly wandered after the dog.

Dave Manuel, with a motion picture camera, had assumed the role of director. "Everybody please be quiet," he called out.

Joanne regarded him with a faint smile. "Why?"

Dave bridled. "So you can walk around undisturbed,

once Joe puts you under."

"I'm not under yet," she said tartly.

Joe was still surveying the area closely, inspecting the crumbling walls, the apple tree growing out of the house, the foundation of an obviously sizable barn across the ravine. "You notice," he said dryly, "that she picked out a house with a terrace and running water." His eyes were on the brook, cutting between house and barn.

"There was a bridge over the brook," Joanne interposed.

"I should hope so," Joe said, "otherwise somebody would get wet."

Dave was ready now. "Everybody back, except Joe and Joanne," he cried, camera poised.

MacIver, strangely quiet, suddenly came to life. "I don't think Joanne should be photographed under hypnosis," he said.

"Why not?" Dave said.

"Because she's very sensitive in trance, and it might upset her permanently."

Dave looked helplessly at Joe, and Joe shrugged noncommittally. "It's up to them," he said indifferently.

I was not particularly interested one way or the other.

Dave was bitterly disappointed. "Posterity should have these pictures," he said warmly.

But MacIver was adamant.

"All right," Dave said, "I'll get a few pictures now, then cut out when Joe gets her under."

It was a June day in September, ideal for hypnosis, or anything else. The sun was pleasantly warm, the breeze invigorating, and the temperature a mild seventy, as Joanne, in a red-striped blouse and blue jeans, stretched out on a clump of grass, Joe squatting nearby on a big stone. In the background were the apple trees, and to the left a muddy pool, resembling an old swimming hole.

"Never before," said Joe sardonically, "has anybody

been regressed in such an atmosphere."

As far as the eye could see, there was but one habitable house, the Johnsons', as Joe proceeded to put Joanne in trance. As she stood up, her eyes suddenly glazed, her lips half-parted, he quickly established her frame of reference. "It is 1849," he said, choosing the year Susan and Tommy married. "Where are we now, Susan?"

Abruptly, she faced south and then north, the remnants of the barn holding her gaze. Surely, she walked across the pathway, toward the brook, Joe jogging to keep up.

"What's in the barn?" he asked.

"Cows."

She leaned pensively against a tree.

"Anything planted?"

"Wheat," nibbling on a blade of grass.

Joe was obviously trying to relax her subconscious.

She now slowly retraced her steps to the house.

"Pick out the garden, Susan," Joe said.

"Vegetable or flower garden?"

"Vegetable."

She moved to the back of the house.

Joe nodded. "That would be about right."

"How big was it?"

She marched off some fifty feet.

In the first visit with me, Joanne had picked out an old well, now at Joe's suggestion, she went to a second well. "Strange," Joe said, "that they should have two wells."

It did seem strange.

"What do you like about the house?"

She walked into the small room she had apparently mistaken for the living room, and picked out a fireplace where there was no sign of a fireplace.

Joe shook his head. "Curious."

He turned her attention to a square slab of concrete,

where a kitchen or pantry must have been. "Where does that go?" Joe asked.

She seemed puzzled at first, then her brow clearing, "There was a stairs there, we kept the food down below."

Joe now asked about neighbors.

MacGregor and Watson were among the few names she reacted to.

"How about Johnson?"

She shook her head.

At seventeen, there was little she could tell us that she hadn't told us before—and so Joe moved on to 1864, with Tommy but recently dead.

The transformation was remarkable. The corners of Joanne's mouth drooped, her eyes slanted like an Oriental's, and her cheeks pinched. She was a woman grieving.

"Where," Joe asked, "was Tommy's body?"

Facing the barn again, she said almost inaudibly, "In the loft, on top."

I saw no point to getting into this unnerving experience again.

"Now where is Tommy buried?"

"I picked it out," she said softly.

"Can you take us there?"

She moved as though sleepwalking, arms slightly raised and forward, her legs stiff. We followed closely, as she pointed for the ravine, stopping just this side of the brook.

"Why there?" Joe asked.

She looked around, frowning. "I could look out my window and see the big tree, and know he was resting."

There was a large tree there now, but perhaps a different one.

Just as her features had changed, so had her voice. It was low, and vibrant, as it had been occasionally under hypnosis at the cottage.

"What happened after that?" Joe asked.

She didn't understand.

"Did anybody come to see you about the farm?"

"Yes, a man came and gave me some money."

"Who was it?"

She seemed to grope for a name. "A—A—L—he was short and wore overalls, with black hair and a beaked nose." It was hardly absentee landlord Alexander Fraser, though possibly an agent.

"Was he sympathetic?"

"Had to be out by next year."

"Sell any stock?"

"To the neighbors."

"Who were they?"

"The McMillans." She pointed south. "They lived down there."

"Were they poor?"

"Medium."

She realized two hundred dollars from her sale, and gave her visitor seventy of it.

"Do you remember his name?" Joe tried again.

Every bit of her seemed to strain. "A . . . L . . . oh, I don't know."

"Have you decided to move?"

Her voice was listless now. "Down the road."

"How did you get the house?"

"I found it."

"Who owns the house?"

"Nobody." She paused. "It's gray stone, not as good as this house, but it will do."

"Was it an abandoned house?"

"Deserted."

"Anybody help you move?"

"Some things I can't move because they belong to the house. I'll take the kitchen table, chairs and bed."

"What church do you go to?"

"The Methodist, up the road."

He advanced her a year in time.

"Do you know the Concession Line?"

She thought a moment. "Twelve."

Apparently, she had already made the move across the town line from Sydenham One to St. Vincent Twelve.

"Do you visit the grave?"

"No more."

"Why not?"

She shook her head wearily. "Stayed where I was."

The collie Jed had broken loose and was excitedly leaping up at Joanne. She looked down through the narrow slits of her eyes. "Is that a dog?"

Obviously she could do no more with names than before, except for McMillan. The most impressive part of the unique session had been her demeanor, as she approached the barn, and again as she stood at the grave.

Now as she came out of her trance, rubbing her eyes, Joe saluted her, "Well, Joanne, you never have to be Susan any more."

As we trooped off to our cars, we noticed a man in the adjacent bee-yard, watching us curiously.

"Having a party?" he called out good-naturedly.

"Digging a few graves," Joe said sourly.

He was harvesting honey himself. He waved an arm at the boxes surrounding him. "This is the biggest bee-yard in Canada," he said proudly. He looked across the narrow dirty road into the Tank Range. "They'll be coming home soon."

Almost as he spoke, swarms of bees, resembling the gyrations of a tornado in their rapid trajectory, buzzed past our heads on their way to the hives. "Don't move suddenly," he warned.

He watched unconcernedly as millions of bees swept

by. "They've had a good time over there in the range with the clover, so they're very good-natured."

"How do you know?" I asked, brushing a few out of my hair.

"You learn about nature, just observing it," he said.

Elmer Showell was a beekeeper like his father before him. "I don't know why," he said, "it just seemed the thing to do."

He eyed me speculatively. "We don't get many visitors up here."

"I'm a writer," I said, "and I don't know why either, except it may have something to do with karma."

Understandably, he looked baffled.

"We're trying to track down somebody who lived here before."

He shook his head over both Marrow and Ganier.

"Is this girl from an old family?" he asked.

A feeling of perverseness suddenly took hold of me. "Ever hear of reincarnation?"

"Oh, sure," he said.

"What do you think about it?"

He plucked a friendly bee out of his eye. "Well, it's like the bees. Man has always known bees, and yet it's only in the last few years he's gotten to know anything about them." He smiled pleasantly. "They have a way of dancing up and down, which we have only just found out, and this is their way of telling each other where the good clover is." The bees kept sweeping past. "So maybe we'll know more about ourselves, when we know more about what God is trying to tell us."

I was to think often of what this stranger had said. Still, I could only proceed evidentially with evidence. After Susan's dramatic manifestation near the range, I decided on a new look through the records in the Owen Sound courthouse. And with young Bob Fournier, still keen on the scent, I hoped for some new resolutions: Was there, for instance, a McMillan to the south of the Marrow place? Was the Susan-Tommy house on the actual site later acquired by Mrs. McDonald's father, Thomas Hughes? Was the house that Mrs. King had carted to Owen Sound the same Susan had lived in? Why had the hypnotized Susan been so puzzled at the arrangement of the rooms, apparently misplacing living room and fireplace, and picking out a sublevel staircase when there was none?

All these problems I discussed with Bob Fournier, as we checked the Susan lot number again. The Kings were the last registered owners, and they had sold to the Johnsons, so that established North 33. Charles King had bought the farm in 1923 from the Hughes family, and it went to his widow, Florence, in 1958. In the period of Tommy's demise, in 1860, it was still Alexander Fraser's, but a few years later the Sheriff, George Sinder, had it, and then in 1867, the Walmsleys held it for thirty-four years until 1901, when neighbor Hughes got it.

The King house had been hauled some fifteen miles to Owen Sound. To Mrs. King, a friendly, pleasant-faced incurious widow of seventy or so, it represented some thirty-five years of connubial bliss. The Kings had built their own house, and she didn't know how much of a house had been there before. "This is the original kitchen," she pointed out, "and the living room."

Neither looked like rooms Joanne had described.

"Were there any unusual features?" I asked.

"We put in a walkway and a terrace, and a little foot-bridge over the brook."

In a few moments we were through the house, and she showed us to the door with a smile. "Perhaps," she said, "the museum will have some useful information about old families."

In the car, Fournier and I exchanged glances. "That takes care of Susan's walkway and terrace," I said shortly.

Fournier shrugged. "Maybe they just put a new one over the old one."

Our stop at the museum was brief. The curator, a Mrs. Menzies, laughed when I asked about the Twin Churches. "Our records of one hundred years ago in this area are like your country's five hundred years ago. In fact, we have to go to your Smithsonian Institution in Washington for information on our early church history."

We had one more stop.

Mrs. McDonald didn't seem surprised to see us.

"Do you know a Walmsley family?" I asked, as she sat straight on her chair, rigidly noncommittal.

She nodded. "They had the farm before my father."

"Could I reach them anywhere?"

She shook her head. "There's no Walmsleys around now."

"Have you any idea where their house was?"

"The Walmsleys had their house just north of the barn," she said, explaining the house nearer the road.

"And your father's house?"

He built in 1903, south of the barn, on the same ground as the King house.

Why had her father built there, when he had a house of his own just to the south, or could have used the Walmsley place?

"His own house was getting old, and the Walmsley place was too small and close to the road."

It seemed logical.

Obviously, something was wrong; Susan could not have lived in a house built long after she had moved off.

"Were there any walkways and terraces?" I asked.

"My father put them in," she said, unhesitatingly.

"And not the Kings?"

She sat rigidly unbending. "I don't know what they did."

"Why did your father build in that particular place?" I asked.

"He picked it out as the best place to live, near enough to his work, and yet with the pleasantest view."

I recalled Susan's sitting out in the late afternoon sun, admiring the view from the terrace.

"Would your father have built over the remains of another house?"

She thought for a moment. "I don't remember any foundation being there."

"Are you sure?"

"I couldn't say for sure, but it seems I would remember."

"If that was the place to build, couldn't somebody else have had the same idea?"

"Who?"

"Some tenant farmer perhaps."

She frowned. "Jim Smith rented the Walmsley house after they left, and then George Baker."

"That would be much later," I said.

"Later than what?"

"The period I'm concerned with, from about 1850 to '65."

"I wouldn't know about that."

Susan had mentioned new people moving in from a nearby farm in 1885. Confused as she was about dates, could that have been Hughes moving up from the farm just south to the farm she once called hers?

Hughes had not built his house till 1903, the year she presumably died, but she once before confused the year 1884 with the year of her death. She could very well have done it again, in a different circumstance.

Mrs. McDonald was watching me passively, not knowing that she had added still another puzzle to the enigma of the Susan house. There was nothing else I could think of, and Mrs. McDonald was not about to volunteer anything. Her daughter, Mrs. Lourie, took us to the door. "If you have any more questions," she said, "don't hesitate to call."

Fournier and I rode silently with our thoughts for a while. "If there was no house there before Hughes—or the Walmsleys" I said finally, "how could Susan have lived there?"

If anything, Fournier was elated. "That explains," he said blithely, "why she wasn't quite right on the house, even looking at it; the foundation was all wrong for her."

"But there should have been some ruins under the Hughes house?"

"How do you know there weren't?" he asked. "Remember she talked of a staircase to a sublevel, and that's where people of that time stored their food, in a sort of subcellar."

"How about the walkway and terrace Susan laid out?" I asked.

He laughed. "Well, Mrs. King thought she did it, and Mrs. McDonald said her father did it, and they're both undoubtedly right. Couldn't Hughes have put the walkway and terrace over one that was there before?"

We passed one crumbling ruin after another. "It doesn't take long in this climate for a house to disappear," he observed.

A few days later, mulling over Mrs. McDonald's report, I checked back on the telephone. Mrs. Lourie, perhaps remembering the optical shop in New York, generously relayed my questions to her mother.

"Was Mrs. McDonald living at home when her father built there?"

"No, she lived away, after her marriage, and wouldn't

have been as familiar with details."

Hughes had built on the land he got from the Walmsleys after his first wife—Mrs. McDonald's mother—had passed on. Like Susan, apparently, he hadn't wanted to live with memories.

I had done all I could in Canada. I was glad to get away, and yet sorry to leave. It reminded me somehow of the old Jimmy Durante song to that effect. A few people, including Joanne and Tag, and Casey Jones dropped over that last night. I had grown fond of the amiable, introspective psychiatrist. He was an intellectual link with my own past, and yet his mind foraged where mine had never been before. His was a gallant soul. Afflicted with a deadly circulatory ailment, his days on earth were limited, perhaps accounting for his interest in reincarnation.

That last night, Casey was his usual cheerful self. Our discussions took a wide range. He pointed out that Somerset Maugham, flirting with the metaphysical, had made a brilliantly plausible case for reincarnation, and then characteristically dismissed it. "I am too sure of the interconnection of my body and my mind to think that any survival of my consciousness apart from my body would be in any sense the survival of myself."

Maugham, not believing in God, drew a rather bleak, but inevitable alternative to a grand design for living: "If death ends all, if I have neither to hope for good to come nor to fear evil, I must ask myself what I am here for and how in these circumstances I must conduct myself. Now the answer to one of these questions is plain, but it is so unpalatable that most men will not face it. There is no reason for life and life has no meaning."

And this was Maugham's "Summing Up."

Accepting determinism, Maugham still failed to equate man's destiny to a definite order in the universe, which even the scientist Einstein had recognized.

All this Casey chewed over, wondering, I suppose, what lay in store for himself. His interest in Joanne stemmed from a feeling that intellectuality itself, in a straitjacket of its own making, could never find man's purpose. "Yet, there must be a purpose," Casey said, "for everything in nature has a reason."

But why Joanne?

Casey smiled wryly. "Doesn't the Bible say something about revelations from the lips of children?"

I had arrived in Orillia with mixed feelings, and so I left, finishing a phase into which I was inevitably drawn, and was as inevitably leaving. The unique familiarity of the town, the *déjà vu*, had given way to the familiarity of conscious awareness. The old and the new were now hopelessly merged. Orillia was like any place, and Joanne like any girl.

And so back in New York, reflecting on recent events, I awaited reports on the minister McEachern; Mrs. O'Leary, neighbor Mr. Thompson, Dr. Black, etc. Meanwhile, there was new information on the Canadian up-country unearthed through research commemorating the Canadian centennial. Joanne was strikingly right about some things. Sugar did come in packages and was ten cents a box, saddles sold for from seven and a half to twelve dollars, and an orange, small and hard as it might be, was a prize indeed. The democrat was a wagon peculiar to the time and place; Owen Sound, the county seat, was Sydenham in the 1860s, changing its name shortly thereafter, when Susan seemed to lose interest in everything around her. The name Toronto may have been unfamiliar because many old-timers clung to the Anglophile York.

Oddly, the most elusive mystery of all—certainly no less apocryphal than the search for the girl with the blue eyes—was cleared up in a few days. The spook of Lake Couchiching, Orillia's own Loch Ness monster, was tragically revealed for what it was in a newspaper clipping sent on by a Canadian friend. The streamer on a Toronto front page read: PLASTER-WRAPPED BODY OF WOMAN FOUND IN LAKE MAY BE MINNIE FORD. Minnie Ford, a wealthy Toronto widow, had been missing for three years. The prime suspect was her son, Wayne, a nineteen-year-old problem boy. The body was found near the Ford cottage, and had presumably been in the lake since June 1963. Apparently, it had floated on the surface after a crate casing had broken apart, and had bobbed about for a while. Ford, it developed, had killed his mother in a dispute over the family car. He was given a life sentence, and that ended that.

The search for records went on long after I was gone. Leslie Levy, a Toronto researcher, covering much the same ground as myself, discovered many McEacherns in early directories and microfilmed census reports. But none was a minister. "Upon checking persons listed in the census reports of 1871," she reported, "I ascertained that all male adult McEacherns were farmers with the exception of a blacksmith and a teacher."

Still, Joanne could have been right. "At that time and that place," a genealogist stated, "most clergymen were farmers, and if they were circuit riders only when crops didn't require their attention, they listed themselves as farmers on the census lists, since that was their chief occupation. In the outlying districts, a lay preacher was probably all that was available for weddings, baptisms and funerals. Most likely, one of the scores of McEachern farmers is what you're after."

There was no Dr. Black in the 1867 medical register of upper Canada. However, with diligence, Leslie had come across a Thomas Black, medically qualified in 1828, and a David M. Black, registered in 1838. They were in the district, but not close. But there were neighboring Blacks, including a James Black of Sydenham Township, who was about thirty-five when Tommy was presumably injured. The microfilm was blurred, Leslie said, but the occupation appeared to be Gent. "Gentlemen," she observed, "could mean that he might have practiced medicine after a fashion." To point up the inaccuracies, she listed another Black, Joseph, a farmer in Sydenham Township. He was forty-eight on the '51 lists, sixty in 1861, and seventy-three in 1871. I was reminded of Susan's difficulty with dates. "The people of one hundred years ago were never sure of their ages, some 'aging' thirteen to twenty years in the ten-year periods between census-taking."

As I had, she checked on the enigmatical Alexander Fraser, a name corresponding to the "A-l" falteringly drawn out of Joanne. There were three Alexander Frasers, all apparently in the wrong place. "The Fraser Clan," Leslie reported, "settled chiefly along the St. Lawrence River and as far inland as Ottawa. They did not apparently move as far west as Meaford and Owen Sound." Had I not myself seen the official correspondence and the land maps, I would have had to conclude that just as there were no Marrows or Ganiers, there were no Frasers.

What was it the Owen Sound curator had said: "Trying to find records in this part of Canada for a hundred years ago is analogous to searching through archives in the United States before Columbus."

Susan's only friend, aside from Mrs. Speedie, had been a Mrs. O'Leary. The librarian in Owen Sound, consulting gazetteers and histories, could turn up no O'Leary. But Leslie, phonetically, had come up with two: J. Oleari (small o), who in 1861 was twenty-one. She was a teacher—a married female; Oleari, Matilda (capital O),

Irish (the Major's Irish block), and nineteen. Her mother would have been a Mrs. Oleari.

One did not disprove anything by not proving it. The investigations, while not fully confirming Susan's statements, did not exclude them as possibilities. There were several Thompsons near the Widow Marrow, in the census for 1861 and 1871: farmers Peter Thompson and William Thompson of Sydenham, or in neighboring St. Vincent, farmer Robert Thompson—or none of these.

For months I considered the whole aspect of reincarnation, scouting about for additional experiences or reflections that might be relevant. One day, Maria Bliecker, the psychic and spiritual adviser, put a book under my nose, *The Rosicrucian Cosmo-Conception,* and said quickly, "Read only two pages—'A Remarkable Story.' "

And a remarkable story it was. A Mr. Roberts, in Santa Barbara, California, was out walking when a three-year-old girl sidled up to him, put her arm around his knees, and called him father. Roberts was considerably upset, until the child's mother came up, equally indignant. The child, however, still clinging, insisted he was her father. She remembered having lived with Roberts, and another mother, in a small house near a brook with a planked bridge. One day her father disappeared, the family ran out of food, and her mother lay down and became still. "I also died," the girl said, "but I came here."

Roberts now told his story. Eighteen years before, in London, he had eloped with an English girl to Australia. There in the wilderness he had cleared a farm and built a cabin by a brook, as described by the child. A daughter was born. When she was two, he was arrested and taken back to England, without getting a chance to see his wife and child, for a robbery committed the day he left the country. There he proved his innocence, and only then was a mission sent out to his cabin. They found only the skeleton remains of a woman and child.

Not everyone thought wishfully of a life beyond. Novelist Taylor Caldwell, melancholy over a husband's illness, had no desire to repeat a life "intolerable in its bleakness, conformity, chrome-plated deadliness and mechanism." Yet, hers was a subconscious, pragmatically psychic, through which visions of past lives constantly flowed.

Besides her recall of the past, she had many psychic experiences, which were readily demonstrable in the present. Once, struck with a painful premonition, she had dashed off a warning of violence to a young President, who was shortly thereafter assassinated. She was herself the central figure in another unusual experience. Her first manuscript, a historical novel, had been unexpectedly rejected by a publisher. Shortly thereafter, disconsolate, she had wandered into a spiritualist meeting in her hometown, Buffalo, New York. The spiritualist, a stranger to her, announced from the platform: "Arthur is here with a message for his daughter."

As Arthur was her father's name, Taylor Caldwell immediately sat up.

The message was remarkably precise, in picking out her disappointment, and made a heartening forecast. It predicted when her book, *Dynasty of Death*, would be published, delineated its success, and reassured her—as no critic or publisher could—that every book of hers thereafter would be an instant best-seller. In the succeeding months, the first part of the prognostication materialized in every respect and in the intervening thirty years, one best-seller after another has tripped off her typewriter.

She had wondered about reincarnation ever since she was a child. At three years of age, in her native England, she had a dream that was to recur down the years. "I was standing at a small, open casement window in a very high building like a tower, and I was looking with anguish down on a roof below the casement which was covered with dirty red tile." There were no such tiles in England.

"The sky," she continued, "was a cold, dull white, and the sea of roofs beyond were all crowded and a jostling red tile, too, and seemingly spread for miles. In the distance, I saw a narrow river and several ornate stone bridges crossing over it. I felt, not a child of three, but a mature woman, say about the middle twenties, looking about the same as I later did when I was really in my mid-twenties.

"I was in a sort of icy stone cell, high over the city, with only a cot, a table, and one chair in it, and there was a wooden door at the rear. I knew the door was bolted, and that I was a prisoner in this city I knew well and in which I had lived and been born. I knew that outside the locked door was a narrow and winding staircase of stone. Then I heard footsteps on the stone, and I knew who was approaching.

"I knew that in the company there were three men in strange costumes, and one was a man I knew very well. I knew his costume, in that awful dream, and now I know it was the white habit and hood of a Dominican monk. All of them were familiar to me, and I knew why they were coming up the stairs—they were going to torture me and kill me. I heard a key grating in the lock and I turned to the window again in despair, and I knew the only way to escape those men was to throw myself out the window. So, as the door opened, I threw myself down onto the sloping roof, very high over the teeming narrow street, with relief and even joy. Then, as I rolled down that cutting tilt of tiles all memory was blanked out, and I woke up screaming in my little trundle bed in England."

The dream kept recurring, until one day it found its sequel in Italy, where the novelist was visiting with her husband. In Florence, they were the house guests of the Count and Countess de Moretti. "On retiring, before drawing the heavy curtains over the big curtain in our bedroom," she recalled, "I looked down with interest at a very huge plaza. In the center of the empty plaza stood a tall pillar surmounted by a medieval horseman.

"All at once a sensation of utter despondency, fear and foreboding came to me and I pulled the curtains across the window and went to bed."

On awakening, she opened the draperies, and looked out on the plaza, hoping the busy daytime traffic would make the scene less bleak. But she was in for another jolt. The plaza she had seen before retiring was gone.

"There was a big broad street outside, and many other streets radiating away from it, but no plaza except for a very small concrete island with a sort of modernistic monument on it."

At lunch, she hesitatingly mentioned the disappearing plaza to her hosts. Count Moretti brought out a large book and showed her a picture of the plaza just as she had seen it earlier. "It was a centuries-old engraving, and there was the prancing horseman high on the pillar, and the gloomy shadowed streets and the blank sides of the buildings."

Later, that day, touring Florence, she apparently had another hallucination. She had been looking at a small concrete island in the heart of the city, when a new vision occurred. "Before my eyes, the island disappeared and there was another if smaller plaza, and crowds of people in strange costumes, and a whole company of white-robed Dominican monks"—now recognizable as the monks of her dream. The vision had the vividness of reality. "In the center of the little plaza a man, also robed in white, wags burning to death on the pile of faggots in the bright sunshine, a small, plump man with a heroic face. Horrified and dazed, I said aloud, 'Savonarola.' "

In the island, unknown to her, there was a monument in Fra Savonarola's honor.

Back in the house, she told the Count of her experience, and he smiled knowingly. "You have been here before," he said. "You lived in Florence at the time of Savonarola, and you must have been one of his followers, and that is why you were condemned to death." He walked to a book shelf and brought out another engraving of medieval Florence. "It was very familiar to me, and terrifying, with the very sort of tall, narrow building in which, in my dream, I had been a prisoner."

Never again did the novelist have the nightmarish dream, for once a dream had fulfilled its purpose it vanished from the subconscious.

This was not the only experience that suggested reincarnation. At six years of age, again in England, she had been shown a copy of *The Mill on the Floss* by George Eliot (Mary Ann Evans), and proceeded to describe the narrative in detail, though she had never heard of the book before. Years later, she bought the book because a teacher had said, "You write just like George Eliot."

As she read it then, a tiny chill ran up her spine. She knew every word in it, where the author had run into problems, and where she had been stuck. Was she the writer she was because of a soul carry-over from a nineteenth-century novelist?

Were distinctive aptitudes or traits a sign of subconscious remembrance? The prodigies, Mozart and Josef Hofmann could be dismissed as musical freaks, but what of Alan Hovhaness, the accomplished American composer? At four, hearing his mother at the piano, he hastily scribbled down a few bars of music and then years later, as a student, realized this first composition was in a style already extinct two hundred years before.

Clairvoyantly, Edgar Cayce had often correctly forecast the careers of newborn babies and small boys, his past-life readings kept from them so as not to influence the choices they made. With adults, too, he had shown the development of qualities from one life to the next, as with Harold J. Reilly, physiotherapist head of Rockefeller Center's health service. "In summing the abilities, the activities that make for both mental and material experiences in aiding individuals to find themselves, will make for that which will bring to self material gains, mental satisfaction and spiritual development in self. While many may look on and consider the entity [Reilly and his cycle of lives] as one of rather material nature and with material desires, yet viewed from soul development the entity is progressing."

It had taken twenty years for me to realize what Cayce had flashed out in a moment—that under his crusty exterior no more generous spirit had ever run a lucrative business in a city of hard knocks. And Cayce had said that Reilly would go on, never giving up helping people, and here he was, well beyond seventy, independently wealthy, treating more people, more successfully, than ever before. "I twice tried to retire," Reilly recalled, "and the need of people twice pulled me back."

Believing in Cayce, did Reilly believe in a concept which had him ministering to people's health in ancient Egypt and Atlantis?

"I've enjoyed this life so much," said pragmatist Reilly, "that I'm all for another."

Curious about my experience in Canada, Reilly was candid as only a dear friend can be.

"Is she on the up and up?" he asked.

"She believes in herself."

"Well, does it stack up?"

He sensed my disinclination to discuss the situation. "You're thinking too much to talk about it," he guessed shrewdly.

"I keep waiting for something, and I don't know what."

I was listless and edgy the day the telephone rang with the same curious insistence it had once before. This time it was not Lee Barker, but Dave Manuel, calling from Toronto.

"Guess what?" he said.

I was in no mood for games.

"Concentrate on Joanne," he said waggishly.

It was now late February '67 (1967, that is), and I hadn't seen Joanne for months.

"Concentrate," Dave persisted, "and what do you get?"

"Marriage," I said.

I seemed to have blown him over.

"How did you get that?"

"From your phone call."

Dave was not easily daunted. "All right, is she marrying Tag?"

"Obviously not," I rejoined.

"Okay," Dave said, "who is she marrying?"

Hadn't we predicted that at eighteen she would marry a man thirty?

"Well," Dave said happily. "Roger is thirty, and Joanne was eighteen last October."

Was this straining coincidence?

The prospective bridegroom, Roger Watson, was a geophysicist—a petroleum geologist—and a first cousin of Tag Watson, to whom Joanne had been virtually affianced.

And the plans of the newlyweds-to-be?

Dave chuckled. "Roger has a plane of his own and they're going to fly out and live in about the farthest urban point they can in Canada—Vancouver."

Not only distant, but for Canada balmy.

They were to be wed at the end of the Lenten season, and, curiously, by my old friend, the Reverend Crighton.

As I considered this turn of events, I recalled a passage from *Life Is for Living,* by the Reverend Eric Butterworth: "The life you once lived can only be found in the life you now express."

I asked Dave for a report on the events up to the marriage, and a fill-in on Roger, and soon heard back.

The pair, Dave noted, had met with all the force and drama one would expect. The meeting, ironically, was at a Christmas week party at Tag's apartment. "For some reason," Dave reported, "Joanne was watching the door when it opened and Roger came in. She had never seen him before, and yet she felt a sharp physical impact, and could hardly breathe."

For most of the evening, Joanne maintained the pretense of not being affected. There had been some group caroling, and she sat on the rug, trying not to look up, when her eyes fell fatalistically on a certain pair of shoes. "This hit her again with a curious numbing sensation. She looked up, in spite of herself, and couldn't help but laugh that even his shoes would do this to her."

It was clearly karmic.

Roger, too, felt the impact, and arranged a skiing jaunt to the Blue Mountains, in Grey County. They made a threesome of it, with Tag still very much unawares. In a few days, Roger broke the news to cousin Tag. And within a week, without his proposing or Joanne accepting, they decided to marry.

Joanne, considerably upset over Tag, turned to her father for counsel. "MacIver," Dave observed, "delineated the conflict between her conscious and subconscious, Roger representing the latter, and said she must let her subconscious come through." Poor Tag!

On their honeymoon, Joanne and Roger stopped off in New York. She had never been more radiant or mature. Roger was as billed: solid, intelligent, pleasant-looking, patient, understanding. He may not have looked like Tommy Marrow, but everything else was there.

They sat down on the sofa, hands entwining, eyes locked in embrace. Roger talked about himself first. His family was from Upper Canada, and had lived in Orillia when he was small. His father, Stanley, was a well-known educator; one brother, Clifford, was a war hero, another, Patrick Watson, a controversial television personality.

As had Joanne, he had known from the first that their union was inevitable. MacIver must have known it, too. The day Roger called at the house, preparatory to the skiing trip, MacIver had looked him over and said, "Welcome into the family."

Theirs was a complete harmony. During a lull in the skiing, when they were momentarily alone, Roger had said, "We belong together, let me tell him."

As they discussed it now, Joanne ran her fingers fondly through Roger's hair. "There actually wasn't much to it," she said. "I could tell from the electric shocks."

"I suppose you'll be having babies soon," I said.

She blushed prettily. "Well, there's nothing stopping it."

When had Roger first heard about Susan?

He smiled. "My mother told me, she thought it strange."

At any time, had Joanne made comparisons to Tommy Marrow?

She looked at me gravely. "I've been trying to forget ever since I remembered."

"But do you see any resemblance?"

Her jaw set squarely. "You can only live one life at a time."

They had expressed a desire to see the still uncompleted manuscript. Each took a section, and Roger, reading rapidly, suddenly exclaimed, "This is wild. Joanne says she will know her husband by his eyes, and that's exactly how we communicated."

He read on, to a frowning halt.

"This must be wrong," he said, turning to Joanne.

She read calmly. "No, it's right."

He blinked, and went back to his reading, occasionally giving me a quizzical glance.

Later, when they were through, I asked about the part he had questioned.

He replied airily, "Where Joanne said she had known you before."

By now, it had been established that I was neither Tommy nor Yancey.

"But you could have been my father," Joanne interposed with a smile. "You know, they were married at Massie, and may have lived there a while, before moving up to what later became the range."

I had remembered this vaguely from one set of notes.

We chatted for a while, the three of us, the impression heightening that here was a marriage that would last and grow stronger. Whether Joanne was Susan or not, and whoever Roger was in that long ago, they had found the rarest commodity in this life—a binding love.

Just as they had arrived, arm in arm, so they left, looking as though it had never been any other way.

That summer, as I was finishing up, saddening news came from Canada. That gay blithe spirit, Casey Jones, had succumbed to incurable leukemia. I had no way of knowing his last thoughts, but I had a feeling that he would get back one day if he could, and soon. I tried to recall anything that would give me a clue as to his final verdict on reincarnation. He had said, as others had, that if this was it, was it necessary? "We eat, sleep, procreate, and deteriorate. All this talk of self-realization, without some overriding universal reason, is hogwash."

And so were Casey's earthly functions interrupted, never to be resumed? He had never remembered another life, nor had an experience of *déjà vu,* yet he questioned only their import. He would be missed.

In my own quandary, I marveled at associates who had no qualms about stating they had lived before and would live again.

"How can you be so sure?" I asked Adela Rogers St. Johns, septuagenarian author of the inspirational *Final Verdict* and *Tell No Man.*

She gave me the smile of the old and wise for those not so old or so wise. "I remember many lives."

My eyebrows went up a notch.

"I remember very well," she went on, "standing on the shore with a company of soldiers awaiting the Spanish Armada as the Queen, Elizabeth, traveled up and down encouraging the troops."

Writers have notoriously active imaginations.

Mrs. St. Johns snorted. "Elizabeth had changed from heavy armor to a special light armor, since she couldn't otherwise have mounted her horse."

"Were you under hypnosis?"

Again she snorted. "I don't go in for dramatics. I just saw it with a vividness as real as anything that had ever happened to me. Sometime later, I was in a London museum, and saw the armor I had visualized. It was a light armor worn by Elizabeth centuries before."

Feeling like Professor Banerjee that reincarnation was essentially a spiritual experience, Mrs. St. Johns now asked, "How has this girl developed?"

I thought for a moment. "She got the husband indicated in her pattern."

"That's not what I asked."

What had my friend Crowley said about soul development?

Susan had had the spiritual experience of communicating with her dead father and describing the heavens as if she were one of its angels.

Mrs. St. Johns shook her head. "How did she develop?"

Joanne had seemed singularly mature at times.

"Where Susan buried herself away in her grief, Joanne stood up bravely to ridicule and adversity. She dared to be a Daniel."

How else had she grown?

Hadn't it taken a certain faith, in herself and God's design for her, to marry a man so much older, more sophisticated, better educated? Moreover, she was a showcase, imperfect perhaps, of the concept that man dies to be reborn again. Did it matter that the Ontario Registrar General, searching his sketchy records, could find no Susan Ganier Marrow, living or dead?

What clear-cut evidence had I that Joanne had lived before as Susan? I could not count heavily on her conscious recall, not knowing its validity. I could grant the Eagles deposition, and still not consider this proof. Joanne subconsciously remembered apple orchards, and there were orchards. She recalled Browns, Blacks, Thompsons, MacGregors, Urquharts, Milligans, Olearis, staples, prices, farms, landscapes, conditions, all of which checked roughly, and there was a McMillan south of her.

Certainly, her description of heaven, in her eerie conversations with her father, was at most evidence of a fertile subconscious. How much more valid was her subconscious than her conscious? In a Toronto negligence trial, a motorist injured in an auto accident testified under oath that only under hypnosis eight years later was she able to remember that accident correctly. There was no questioning Joanne's sincerity, but could it have been the sincerity of the misguided? Had he been concocting a hoax, MacIver could certainly have arranged matters better. Still, Joanne's winding up on the lot where Mrs. McDonald had lived as a child had a certain poetic retribution, confusing the picture just as it seemed to be clearing.

True, she picked out the Twin Churches (correctly 25 by 15 feet), and we found bits of headstones there, and no map had shown the churches, just as no map she had ever seen had shown her Massie. Still we had not proved Susan Ganier's grave, any more than we had Tommy Marrow's. We had only Susan's subconscious to answer for it. Yet again on the St. Vincent Ninth Line, as she had said, near the Ganiers', a librarian reported, "A commodious chapel (Wesleyan Methodist)."

At the end, she was a recluse on property once briefly held by Archibald Marrow, in an abandoned shack. She had traveled to Sydenham or Owen Sound occasionally in the declining years, and once, visibly agitated, ventured up the road to witness a neighbor moving from one property to the next, possibly her own. She was not grateful, as one might have thought, to Thompson, MacGregor, Eagles, or any of those that may have helped her. She was too out of it to be anything but resigned or acceptive. One day dragged endlessly after another, as she waited for whatever end her fancy led her down. In the spell of her subconscious, Joanne was clearly Susan, but how much of Susan was Joanne? So far, the predictable pattern of her marriage choice was the truest clue; the marriage itself, with motherhood, would now bear scrutiny.

Watching her near the range that day, I could have sworn her personality changed under hypnosis. There could have been no trick about the slanting of her eyes, nor the pinching of her cheeks, the change of voice. She looked like another person, and that person may have been Susan, subconsciously certainly, real perhaps.

Many apparently remembered: Shelley, Thoreau, General Patton, my friends Dr. Crowley and Adela Rogers St. Johns—some remembered events and places, and others, like Thoreau, "walked with Christ." Cayce had said that people often felt at home when they remembered from another life without specifically remembering what they remembered. What else, he asked, was love at first sight, the soul phenomenon poets had been pressed to define since the beginning of time?

"What more likely," supposed the Reverend Leslie Weatherhead, "than that the formation of a new body means for most people the obliteration of the memories of an earlier life?"

But there was nothing apocryphal in Christ asking His disciples, "Who do men say that the Son of man is?" And their answer: "Some say John the Baptist; some Elijah: and others, Jeremiah, or one of the older prophets."

Constantly, I was asked how I felt about reincarnation. I neither accepted nor rejected it. There were times in the search when I wondered . . . is it possible? We were so limited in understanding and God so unlimited, and yet man attributed his own limitations to Him.

There was something more than met the eye, that I knew. Some glimpse of it had been imparted to the ancient prophets, much more to Christ, and certain psychics, gifted with extraordinary sensitivity, had a smattering of a world beyond.

Was death so final and unrelenting? Was it merely a cessation of consciousness, a rest, and then a resumption? Was the body, which seemed so weak, yet so powerful that it could subdue the same spirit which had driven and guided it during life?

Essentially, what was Joanne's message? As Adela Rogers St. Johns had suggested, what was the soul development? What was the point of her coming back? Was it just to marry and have children? This seemed hardly the lesson that Joanne herself had said was the purpose of it all.

So I puzzled, wondering about the spiritual transformation that would make another life cycle worthwhile. And then one day, a young girl who knew the Susan story looked up in surprise, and said, "Perhaps you are too close."

And what did that mean?

"Joanne was not frightened of life—or death—because death was no longer the Great Unknown."

Was that all?

The girl smiled.

"She was unafraid, she knew where she had been and where she was going, and there she went."

Death was no longer oblivion but a promise. This was the message of Joanne, if there was a message, and this, too, was the message of One greater, who, two thousand years before, said to a still unheeding world: "I say unto thee, Except a man be born again, he cannot see the kingdom of God."

A.R.E. PRESS

The A.R.E. Press publishes quality books, videos, and audiotapes meant to improve the quality of our readers' lives—personally, professionally, and spiritually. We hope our products support your endeavors to realize your career potential, to enhance your relationships, to improve your health, and to encourage you to make the changes necessary to live a loving, joyful, and fulfilling life.

For more information or to receive a free catalog, call

        1-800-723-1112

Or write

        A.R.E. Press
        P.O. Box 656
        Virginia Beach, VA 23451-0656